Human Resources Management Systems

Human Resources Management Systems

Glenn M. Rampton

—

Ian J. Turnbull

—

J. Allen Doran

—

Monica Belcourt, Series Editor

 I(T)P Nelson

an International Thomson Publishing company

Toronto • Albany • Bonn • Boston • Cincinnati • Detroit • London • Madrid • Melbourne •
Mexico City • New York • Pacific Grove • Paris • San Francisco • Singapore • Tokyo • Washington

I(T)P™
International Thomson Publishing
The ITP logo is a trademark under licence

I(T)P Nelson
A division of Thomson Canada Limited, 1997

Published in 1997 by
I(T)P Nelson
A division of Thomson Canada Limited
1120 Birchmount Road
Scarborough, Ontario M1K 5G4

Canadian Cataloguing in Publication Data
Rampton, Glenn M.
   Human resources management systems

(Nelson Canada series in human resources management)
Includes bibliographical references and index.
ISBN 0-17-604825-1

1. Information storage and retrieval systems – Personnel management. 2. Personnel management - Data processing.
I. Turnbull, Ian J. II. Doran, J. Allen. III. Series.

HP5549.5.D37R3 1996   658.3'00285   C96-930653-9

Publisher	Jacqueline Wood
Production Editor	Jill Young
Project Editors	Anita Miecznikowski and Jenny Anttila
Senior Production Coordinator	Carol Tong
Assistant Art Director	Sylvia Vander Schee
Interior Design	Holly Fisher
Lead Composition Analyst	Zenaida Diores

Printed and bound in Canada

1 2 3 4 (BBM) 99 98 97 96

Brief Contents

Contents

About the Series

There is one asset within organizations that provides the competitive advantage for many organizations: human resources. While the purchase of facilities and the adoption of technology are considered major long-term decisions, and accorded the appropriate time and money, senior executives do not give the same consideration to the investment in human resources. Yet, many studies in human capital suggest that investments in human resources do provide a good return, and unlike other resources, are renewable. Because knowledge about the effective management of an organization's employees is critical, ITP Nelson is publishing a series of texts dedicated to those managers and human resource professionals who are responsible for the productivity and satisfaction of employees.

The texts in the ITP *Nelson Series in Human Resources Management* include *Managing Performance Through Training and Development, Occupational Health and Safety, Human Resources Management Systems, Recruitment and Selection in Canada, Compensation Management in Canada,* and *Human Resources Planning.*

The ITP *Nelson Series in Human Resources Management* represents a significant development in the field of HR for many reasons. Each book in the series (except for *Compensation Management in Canada*) is the first Canadian text in the functional area. Human resource practitioners in Canada must work with Canadian laws, Canadian statistics, Canadian policies, and, Canadian values. This series serves their needs. It also represents the first time that students and practitioners have access to a standardized guide to the management of many HR functional areas. This one-stop resource will prove useful to anyone involved with the effective management of people.

The publication of this series signals that the HR field has advanced to the stage where theory and applied research guide practice. Because the field is still emerging, and new tools and methods are being invented, theory and research are discussed along with common practices used by Canadian HR professionals. The books in the series present the best and most current research in the functional areas of HR. This research is supplemented with examples of successful practices used by Canadian companies who are leaders in the HR area. Each text identifies the process of managing and implementing effective strategies, thus serving as an introduction to the functional area for the new student of HR and as a validation manual for the more experienced HR practitioner. Cases, exercises, discussion questions, and references contained at the end of each chapter provide opportunities for further discussion and analysis.

As you read these texts, I hope you share my excitement at being involved in the development of an important profession, one that affects daily interactions with our own employees as well as those in organizations with whom we conduct business.

Monica Belcourt
SERIES EDITOR
AUGUST 1996

About the Authors

GLENN M. RAMPTON

Glenn Rampton is currently chief executive officer of Community Living Algoma. Previously, Dr. Rampton held senior human resources positions in a variety of settings. He retired as senior psychologist of the Canadian Forces in 1983, after a distinguished career as a military behavioural scientist. During his tenure with the Forces, Dr. Rampton was responsible for a number of innovations that led to the more effective and efficient staffing and utilization of human resources within the Department of National Defence.

Prior to his appointment as senior psychologist, Dr. Rampton served as commanding officer of the Canadian Forces Personnel Applied Research Unit, and as an associate professor of leadership and management at the Royal Military College. Dr. Rampton represented Canada on a number of international committees and working groups, including the Steering Committee of a prestigious panel of senior scientists from the United States, Great Britain, Australia, and New Zealand. He also served as president of the Military Testing Association (MTA), representing more than 1000 scientists engaged in applied research in 15 research institutes from eight countries in Europe, Australia, and North America. In this capacity he acted as chair of the MTA's 22nd Annual Conference in Toronto.

Dr. Rampton has also held appointments as the director of Human Resources Planning and Development for Canada Post Corporation, and as assistant vice-president (human resources) for York University. In both of these positions, he was responsible for overseeing the development and implementation of corporate human resources programs in the context of great organizational change.

In the summer of 1993, Dr. Rampton agreed to oversee the amalgamation and rationalization of supports and services for individuals with developmental disabilities across the District of Algoma in Northern Ontario. This new organization is one of the largest of its kind in Ontario, and may serve as a model for others in the province.

Ian J. Turnbull

Ian Turnbull is currently a consultant for Sierra Systems Consultants Inc., to which he brings over 20 years of management experience. Using a business-wide value-added focus, Mr. Turnbull assists organizations through a wide variety of services, including change management, strategic planning, requirements definition, system assessment and selection, project organiza-tion/management/implementation, and engineering of business processes. Specializing in human resources, payroll, and time and attendance, he has also dealt with general management and operational issues. Mr. Turnbull has worked throughout Canada and the United States in such industries as consulting engineering, distribution, education, energy, health care, govern-ment, manufacturing, mining, forestry, and retail.

Mr. Turnbull is a founding director of the International Association of Human Resources Information Management (IHRIM), a past president of the Association of Canadian Human Resources Systems Professionals (CHRSP), a director of the Canadian Council of Human Resources Associations (CCHRA), a past director of the Edmonton Personnel Association, and past president of the Alberta Society of Human Resources and Organization Development (ASHROD). He represented the province of Alberta on the Canadian Engineering Manpower Task Force, and has developed and delivered several management training programs.

Mr. Turnbull also developed and taught a graduate course in HRMS at the Centre for Industrial Relations at the University of Toronto, and has spoken at numerous professional conferences throughout North America and in Europe on general management, human resources, payroll, and systems issues.

Mr. Turnbull's previous employers include Noranda, Canada Post Corporation, the Edmonton General Hospital, Athabasca University, Kaiser Resources, and the Hudson's Bay Company.

J. ALLEN DORAN

Al Doran is currently president and chief executive officer of Phenix Management International, a consulting firm headquartered in Toronto and specializing in assisting organizations of all sizes develop and maintain effective human resources management systems.

Previously, Mr. Doran was director, Human Resources Management Information and Payroll at York University, Toronto, Ontario. He has more than 25 years of experience in the design, development, and application of computer-based information systems, with particular emphasis in personnel, payroll, and human resources planning functions.

While at York, Mr. Doran was responsible for the development and implementation of a "state of the art" human resources information system for the university. He was also responsible for an annual payroll in excess of $200,000,000. Using the latest methodologies, Mr. Doran worked on the re-engineering of current human resources practices to streamline operating procedures, reduce paper, and distribute management information to line managers.

In his previous assignment, Mr. Doran was responsible for directing the development of all personnel and labour relations systems for one of Canada's largest Crown corporations, Canada Post. He was responsible for coordinating a major project to develop a comprehensive and coherent structure that will be used as the blueprint for all future HR systems development.

As manager of the Research Information Systems at the Canadian Forces Personnel Applied Research Unit in Toronto, he developed one of the most comprehensive people databases in Canada.

Mr. Doran is vice-president of the Greater Toronto Chapter of the International Association for Human Resources Information Management (IHRIM) and is vice-chair of the Higher Education Significant Interest Group (HESIG) of IHRIM. IHRIM has more than 5000 members worldwide. He is a past president of Canadian Association of Human Resources Systems Professionals (CHRSP) and was a member of its board of directors from 1989 through 1995.

In June 1996, at Orlando, Florida, Mr. Doran was the first Canadian recipient of the "Summit Award," IHRIM's highest honour, for "his significant, long-standing contributions to the Association's mission and goals."

Mr. Doran is a regular speaker at IHRIM and personnel/payroll conferences in Canada and the U.S. and he often contributes articles on the effective use of technology in managing human resources information to a variety of publications. He is the founder and list-owner of one of the most popular Internet HRMS discussion groups in the world: HRIS-L. Mr. Doran frequently speaks on the use of the Internet in human resources.

Preface

A human resources management system (HRMS) is more than a human resources information system (HRIS). It is what the name implies; an information management system accessible to staff at all levels, designed to ensure that the organization's most important resource—its people—are recruited, selected, developed, employed, deployed, and supported most effectively.

Texts on human resources information systems commonly focus on developing and implementing systems that gather, store, and report human resources data in a timely fashion, in forms that are useful to human resources personnel, line management, and other users. In writing this book, we have attempted to go further than this, by focusing as well on the uses of an HRMS as a critical management tool.

While this book is designed as a text for students specializing in human resources programs at community colleges and universities, it should also be of value as a practical manual for human resources practitioners and line managers. That is, the book will also appeal to:

1. post-secondary school students taking a general HRMS course;

2. human resources and/or payroll managers and functional specialists who want to know more about what an HRMS can do, or who are involved with, or contemplating the development of a new HRMS;

3. information systems professionals who will be working on an HRMS project and want to learn more about the business and user perspective on such systems;

4. executives and general managers who understand that their human resources are their most important resource and are looking to the strategic and pragmatic value of an HRMS in terms of helping them manage their human resources.

The content of *HRM Systems* is based on advancements in the professional literature, together with the authors' combined first-hand experience in developing, implementing, and using numerous human resources management systems in private and public sector organizations. The perspectives of human resources, payroll, operations, human resources information specialists, and management systems specialists are all addressed, as are the different issues facing small, medium, and large organizations.

The text begins with the history of HRMS. Chapter 2 "The Need for an Effective HRMS," discusses the typical reasons why organizations begin a search for an HRMS. Using examples, Chapter 3, "Return on Investment," explores the value that an HRMS can add to an organization's efficiency and effectiveness. These two chapters together provide a framework by which practitioners can develop their own business cases for an HRMS.

Chapter 4, "Planning a New HRMS," outlines the planning processes to be considered in researching the requirements of a new HRMS, with emphasis on the importance of a complete, realistic, and documented plan. An experienced human resources practitioner should be able to use the processes outlined to arrive at an HRMS plan. At the beginning of an HRMS development project, those responsible are generally faced with the decision of whether to upgrade the existing system, to build a new one from scratch, or to buy one.

Chapter 5, "Designing and Developing a New HRMS," describes the steps involved in building (designing/developing) a system in-house, or in adapting existing commercial software packages to meet the needs of the organization. The strengths and weaknesses of each approach are discussed. There are currently many sophisticated, reasonably priced HRMSs on the market. Consequently, most organizations find it more cost-effective to buy a new HRMS "off the shelf." This chapter therefore also outlines the steps involved in identifying the best software packages, including preparing requests for proposals, short-listing proposals, how to approach systems demonstrations, hidden issues surrounding the decision, and the final choice. Chapter 5 also discusses what is required to prepare a feasibility report and a business case to present the options, arguments, and recommendations so that an informed decision may be made. Many organizations have existing manual, semi-automated, or automated processes and systems in place. This chapter examines how to determine whether opportunities exist to better use or improve on those systems and processes and, thus, avoid the expense of buying or building a new HRMS.

The many issues involved with implementing an HRMS are discussed in Chapter 6. We believe that most texts do not give adequate attention to this important subject.

Once implemented, an HRMS must be maintained, or it, and the information the system contains, will soon become out-of-date. Chapter 7, "Maintaining the HRMS," discusses the ongoing requirements of an information system's maintenance, as well as who should be involved. The "users," whoever they may be, must be schooled in both the concept and operation of an HRMS to fully and successfully integrate it into their everyday work.

Continuous systems testing is required in the development, implementation, and operation of an HRMS. It is better to test and retest rather than to allow errors to go unidentified and uncorrected, resulting in a lack of confidence that would take much longer to correct than any testing process.

Without giving users the ability to generate information, an HRMS is simply a bucket for data—*and data are not necessarily information*. This chapter points out that on-line and hard-copy reports, graphics, and analysis, are the keys for successful system use. Adapting the HRMS to new legal requirements, changing business needs, turnover in personnel, and new technology is a challenge requiring continuous improvement. A successful HRMS will never be "finished": it must be flexible enough to grow and change with the needs of the organization. Included is a discussion of who should do what, when an HRMS is "live."

Using actual examples drawn from the authors' experience, Chapters 8 through 13 describe how an effective HRMS can be used to further the work of the core human resources functions. Chapter 14, "Trends in HRMS," discusses the impact that the ever increasing technological and organizational change is having on HRMSs, as well as how this technology may be used to support the human resources function, and in turn, the larger organization which the human resources function supports.

Acknowledgments

The authors would like to thank Dr. Monica Belcourt, who went far beyond her role as senior editor of both this book and the series of which it is a part, in offering encouragement, pressure at appropriate times, and professional support. Her support has been critical. We would also like to thank Barbara Rampton, who served as our lay critic and helped to edit the book, and Laurie Murray, who provided insightful feedback on early chapters.

We appreciate the excellent support that we have received from Edward Ikeda, Anita Miecznikowski, Jenny Anttila, Jill Young, and the others at ITP Nelson, who have made publication of this book possible. They have shown great tolerance.

Thanks as well to the anonymous reviewers who provided extremely useful feedback on early chapters of the book.

We would like to offer a special tribute to our many friends in IHRIM (formerly CHRSP/HRSP), who daily contribute to our knowledge and make this business fun to work in.

Glenn Rampton would like to thank Barbara and Sherene for all the sacrifices that they made while he was preoccupied with this project. He would also like to acknowledge that his interest in the "human condition" came from long discussions with his mother over the kitchen table when he was a young farm boy. He now has more education, and is a long way from the farm, but she probably remains the better psychologist.

Ian Turnbull would like to thank his wife Susan for her continued loving support, his daughters Katherine and Elizabeth for their forbearance, his parents for giving him the love of the pursuit of knowledge, and Bob Grose, who was his mentor in HRM.

Al Doran would like to dedicate this work to his children, Wendy and Michael, who make it all worthwhile. He would also like to thank his co-authors for their patience, and Glenn for being his mentor in HRM and in life.

Introduction

◆ ◆ ◆

INTRODUCTION

The information age is here. Automation and information technology are revolutionizing the way we do business and, as the following example illustrates, Human Resources Management is no exception.

◆ ◆ ◆

Suppose you are an operational manager in a large organization. The planning committee has determined that a need exists for an industrial systems engineer in your area; you have advertised the vacancy in the newspaper, trade journals, in relevant on-line publications, and on your company's World-Wide Web home page. Several candidates have responded via e-mail. By accessing the on-line HRMS on your office computer, you compare each candidate's qualifications against the job requirements and determine what testing procedure will be used to demonstrate each qualified individual's abilities. The test is administered via computer, and the results, along with all other recruitment and selection information, are automatically collected, edited, stored, and made available to those who have authorized access to it by the on-line HRMS. Using these results, you determine which candidate is best suited for the job, and make a formal offer of employment to Ms. Mary Smith.

Once the successful candidate, Mary Smith, has been hired, a file is opened in the HRMS computer and all key information (address, education, etc.) is automatically transferred into it from the applicant file. On her first day at work, Ms. Smith is assigned a log-in name and selects a password; from now on, she will be able to log in to her HRMS file directly from any terminal. This will allow her to access the HR data files in order to find and retrieve information on her company benefits and pension account and update her biographical information. On-line access also allows Ms. Smith to use title or name keywords to find out who is responsible for various functions within the multinational organization, where they are located, and how they may be reached by telephone or e-mail.

As Ms. Smith's role and responsibilities change to adapt to the growing needs of your organization, her HRMS file is continually updated; throughout her tenure, these responsibilities are translated into goals and priorities which are updated monthly on the HRMS. Ms. Smith reports on these goals, and on the status of various projects within her portfolio, by submitting a monthly report to you which she simply uploads into your office terminal on the first Monday of every month.

One morning, you are scheduled to meet with Ms. Smith to discuss a new department initiative; however, when you sign on to your office terminal you find an e-mail message addressed to you marked "Urgent." Due to an accident, Ms. Smith will be unable to attend the meeting. She reported her absence by phone to the Interactive Voice Response attachment of the HRMS, which recorded her absence, deducted the day from her sick leave balance, checked the employee scheduling and calendar system and automatically sent you an e-mail message notifying you that the meeting will have to be rescheduled.

The HRMS also automatically prompts you to schedule regular work planning and career development sessions, including quarterly reviews, with each of your employees. The work planning process involves the translation of company goals into individual achievement objectives, which form the basis for quarterly job performance reviews; all of this is documented on the HRMS for easy reference by yourself and the employees, and is linked by the HRMS with the organization's individual and department-based merit (or bonus) pay programs. Career development information stored on the HRMS might include vocational interests entered by the employee, career development objectives entered by both the employee and the manager, and the results of training or qualifications gained during the employee's tenure, all of which will assist you in making decisions concerning employee promotions, transfers, and pay raises.

The HRMS also provides a forum for employee feedback. Just as the performance of each employee is evaluated each quarter, so too does each employee have the opportunity to provide his or her views on organization culture, leadership, and initiatives through specially formatted HRMS screens. This data is then grouped together by the HRMS to provide a comprehensive and detailed portrait of the company to management. Using this information, management is able to track changes in employee attitudes, assess reactions toward current organizational programs, identify strengths and areas for improvement, and design programs leading to greater employee satisfaction and increased productivity.

The technology described above exists. Although not yet available as one seamless software package, each element is available to be acquired and implemented. This book discusses the issues that must be taken into account by the human resources practitioner or HRMS specialist when developing, implementing, and maintaining a leading edge HRMS such as the one described here.

◆ ◆ ◆

The electronic management of human resources information is referred to as "human resources management systems," or "HRMS." The term used to describe the HRMS of any particular company many vary: HRMS is often used interchangeably with a number of other terms, including Human Resources Information Systems (HRIS), Employee Data Base (EDB), Personnel Data Base (PDB), and Personnel Management Information System (PMIS). Whatever they are called, however, HRMSs have evolved to the point where they have become essential business support tools for today's progressive organizations (Berry, 1993; Broderick and Boudreau, 1992; Mueller, 1994; Richards-Carpenter, 1994).

This chapter provides a brief outline of the historical context of human resources management systems and related issues. It then introduces current HRMS issues and trends, and presents a model showing the relationships between an HRMS and other human resources programs. (This model will appear in subsequent chapters in modified forms, adapted to specific functions.)

◆ ◆ ◆
HISTORICAL BACKGROUND
PRE-WORLD WAR II

In the first half of the twentieth century, human resources, or personnel, as it was then known, was undervalued. Prior to the mid-1940s, the *personnel* function was often regarded as a reactive, caretaker activity that provided very little to the bottom-line of the corporation. Seen as "paper pushers," those in the personnel department were generally regarded as caretakers of employee records and such. At the time, these functions ranked below those of operations, marketing, and finance.

HUMAN RESOURCES MANAGEMENT SYSTEMS

During this period, there was no significant automation of any personnel or payroll function: the technology available was limited, and that which did exist was not generally applied. However, the fact that the personnel (or human resources, as it is now generally known) came late to applying automation technology is a little ironic, given that the first large-scale application in information automation was, effectively, a human resources application (Encyclopaedia Britannica, 1975).

In the 1880s the United States Census Bureau discovered that it could not publish the 1880 census on time using manual techniques. Consequently, the United States government commissioned Herman Hollerith to adapt technology invented in the 1820s by the Englishman, Charles Babbage. This technology made use of punched cards and a variety of equipment—card punchers, sorters, tabulators, printers—to process the cards and the data they contained. Application of this technology was very successful and, with refinements, it was used for more than 50 years.

The "Hollerith" punched card continued to be widely used (until the 1970s) to input data into the electronic computers that eventually replaced mechanical equipment in data automation, thus forming the main link between the eras of mechanical and electronic automation. In fact, the standard "IBM card," so familiar only a few decades ago, was the same size as the United States currency of the 1880s because the equipment that Hollerith used to produce the "blanks" for his punch cards was the same as that used to produce American bank notes of the day.

THE POSTWAR PERIOD

The first computerized personnel systems were the payroll systems that evolved in the 1940s and 1950s. These were very basic recordkeeping files maintained on tabulating and electrical accounting machinery (EAM). These early payroll systems met the requirements of the time, which, from a human resources point of view, were really limited to what we now think of as staffing or employment data. The "data dictionary" of the 1950s would have included only such basic information as the name, address, sex, work location, and department code (for budget purposes) of employees.

Payroll systems did not evolve until the demand for information could not be met with simple paper ledgers. As the demand for industrial products and services grew, so did the numbers of workers. Employees worked in shifts, in different locations, at different jobs, and for varying rates of pay. In addition to the sheer volume of information that had to be kept, there was the additional complexity of collecting enough information to comply with labour laws. In the United States, for example, the Fair Standards Act of 1934 and subsequent amendments provided the stimulus for time clocks and payroll systems (United States Department of Labor, 1967). In Canada, the equivalents to the Fair Standards Act are the Employment Standard Acts of the provinces and the Canada Labour Code for the federal government. These acts do not generally require either time clocks or payroll systems, but do typically require specific records retentions and accurate pay.

THE MID-1950s AND EARLY 1960s

Computer technology began to accelerate by the early 1960s. Unfortunately, the availability of these tools was not generally taken advantage of by those working in Personnel, but there were notable exceptions in the aerospace and defence industries, where the first known nonpayroll personnel systems were developed. These industries were leaders in the use of technology. They identified the need for information on employees and potential employees with specific skill sets, and then developed automated systems to gather, store, and access it. The first known human resources inventory applications were developed in the late 1950s (Walker, 1982).

These particular industries had to be ready to respond to a rapidly growing demand for special skills for projects. Behavioural scientists developed instruments to survey existing employees who were already working on projects. These instruments determined levels of, education, experience, etc., for each special skill. The information gathered was recorded on computer cards. Once analyzed, it told the Personnel department which of their employees had specific skills; they could then be identified for new projects, as required. As well, surveys and tests were developed for applicants that would help indicate whether an individual had a specific skill.

The computers available, although offering capabilities only previously dreamed of, were cumbersome to program. Many of the programmers and analysts of the time were engineers and scientists, and the applications they developed tended to serve the areas they knew, or which were pressing for assistance. During this period, only the larger companies could afford programmers. But some of these companies began to recognize the value of having information available on their employees. They learned over time that collecting and analyzing such information was expensive but sometimes necessary. Gradually, new applications were developed; however, these occurred in a piece-meal fashion rather than as a total solution.

Much of the data was collected on Hollerith cards. These 80-column paper cards were punched with code to record basic information. Often, several cards were required to record all of the information on one employee. When it was determined that additional information was required, new cards were often needed. Even with the use of magnetic tape, only a "card image" was available to store information. Since the storage media was so inflexible, most new applications were developed to handle specific needs. One file might hold basic personnel biographical data, while another contained skill information, and still others time information, training information, etc. Very few applications were developed where the full picture of an employee was available. This was the era of the second generation computer.

THE MID-1960s

As organizations realized the power of the computer, more and more applications were developed, and inefficiencies corrected. Computer storage was relatively expensive, yet there was much duplication of information. Dozens of personnel records could exist for each individual, each having an employee identifier recorded as well as name and department. Eventually it was realized that this duplication could be prevented if the records could be longer. As well, it was realized that information, if properly captured once, near the source, could potentially be accessed for a variety of uses. Time worked, for example, was generally captured to determine the amount to pay the employee. In many cases, other applications were developed separately to capture labour distribution and product costs. It would clearly be beneficial to tie these records together, and when possible, link them to one employee record.

The adoption of this "longitudinal file" concept coincided with the development and introduction of the IBM/360 and related mainframe computers. Management Information Systems (MIS) departments became involved in massive projects to track information flow and create new applications that managed whole business events. Some of these projects included payroll and personnel applications, but generally speaking, payroll received more attention. This was a trend that would continue for some time, as it was seen to be more important to pay people accurately and on time than to use automation for other human resources management purposes.

During the 1960s, a number of very large projects were initiated to develop systems to manage all of an organization's business information needs in one application, including personnel and payroll. While conceptually feasible, the technology did not exist to support the complexity of these systems, so that these initiatives were generally not successful.

The American Equal Pay Act of 1963 is said to have provided the most significant business case of all for developing an automated personnel system (Walker, 1993). This legislation was designed to ensure equality in pay between men and women for work that was substantially equal. To comply, companies needed data and statistics. Employers needed to collect large amounts of data about their employees, including job content, pay levels, and so on. Existing personnel systems were generally unprepared to meet these needs. The Equal Pay Act of 1963 was followed by Title VII of the Civil Rights Act (1964). This act forbade discrimination in employment (as well as housing, education, and other areas) and subsequent amendments were enacted to remedy these deficiencies. An Equal Opportunities Commission (EOC) was established, and it brought a new discipline to personnel processes. It also set forth recordkeeping rules for employers with 25 or more employees.

There were some success stories in the 1960s. White collar and clerical labour costs for processing paper-handling tasks in the larger banks and insurance companies were high. These resources were not unionized, and management consequently saw opportunities to save by paring administrative and turnover costs. They saw benefits in automating the processing of personnel documents, and in reducing turnover and training costs. This was accomplished with automated systems that tracked skills and assisted in the selection of the "right person for the right job" (Walker, 1982).

It was in the 1960s that the first commercial HRMS packages were developed. In May 1965, several individuals who worked at IBM got together and formed a new company called Information Science Incorporated (known as INSci); this company was to develop the first packaged personnel system. Their first product, PICS (Personnel Information Communication System), used the concepts of skills systems. InSci developed a system to match jobs with people: résumés were coded and matched against existing job criteria to assist employers in filling jobs.

Although the first InSci system was not a tremendous success, it generated some interest with employers who were experiencing problems with their personnel records functions. InSci responded by developing a number of customized personnel systems to meet the specific needs of individual companies. In 1970, for instance, it developed HRS II, a mainframe-based HRMS system designed for banks.

Western military forces quickly became leaders in applying the development and implementation of computer technology to human resources. In an early example, the United States Air Force Human Resources Laboratory (AFHRL) distributed thousands of task inventories to airmen in all enlisted jobs in the Air Force (Christal, 1974). Through the use of computers and statistical software, called the Comprehensive Occupational Data Analysis Programs (CODAP), these data were analyzed to identify different jobs, job families, and the requirements for each. Such efforts not only established the most effective and comprehensive approach to job analysis yet attempted, but clearly identified the potential power and impact of the use of computers in personnel.

Many of the programs put into place by military forces to select the right people for the right job were copied by their civilian counterparts, expanded to include attitudinal surveys and other human resources tools. For instance, Ontario Hydro, a Canadian company, successfully used CODAP in the 1970s and 1980s (Haltrecht, 1980).

These developments resulted in a heightened awareness of the fact that human resources was an increasingly significant part of a company's budget. By controlling these costs, a company could be more competitive. Further, the importance of employee morale was recognized as crucial to retaining the best people. Motivational and opinion surveys consequently evolved.

New human resources programs were developed to ensure that a supply of properly skilled and motivated employees were available (for an overview of state-of-the-art human resources practices during this period, see French (1974)). Job evaluation systems were created to rate jobs according to established criteria. Salary ranges were established; so too were performance criteria, and performance evaluations were developed to track progress. Pay was thus linked to performance.

THE 1970s

In the United States in the early 1970s, government legislation related to Equal Employment Opportunity (EEO) and other employee programs forced most companies of a few thousand employees or more to develop automated personnel systems. During this time, the cost of storing and processing information started to fall, and pre-programmed commercial HRMSs made personnel systems less expensive.

Amendments to American EEO legislation in the 1970s established the concept of "affirmative action." This new legislation created requirements for calculating "availability," setting goals and targets, producing utilization reports, and generating workforce analysis. This level of legislation was the strongest to date and American business began to seriously monitor their workforce in order to comply with the recordkeeping requirements. Computerization was the most efficient way for many larger companies to comply with the legislation. Many organizations added new data elements to their existing payroll systems, as this area had already been automated.

In the late 1970s, the scope of systems was expanded greatly for many organizations. Many HRMS projects were completed, but many others were abandoned along the way. Some were halted when they ran out of funding while others simply ran out of time, and a new project was started. This was a frustrating period for those involved with HRMS projects. The human resources function turned out to be much more difficult to automate than many people anticipated.

THE 1980s

In the late 1970s and early 1980s, personnel functions went through a transformation (Walker, 1980, documented "leading edge" human resources management practices from this era). The number of functions and services offered grew: job analysis became more rigorous; compensation became quite complex; employment equity programs were put in place; large investments were made in staff development; employee testing became quite common; and organization development arrived. Each area required specialized expertise. Even mid-size companies (those with 1000 to 4000 employees) found that they could justify their own HRMS. Many did not need the power of a mainframe, and chose instead to utilize a mid-size computer. Packaged HRMS products were utilized that did not take a lot of time to customize, install, and maintain.

The early HRMS packages had many limitations, and by the early 1980s many organizations were experiencing problems. The number of processes to be automated were growing in number and complexity and the available packages could not readily accommodate them. Seemingly straightforward applications such as recruitment and selection left vast gaps in what could easily be automated. This reflected the recordkeeping basis of the HRMS systems in place at the time.

Existing HRMS were generally not as effective as they might have been because they were not designed to meet the specific requirements of the host organization. For example, the process of transferring an existing employee from one job to another in the same organization may sound simple. But this is generally not the case, as company policies and labour agreements can come into play. Each process must be fully reviewed and agreed upon before it can be decided that a process is correct and work can commence in automating it. Another example is defining an "applicant." The definitions may differ by union affiliation or by plant site.

THE LATE 1980s AND EARLY 1990s

The introduction of the microcomputer or personal computer (PC) had a dramatic impact on human resources (Pasqualetto, 1993), for it offered some relief for the problems created by rapidly changing requirements. This relief came in several ways:

♦ Microcomputers were a lot less expensive than mainframes and mid-ranges.

♦ Micro-based systems could be installed in a few short months whereas larger systems could take years.

♦ Micro-based systems could be maintained by the HR user.

♦ They were easy to modify.

♦ They were easy to use.

♦ They could be used in conjunction with office productive tools such as spread sheets, document processing, other databases, and electronic mail.

When microcomputers first became available to the business community, HR applications had to be built by the user. Few, if any packages were available, and local MIS resources were not yet trained to program the microcomputers. The use of microcomputers in many organizations was originally banned or severely restricted: MIS departments put such strong impediments in the way that most users could not acquire a micro without going through impossible roadblocks. A number of reasons for restricting access to computers were provided, but many micro-users today believe that the primary explanation lies in the insecurity of the then mainframe-oriented MIS department, which feared loss of control and of jobs.

However, many of the concerns voiced have actually turned out to be valid. Some of these include:

- Inadequate or no routine back-up of important files

- Data not secure

- Lack of standards when developing supplementary databases in-house, incompatible files

- Lack of adequate documentation for user-built systems and subsystems

- Databases not integrated, resulting in redundancy of data, inconsistent or outdated data, or data in multiple systems that do not match

This revolution continues, however, and MIS resistance has given way to reluctant acquiescence or to enthusiastic support.

During the late 1980s, the major issue facing HRMS was the marriage of microcomputers to mainframes. Connectivity was an issue. In large companies, some of the business applications remained on mainframes and the microcomputer was used like a "dumb terminal," merely to access the HRMS on-line to the mainframe. There were many problems related to complex access protocols and data standards. Moving data back and forth between mainframe databases and micro-based productivity tools was very difficult. Downloading a subset of HRMS data to a spreadsheet such as LOTUS for analysis, for example, was very difficult. Users found it difficult to enjoy the full benefit of the information resource available only on the mainframe HRMS. Also, microcomputer users found it difficult or impossible to share information that was only resident on their micro-units.

During the late 1980s great improvements were made in linking computers together into networks. Wide Area Networks (WANs) and Local Area Networks (LANs) became possible after improvements in the technology (Miracle, 1993). LANs, both independent from or connected to the mainframe, provided access to common data for users who had common interests, such as HR. Human Resources, however, was seldom the first, or even the second function in a company to take advantage of this new technology (Wetherbe et al., 1994).

Some of the reasons for Human Resources being slower in utilizing networks were related to the following considerations:

1. In large companies, the HRMS was already established on the mainframe and provided some level of satisfactory service.

2. Moving the HRMS off the mainframe and onto a LAN, or at least integrating the two, had to be "cost-justified" before closing down the mainframe-based HRMS.

3. There was a distinct lack of micro- or LAN-based HRMS applications available.

4. The first applications were generally "stand alone applications," for use on one microcomputer, which would deny access to others in Human Resources and to line management.

5. Customizing a stand-alone micro-HRMS application to work on a network was expensive and time-consuming.

6. Most human resources practitioners were not as computer literate as their colleagues in Finance and Operations. As a result, they often failed to convince management to invest in the new technology.

7. There were many technical problems associated with HRMS installation. End users were simply not prepared to contend with the numerous problems with downtime, hardware problems, lost data, and new releases of software. These were not sophisticated technology users; they were HR users with little technical training and a low tolerance for paving new ground.

Basically, there was a reluctance to try new solutions even when they did become available, especially when it was widely believed that LANs were unreliable and that a mainframe offered more stability. This issue was not really resolved in many organizations until employees who were more comfortable with computers entered the HR workforce (Pasqualetto, 1993; Richards-Carpenter, 1994).

In the past, human resources practitioners were generally not knowledgeable or skilled in data automation or computer-related areas, and so were dependent on systems analysts and other "experts" to design and implement systems for them. However, these systems/computer experts frequently did not understand the content areas for which they were designing the systems, leading to communications problems. This in turn led to the design and implementation of systems that were not as effective or as efficient as they otherwise might have been. Because the human resources generalists did not understand the potential inherent in automation, and the systems specialists generally did not understand human resources requirements at anything but a superficial level, many such systems wound up being little more than an automation of existing paper files and practices (Rampton and Doran, 1994).

To bypass these communications problems, the systems people developed and adopted an extensive, complicated set of needs analysis and project management protocols designed to obtain user-input and feedback at various stages. The problem with this process was that it was "owned and operated" by the management information specialists. Too often it was not applied under the direction of someone knowledgeable in both human resources and computer applications and ended up automating current or even past practices rather than allowing for future innovations. Adding to this the fact that the process was long and inefficient, it is no wonder that many of the systems developed were verging on obsolescence before being implemented (Stright, 1993).

Because human resources practitioners have not traditionally been computer experts, and especially in small organizations purchasing a human resources management information system for the first time, the following problems may be encountered:

1. Practitioners may go with what they are comfortable, in terms of implementing a system that merely automates existing paper and labour-intensive practices.

2. Management information specialists may be given the job of conducting needs analysis, choosing software, and implementing the system, without adequate awareness of human resources requirements.

3. Human resources practitioners and others in the organization may be persuaded to purchase and implement a system that is more or less sophisticated than the organization requires at its current level of technical evolution.

Thus, the marriage of Human Resources (HR) and Information Systems (IS) has not always been as smooth as it might have been. Human resources and information systems professionals tended to have very different approaches and philosophical outlooks and, as a consequence, neither understood each other nor communicated well. However, in the early 1980s an organization dedicated to bridging this communications gap began to gain prominence.

The International Association for Human Resource Information Management (IHRIM) was formed in 1996 after CHRSP and HRSP joined to form one international association. The Canadian Association of Human Resource Systems Professionals (CHRSP) was an organization of about 800 members across Canada. The Association of Human Resource Systems Professionals (HRSP) had over 4000 members in the United States and had been affiliated with CHRSP for a number of years. In 1996, with the formation of the new international association, IHRIM has over 6000 members in 30 chapters in Canada and the United States. Chapters are being formed in a number of other countries as well.

Members of IHRIM meet both regionally and annually on a regular basis. Each chapter holds four or more meetings annually, with some chapters meeting monthly to discuss issues related to the effective management of human resources information. Each spring a large conference is held in a major U.S. centre where a large vendor exposition is held in conjunction with key note and educational events. A similar vendor expo is held each fall in a major Canadian centre. Professional development seminars are also offered on a regular basis in many major North American centres.

IHRIM has a professional magazine that is published every two months called *IHRIM.link*, which replaces the former publication of CHRSP and HRSP, *Resource and Review*. IHRIM hosts a home page at http.//www.ihrim.org/, which offers extensive information on the association, its goals and objectives, and chapter events.

◆ ◆ ◆

EVOLVING HUMAN RESOURCES MANAGEMENT INFORMATION REQUIREMENTS FOR THE LATE 1990s AND BEYOND

Flexibility and effectiveness in the strategic structuring and managing of human resources is becoming increasingly important (Hennecke, 1984; Kazanas, 1988; Niehaus, 1987; Rummler and Brache, 1991). While we are in a period of great change, and there is uncertainty as to how best to achieve these goals, it is clear that doing so requires data gathering, storage, retrieval, and analysis from an appropriate HRMS (Ceriello, 1991; Lederer, 1991).

Valaskakis, Coull, and Clermont (1991) have pointed out that, for most organizations, corporate success will increasingly depend on the coordinated, strategic management of the organization's human resources and information technology. These authors state: "The management challenge of the 90's will be to develop a close partnership between the strategist and the information technologist. People and information management will be done in concert (p. 20)."

◆ ◆ ◆
BUSINESS/TECHNOLOGICAL TRENDS

In the future, those responsible for developing, implementing, operating, and maintaining an HRMS must have a broad knowledge of: the organization's human resources programs; the relationship between human resources programs and other organizational functions, particularly strategic planning and operations; the potential inherent in computer and data automation; and how to capitalize on this potential, and explain and "sell it" to others in the organization (Bloom, 1991; Mackey, 1991; Ceriello, 1991).

An HRMS must therefore be geared to the strategic and business requirements of the organization, and harmonized with its other systems (Mackey, 1991). It must also be sufficiently flexible to adapt and grow with evolving requirements and technology (Stambaugh, 1991). Those responsible for designing and implementing new systems must understand the evolving strategic, business, and techological trends of the organization, and its external environment (Bloom, 1991).

For many organizations, these evolving trends may be summarized as follows:

1. Office and process automation technologies are profoundly modifying the organization of work with the following outcomes:
   - the information-based organization is flatter, requiring significantly fewer levels of management; and,
   - the nature of management is changing, emphasizing technical knowledge and facilitation rather than supervision.

2. Managerial, professional, and administrative occupations are increasingly relying on distributed computing as an essential part of their business.

3. Computers are increasingly used to gather, analyze, and communicate or report crucial information, facilitated by electronic mail and local area networks.

4. Information technology can increase the speed and quality of managerial decision making.

5. There has been a shift in office automation from support staff to business professionals.

6. Office automation has become a continuing, dynamic process of combining all the interactive elements of the office: people, information, functions, and procedures (Valaskakis et al., 1991).

◆ ◆ ◆

MODELS OF THE HUMAN RESOURCES FUNCTION

Many human resources practitioners begin as employment counsellors, compensation and benefits clerks, or labour relations officers, whether directly from university or college, or on transfer from other functions (Schuler, 1984). They may spend their careers administering or managing human resources programs such as those outlined below.

- ◆ Recruiting and Selection
- ◆ Training and Development
- ◆ Time and Attendance
- ◆ Payroll
- ◆ Compensation and Benefits
- ◆ Employee/Labour Relations
- ◆ Employee/Performance Problems
- ◆ Employee Assistance
- ◆ Equity Programs
- ◆ Retirement/Pensions

As organizations mature, they generally find that they require more effective means for assessing, keeping track of, and managing their human resources (Ceriello, 1991; Kavanagh et al., 1990). Recently, the impetus for this has come from the need to develop tools to satisfy legislative requirements, as well as the need to respond more effectively and efficiently to evolving strategic/business pressures (Doran and Rampton, 1994). These tools include job analysis, work planning and review, performance/personnel assessment, and an HRMS (Cascio and Thacker, 1994).

FIGURE 1.1 A Human Resources Model

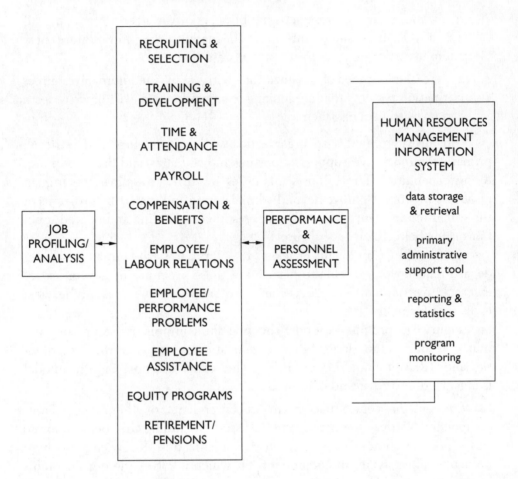

With respect to HRMSs, Lederer (1991) argues that a broader range of organizations are finding that they require automation to handle their human resources information management needs. Furthermore, as discussed in succeeding chapters, there are many new developments in HRMS software and hardware. This means that many systems that have been in place for five or ten years are now obsolete, particularly if they were not originally based on sound needs analysis or on state-of-the-art technology existing at the time of implementation. A combination of circumstances, therefore, have conspired to make this a time when many organizations are looking to obtain a new HRMS. Included among these are:

1. relatively small but growing organizations looking for their first system;

2. organizations that are restructuring because of the need to be competitive in the increasingly international marketplace, and require new systems as strategic tools in support of this goal; and

3. an increasing number of organizations with established human resources information systems that are looking to upgrade their existing systems to keep up with evolving technology.

An HRMS provides an organization with data storage and retrieval, primary administrative support, reporting and statistics, and program monitoring capabilities. These four capabilities in turn may allow the human resources function to move beyond administering and managing programs of the sort listed in Figure 1-1, to human resources planning and related functions (Horsfield, 1991—see Figure 1-2).

As noted by Cascio and Thacker (1994), progressive Human Resources departments have been able to place all of these programs in the context of external environmental influences and the organization's strategic/business focus (see Figure 1-3).

Figure 1-3 provides a model showing the components comprising the human resources functions of most organizations, along with their interrelationships (Rampton and Doran, 1994). The reader will note that this model is organized into rows and columns.

ROW 1 contains contextual, strategic components of the model. Thus, component C1 deals with the external issues, including the socioeconomic and legislative context impinging on the organization. Knowledge of these influences affect issues in component A1, which involves the organization's strategic, business planning processes.

ROW 2 contains forecasting and planning processes required to identify the need/potential inherent in Row 1, and translate these into effective human resources programs.

ROW 3 contains the programs that most practitioners recognize as the traditional human resources functions, including job/position evaluation, recruiting and selection, training and development, labour relations, compensation and benefits, performance management and evaluation, etc.

ROW 4 involves the program evaluation or auditing function required to ensure that the previous components are working as they should. Thus, the

FIGURE 1.2 **Addition of Human Resources/Succession Planning to the Human Resources Model**

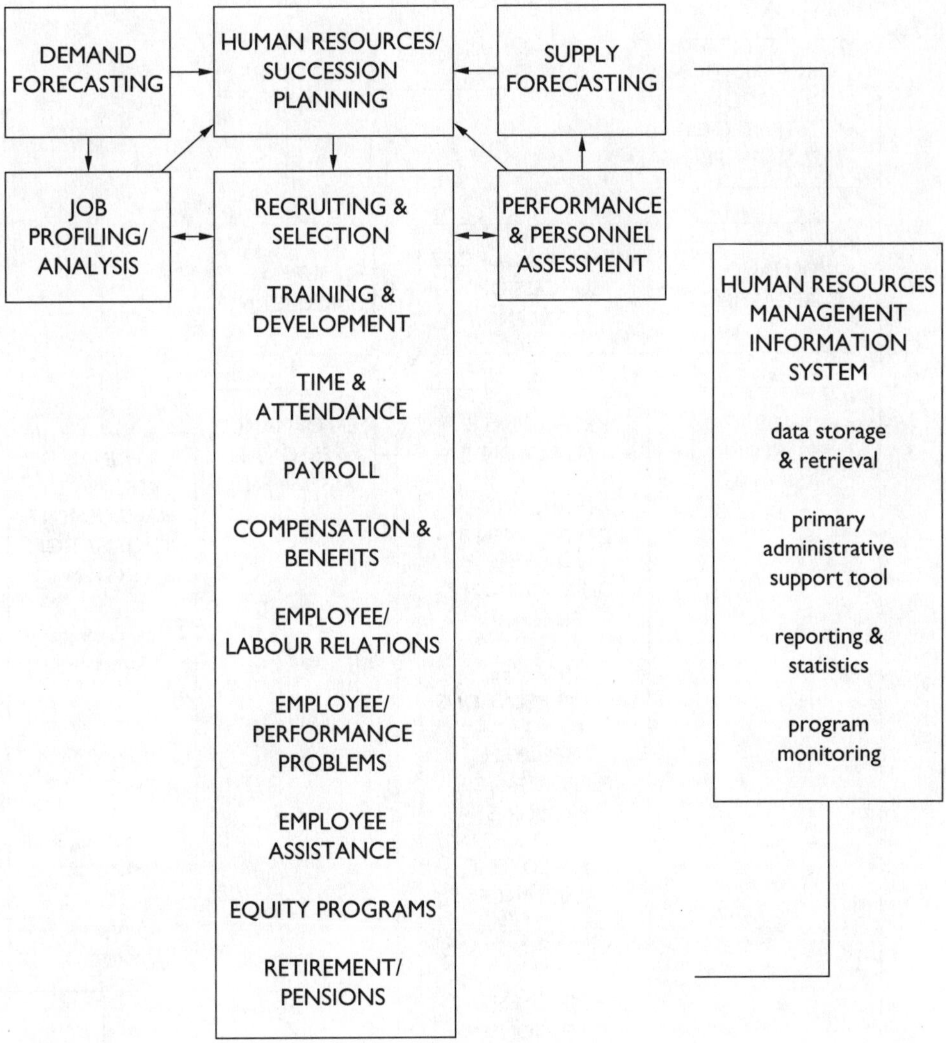

```
┌──────────────┐   ┌──────────────────┐   ┌──────────────┐
│   DEMAND     │   │ HUMAN RESOURCES/ │   │    SUPPLY    │
│ FORECASTING  │──▶│   SUCCESSION     │◀──│ FORECASTING  │
│              │   │    PLANNING      │   │              │
└──────────────┘   └──────────────────┘   └──────────────┘
```

| DEMAND FORECASTING | HUMAN RESOURCES/ SUCCESSION PLANNING | SUPPLY FORECASTING |

| JOB PROFILING/ ANALYSIS | RECRUITING & SELECTION | PERFORMANCE & PERSONNEL ASSESSMENT | HUMAN RESOURCES MANAGEMENT INFORMATION SYSTEM |

TRAINING & DEVELOPMENT

TIME & ATTENDANCE

PAYROLL

COMPENSATION & BENEFITS

EMPLOYEE/ LABOUR RELATIONS

EMPLOYEE/ PERFORMANCE PROBLEMS

EMPLOYEE ASSISTANCE

EQUITY PROGRAMS

RETIREMENT/ PENSIONS

data storage & retrieval

primary administrative support tool

reporting & statistics

program monitoring

model is not just driven from the top down. This and other components should feed back to and influence functions higher in the model, so that problems are self-correcting.

COLUMN A consists of components that assess or reflect the "demand" or requirements for human resources. That is, the global requirements of the

FIGURE 1.3 General Human Resources Model

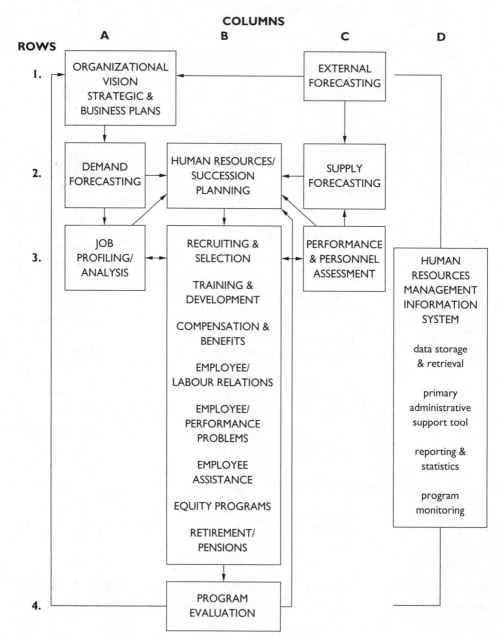

organization should be reflected in its strategic and business plans; these, in turn, are further analyzed and planned for in the organization's demand forecasting. The organization's strategic/business plans should also drive the structure of the organization, which are then reflected in the job description/job evaluation process.

COLUMN B consists of what one commonly thinks of as the "traditional human resources functions." These are the functions and processes that serve as the link, interface, or means of satisfying gaps between the requirement for human resources at various levels and its supply.

COLUMN C consists of components that assess or reflect the "supply" of human resources. That is, external conditions determine the skills and availability of individuals that might be recruited, as well as socioeconomic and legislative influences on other components in the model. These, in turn, can be further analyzed and planned for the organization's supply forecasting. Performance management and evaluation processes not only represent the means of planning for and getting the work of the organization done through the efforts of its employees, but also reflect and provide an inventory of the skills, expertise, and qualification of the internal workforce.

COLUMN D represents the various modules and tools that, together, comprise the HRMS.

Not all of the components of this model may be included in every human resources department. All of them exist, however, whether explicitly or implicitly, in every organization.

The challenge of the human resources professional is to understand the relationships among the various components of the model and to become proficient in using them effectively. As mentioned above, many human resources practitioners do not understand that their role could extend beyond programs outlined in row 3, column B of the model. Others understand the need for demand and supply forecasting cum human resources/succession planning (row 2, columns A, B, and C), but are unable to use this knowledge to provide input into and influence the organization's strategic plan (row 1, columns A, B, and C). Furthermore, they are unlikely to gain this influence and the status that comes with it without a sound working knowledge of how to use an HRMS effectively (column D) in support of the remaining programs (Broderick and Boudreau, 1992; Kossek et al., 1994).

◆ ◆ ◆
SUMMARY

This chapter began by providing an historical overview of HRMSs, from their earliest beginnings, as a means of compiling the first United States Census, through the evolution of Hollerith computer cards, "batch" payroll application, mainframe driven, tape-resident longitudinal files to today's direct-access, PC-networked systems.

The chapter went on to describe how, in today's dynamic business environment, those responsible for planning for and developing a new HRMS are faced with many challenges. A new or updated HRMS must be fully capable of adapting to new requirements. These trends have been reviewed to set the stage for more detailed discussion on how process re-engineering and other methods discussed later in the book may be used to define requirements, and then to plan, develop, implement, and maintain an HRMS.

EXERCISES

1. It was suggested in this chapter that, to be effective, those responsible for designing and implementing new information systems must understand the strategic context of the organization. Why is this so important? How might one undertake to develop this understanding?

2. Suppose you were put in charge of an HRMS with all the capabilities depicted in Figure 1-3. Describe how you might use these capabilities to convince senior management to accord the human resources function generally, and your role more specifically, more influence in strategic/business planning. What do you think would be the biggest problems you would face? How would you overcome them?

3. In the past, human resources professionals have often defined what they felt they required in a new HRMS and then left it to information systems professionals to develop the technical specifications for a new system, develop or purchase the appropriate software, and implement the system. What are some of the strengths and weaknesses inherent in this division of responsibilities? Is there a better way? Please explain.

References

Berry, W.E. 1993. "New Role for HR Requires a New Vision for Management Systems." *HR Focus* 70, no. 3 (March): 22.

Bloom, N.L. 1991. "Corporate Needs for HR Information." In A.L. Lederer, ed., *Handbook of Human Resources Information Systems*. New York: Warren, Gorham and Lamont.

Broderick, R., and J.W. Boudreau. 1992. "Human Resource Management, Information Technology, and the Competitive Edge." *The Executive* 5, no. 2 (May): 7–17.

Cascio, W.F., and J.W. Thacker. 1994. *Managing Human Resources*. Toronto: McGraw-Hill Ryerson.

Ceriello, V.R. 1991. *Human Resource Management Systems: Strategy, Tactics, and Techniques*. Toronto: Maxwell Macmillan.

Christal, R.E. 1974. *The United States Air Force Occupational Research Project, AFHRL-TR-73-75*. Lackland Airforce Base, Texas: Airforce, Occupational Research Division.

CHRSP Resource Magazine 5, no. 3, 1995.

Doran, J.A., and G.M. Rampton. 1994. "Making a Business Case for a New Human Resources Management Information System." *Canadian Human Resources Systems Professionals Resource Magazine* (June): 4–8.

Encyclopedia Britannica (Micropaedia, vol. V). 1975. Toronto: Helen Hemingway Benton, p. 92.

French, W. 1974. *The Personnel Management Process: Human Resources Administration*, 3rd ed. Boston, Mass.: Houghton Mifflin.

Haltrecht, E. 1980. "CODAP: Introduction and Uses in a Large Public Facility." In G.M. Rampton, ed., *Proceedings of the 22nd Annual Conference of the Military Testing Association*. Toronto: Canadian Forces Personnel Applied Research Unit, ha10 - ha115.

Hennecke, M. 1984. "The People Side of Strategic Planning." *Training* (November): 25–34.

Horsfield, D. 1991. "Human Resources Planning Applications." In A.L. Lederer, ed., *Handbook of Human Resources Information Systems*. New York: Warren, Gorham and Lamont.

Kavanagh, M.J., H.G. Gueutal, and S.I. Tannenbaum. 1990. *Human Resource Information Systems: Development and Application*. Boston, Mass.: PWS-Kent.

Kazanas, H.C. 1988. *Strategic Human Resources Planning and Management*. Englewoods Cliffs, N.J.: Prentice-Hall.

Lederer, A.L. 1991. *Handbook of Human Resources Information Systems*. New York: Warren, Gorham and Lamont.

Mackey, C.B. 1991. "Conducting a Preliminary Study for an HRIS Project." In A.L. Lederer, ed., *Handbook of Human Resources Information Systems*. New York: Warren, Gorham and Lamont.

Miracle, M. 1993. "The Trend to Client/Server is Maturing into Acceptance." *National Underwriter Life/Health/Financial Services* 97, no. 45 (November): 2–8.

Mueller, B. 1994. "Changing Attitudes Help Shape HR Systems." *Systems Management* 22, no. 3 (March): 82–89.

Niehaus, R.J. 1987. *Strategic Human Resources Planning Applications*. New York: Plenum Press.

Pasqualetto, J. 1993. "New Competencies Define the HRIS Manager's Future Role." *Personnel Journal* 72, no. 1 (January): 91–99.

Rampton, G.M., and J.A. Doran. 1994. "A Practitioner's Guide for a New

HRIS." Paper presented at the 9th Annual CHRSP Conference (October 4–7).

Richards-Carpenter, C. 1994. "Personnel takes Pragmatic Approach to Technology." *Personnel Management* 26, no. 7 (July): 55–56.

Rummler, G.A., and A.P. Brache. 1991. "Managing the White Space." *Training* (January): 55–70.

Schuler, R.S. 1984. *Personnel and Human Resources Management*, 2nd ed. New York: West Publishing.

Stambaugh, R. 1991. "Determining HRIS Requirements." In A.L. Lederer, ed., *Handbook of Human Resources Information Systems*. New York: Warren, Gorham and Lamont.

Stright, J.F. 1993. "Strategic Goals Guide HRMS Development." *Personnel Journal* (September): 68–78.

United States Department of Labor. 1967. "Equal Pay for Equal Work under the Fair Labor Standards Act." *Interpractices Bulletin*. Title 27, Part 800.

Valaskakis, K., R. Coull, and R. Clermont, R. 1991. *Information Technology and Human Resources: Prospects for the Decade*. Report prepared for the Canadian Human Resources Scanning Association. Toronto (April).

Walker, A.J. 1982. *A Project Team Guide to Building an Effective Personnel*

Information System. New York: Van Nostrand Reinhold.

Walker, J.W. 1980. *Human Resource Planning*. New York: McGraw Hill.

Wetherbe, J.C., N.P. Vitalari, and A. Milner. 1994. "Key Trends in Systems Development in Europe and North America." *Journal of Global Informations Management* 2, no. 2 (Spring): 5–20.

2

The Need for an Effective HRMS

INTRODUCTION

To be competitive in today's demanding and rapidly changing business environment, management needs accurate and timely information on the organization's most important resource—its employees. Many organizations are finding that the traditional ways of managing human resources information are not up to the challenge, and must be updated or completely revamped. This chapter begins by discussing some of reasons why organizations are coming to this conclusion. Included is a discussion of the organizational information needs that a modern HRMS can satisfy (Berry, 1993; Mueller, 1994).

Human resources information requirements are becoming more complex and demanding for most organizations (Broderick and Boudreau, 1992; Rampton and Doran, 1994). This is due, in part, to the need to comply with greatly increased requirements for information to satisfy government legislation in such areas as employment equity, pay equity, pensions, payroll, and taxation (Cascio and Thacker, 1994; Fogel, 1984; Hunter, 1986; National Committee on Pay Equity, 1987). It is also due to the fact that more effective access to workforce information is becoming more and more necessary if organizations are to be competitive in today's rapidly changing business environment (Burak, 1980; Ceriello, 1991; Director, 1988; Kazanas, 1988).

Information technology has evolved to the point where organizations with as few as 50 to 100 employees are finding it cost effective to implement and maintain an HRMS (Lederer, 1991). Companies that have never had an HRMS are exploring the feasibility of implementing their first system. In larger organizations, line managers and human resources practitioners are discovering that technological advancements have rendered existing systems obsolete, leading them to believe that their organizations would benefit from either modernizing an existing HRMS or purchasing a new one (Rampton and Doran, 1994).

Organizations will often decide to implement a new HRMS either to develop the capability to do the applications described below, or to do them better than is possible using the technology currently available to the organization.

◆ ◆ ◆
EMPLOYEE LISTS

This is a simple but very common and important application (Doran and Rampton, 1994). Most organizations have accurate information on each employee in paper files, including his or her work or home address. Such information may also be available in automated form in payroll files, but it may not be readily accessible to identify different groups of employees or to communicate with them for a variety of purposes, such as:

1. distributing surveys to assess employee attitudes to proposed changes in administrative policies or benefits programs;

2. communicating widely regarding employee recognition programs;

3. advising employees about changes regarding administrative or operational programs; or

4. saving money on postage by sending payroll tax returns to each individual's work address rather than to their homes.

There are many occasions during the course of a year where managers at all levels are required to identify employees with specific characteristics, and to produce tables of the numbers of individuals having these characteristics. These lists should be simple to produce, but many organizations do not have the means of doing so quickly and accurately (Doran and Rampton 1994). Such lists should allow employees to be grouped by plant, department, sex, age, years of service, grade, salary, employee affiliation, employment status (part-time/full-time), etc., for such purposes as:

1. providing a record of all the employees reporting to a new manager;

2. documenting all employees in Department A, age 60 and older, listing name, job title, grade, age, length of service, as background information for a human resources planning exercise;

3. producing a list of casual employees by time in position to monitor violations of a collective agreement; and

4. producing a list of full and vacant positions by department.

◆ ◆ ◆
ATTRITION REPORTING/MONITORING

If Canadian organizations are to compete successfully in the increasingly international marketplace, employees must be regarded as a renewable resource to a much greater extent than they are now (Berry, 1993). This means attracting well-qualified applicants, making the most of their talents through progressive training and effective employment practices, and retaining the individuals that you want to keep. There is a considerable body of research evidence that suggests that North American organizations lag behind others in the industrialized world in making the most of their human assets (Downey and McCamus, 1990; Larson and Blue, 1991).

As automation and information technology become more pervasive, investment in associated skills in a broader range of employees increases (Valaskakis et al., 1991). The generic skills of typing or shorthand for secretaries or administrative assistants, for example, have largely been replaced by word processing, spreadsheets, electronic mail, and electronic information and storage devices, all resident on local area networks (Miracle, 1993). Further, these applications are often tailored to the specific organization, so that individuals with experience in one organization may require retraining before they can be fully productive in a new organization.

Thus, in today's competitive environment, an organization requires effective recruiting, selection, training, compensation, and employment programs, along with effective information systems to support them (Kavanagh et al., 1990; Niehaus, 1987). It also requires the means of monitoring who is leaving the organization, and for what reasons (see Murray and Rampton, 1986). Depending on an analysis of the reasons for attrition, its consequences, and the options available to the organization, the company could:

1. accept the situation and
   a. do nothing; or
   b. respond to the high turnover by increasing recruiting and training costs; or
2. try to decrease attrition by:
   a. increasing compensation and benefits in an effort to make it more attractive for individuals to stay; or
   b. addressing motivation problems by examining leadership practices, increasing employee empowerment, quality of working life, etc.

◆ ◆ ◆
EMPLOYMENT EQUITY TRACKING/MONITORING

For many years employment equity legislation of one sort or another has applied to all employers and employees in Canada and the United States (National Committee on Pay Equity, 1987; Rampton, 1989). Corporations are finding that minority group recruiting is good business, as it broadens the population from which to select individuals with hard-to-find skills (Bozman, 1993). As documented in Chapter 1, legislation has made it absolutely essential for organizations to develop accurate information gathering, retrieval, and analysis systems capable of:

1. reporting on the numbers and status in the organization of individuals from four designated groups (women, visible minorities, individuals with disabilities, and aboriginal people);

2. supporting the development of action plans for ensuring that individuals from the designated groups are approximately represented in all functions and levels in the organization in the same proportion that they are represented in the population from whence employees are recruited; and

3. monitoring the effectiveness of these action plans and modifying them as required.

A complication for those organizations covered by both federal and provincial legislation is that the reporting requirements for each, while similar in principle, differ significantly in format and detail.

Over the past few years, legislative changes have led to increasing pressures and constraints for most employers. Pay and employment legislation, for example, have had a significant impact on the field of human resources generally, and HRMS specifically, as systems must be adapted to provide for data and reporting requirements.

◆ ◆ ◆
SALARY/BENEFITS BUDGET REPORTING

These reports must be able to be integrated into routine budget and monitoring processes (McCaffrey, 1988). As with other assets, it is important to be able to accurately and efficiently track salary and benefits costs to date, and to make projections against authorized budgets, given staffing levels and authorized staff complement. This capacity is crucial to budget management and budget planning.

◆ ◆ ◆
SALARY/BENEFITS MODELLING

The compensation (salary and benefits) structure of most organizations having more than one or two hundred people can become quite complex. Yet situations arise (e.g., contract negotiations, pay equity planning, corporate restructuring, social contract planning) in which it is essential to be able to quickly estimate the costs of various changes in salary and benefits plans (Belcher and Atchison, 1987; Burgess, 1984). In a typical application, the organization might have a total amount of money that can be divided between salary and benefits in different ways (McCaffrey, 1988). A series of quick but realistic "what-if" analyses might have be done to demonstrate that whatever is negotiated does not exceed budget limitations. Horror stories exist in many organization about the lasting effects of agreements that were not accurately costed.

◆ ◆ ◆
SENIORITY LISTS

Seniority is an important consideration governing employment conditions in many union contracts. Included are rights to:

◆ Overtime

◆ Vacation scheduling

◆ Bids for new positions where more than one employee meets the qualifications

◆ Bumping when positions are declared redundant

Employers are typically responsible for producing accurate seniority lists to be sent to the union and posted to be seen by the union membership. Errors or omissions in such lists are then open to grievance/arbitration processes.

In situations where seniority can be affected by different kinds of leave or working relationships, calculating seniority can be complicated. However, being able to produce accurate lists is very important to the organization, the union, the individuals concerned, and the relationships among all three.

◆ ◆ ◆
APPLICANT TRACKING

In the current economic climate there are typically many applicants for each job advertised. It is important to be able to cross-reference applicants from one competition to another, and to be able to track each applicant through the selection process. Frequently, applicants passed over from one competition may be a good match for another. If this matching can be done effectively and efficiently, it is possible to save significantly on recruiting costs, such as advertising and administration.

It should also be possible for the information that is collected to be passed on to other human resources systems modules. For example, biographical information should not have to be collected more than once, and information on applicant characteristics should be available for employment equity reporting.

◆ ◆ ◆
GRIEVANCE TRACKING AND ANALYSIS

In unionized settings there is an obligation on both management and unions to process grievances according to steps and timing stipulated in union contracts. An effective automated grievance management information system can save money, avoid unnecessary ill-will, and avoid the prospect of losing grievances or arbitrations for technical reasons.

The information gathered to manage grievance processes is also very important in providing a picture of the "who, why, what, where," and of the incidence of grievances and arbitrations. By analyzing trends one can often identify problem areas that can be worked on to reduce grievances and effect better employee relations. An important aspect of this process is to feed back to managers the types of grievances that have arisen over particular time periods, as well as their disposition and cost to the organization (see Ceriello, 1991).

◆ ◆ ◆
WORKERS' COMPENSATION (WCB) AND LONG-TERM DISABILITY (LTD) TRACKING

Organizations that have established effective means of managing WCB and LTD costs can save hundreds of thousands of dollars annually (Rampton and

Doran, 1994). To be able to manage these costs effectively, the organization must be able to track the incidences and reasons (who, what, where) for accidents or illnesses. Effective management of WCB and LTD means: determining what kinds of accidents or illnesses are happening, and where and when they are happening, to provide the basis for identifying and addressing problem areas; identifying potential fraudulent claims and taking corrective action; and getting individuals back on the job as quickly as possible, even if this means appropriate workplace accommodation.

WCB provides financial inducements to employers that are successful in reducing workplace accidents and minimizing costs. The situation for LTD is similar except that, instead of being funded through an agency like the Workers' Compensation Board, LTD is self-funded (in the case of large organizations for whom this is economical), or funded indirectly through the payment of premiums to an insurance carrier.

While WCB has traditionally focused on workplace accidents, stress-related illnesses have recently begun to be funded. If the analyses shows that these or similar ailments funded by LTD are prevalent, wellness programs or employee assistance programs may be useful in reducing costs by either preventing them from developing, or stopping them from getting worse.

◆ ◆ ◆
HRMS REPORTS

Regular HRMS reports can include population snapshots or overviews, including such important variables as present employee make-up, population flows, population forecasts, and the implications that these have for staffing, human resources planning and development, and other personnel programs. These reports can serve as important benchmarks for the monitoring of population shifts and the identification of trends, potential problems, and areas meriting more detailed analysis (Murray and Rampton, 1986).

◆ ◆ ◆
HUMAN RESOURCES/STRATEGIC PLANNING

Business is carried out through and by people. The role of human resources planning, supported by an effective HRMS, is to provide managers with human resources data to influence and aid them in decision making, so that the right quantity and quality of people are available in the future to carry on sound and effective business (Niehaus, 1987).

Business decisions made today affect present human resources availability and the balance between future human resources demand and supply (Director, 1985). An effective HRMS is required to support the following important human resources functions: strategic planning, succession planning, and internal population analysis (Kavanagh et al., 1990). Each of these is discussed in more detail below (see also Walker, 1980).

STRATEGIC PLANNING

Planning the future activities of the organization generates specific human resources needs and requirements to carry out the planned operations. A sound understanding of external and internal human resources trends is required to anticipate their potential impact on the supply/demand balance (Hennecke, 1984). This is particularly true in today's rapidly changing environment.

One objective of human resources planning is to monitor business plans closely and to integrate upcoming human resources requirements with strategic business and operating plans to avoid unanticipated imbalances between labour force supply and demand. The quality of an organization's adaptation to human resources needs generated by business plans is dependent on the quality of the information received. The role of human resources planning must have a proactive effect on strategic business planning, in terms of providing an appreciation of the organization of the labour force and its capacity to accommodate changes in business requirements.

SUCCESSION PLANNING

Human resources planning is oriented towards achieving a balanced state between human resources demand and supply, where shortages and surpluses are anticipated and dealt with to harmonize the flow of human resources throughout the organization (Walker, 1980).

All organizations must cope with the fact that employees, regardless of their positions, move internally and eventually leave the organization. To ensure stability and continuity in its operations, an organization must examine mobility, turnover, and separation statistics, and be prepared to allocate human resources to best satisfy the requirements of vacant positions.

Succession planning is a special case of human resources planning in which real or probable vacancies in specific key or vulnerable positions are identified, often with the assistance of specially designed HRMS modules. The next step is to identify potential in-house candidates, and to provide them with opportunities to prepare for and acquire skills to suit them for the key and/or vulnerable positions when vacancies occur.

INTERNAL POPULATION ANALYSIS

Factors to be monitored through internal population analyses may include mobility of the labour force within the organization, aging of the employee population, hiring and promotion practices, and surplus of resources. (Murray and Rampton, 1986).

The development of a systematic capability for modelling (forecasting) attrition/retention can provide management with an effective tool for planning staffing needs. Techniques such as Markov analyses (Cascio, 1978) can be incorporated into the HRMS to do "what if" scenarios to evaluate such issues as promotion rates, transfer rates, hiring rates, reorganization, and downsizing, on the distribution of employees.

Effectively anticipating supply and demand problems, developing people to fill key or vulnerable positions, and recognizing the potential that different types of people bring to the organization are becoming increasingly important to ensuring long-term organizational success.

◆ ◆ ◆
SUMMARY

Recent technological changes, together with greatly increased demands for human resources information, have converged to make it cost-effective for organizations with as few as 50 employees to develop and implement a new HRMS. Parallel trends have contributed to HRMSs in larger organizations becoming obsolete, so that many of these organizations are in the process of replacing or upgrading their current systems. This chapter has discussed some of the human resources management needs that may lead an organization to develop a new HRMS or to upgrade their old one. The next chapter discusses issues relative to cost-justifying human resources management systems in modern organizations.

EXERCISES

1. For the better part of two years, the two-person human resources team in a small but dynamic manufacturer of precision electronics and mechanical equipment, located in a suburb of Toronto, had been advocating for the resources to purchase a new HRMS. The existing system consisted of an older generation payroll system to which a number of in-house developed, HRMS database modules had been added over the years. Files were stored on tape and the preparation of anything but the most routine reports was complicated and time-consuming.

   Senior management seemed to appreciate the need for a new HRMS, but was not willing to accord it sufficient priority over the many other competing automation needs of the organization. However, one year the president of the company was not able to get his employee Christmas card list printed as quickly as he wanted. This leverage was used to obtain authority for a new HRMS.

   How typical do you think that the dynamics were in this situation? What do you think that this example implies for the value that the organization holds for the HRMS, or the human resources function? If you were one of the individuals in the function, what strategies might you devise to change this?

2. This chapter has provided a number of examples that might lead an organization to begin the search for a new HRMS. Can you think of additional examples, either hypothetical or from your own experience? For each example, describe what organizational function or authority might be the most important user of the information.

3. Many organizations required to implement pay or employment equity have found this to be very labour intensive without the support of an effective HRMS. Why do you think this might be so? What might these organizations have done to better prepare for the advent of equity programs? Could ensuring that the organization's HRMS was able to support such programs effectively have broader advantages for the organization? If so, in what ways?

4. Would an organization of between 50 and 100 employees have to acquire an HRMS with the same capabilities required by one with more than 1000 employees? What similarities might the HRMSs of small, medium, and large organizations share? What differences would you expect to find among them?

References

Belcher, D.W., and T.J. Atchison. 1987. *Compensation Administration.* Englewood Cliffs, N.J.: Prentice-Hall.

Berry, W.E. 1993. "New Role for HR Requires a New Vision for Management Systems." *HR Focus* 70, no. 3 (March): 22.

Bozman, J.S. 1993. "Minority Hiring Getting More Attention, Help." *Computerworld* 27, no. 44 (November): 101.

Broderick, R., and J.W. Boudreau. 1992. "Human Resource Management, Information Technology, and the Competitive Edge." *The Executive* 5, no. 2 (May): 7–17.

Burak, E.H. 1980. *Creative Human Resource Planning and Applications: a Strategic Approach.* Englewood Cliffs, N.J.: Prentice-Hall.

Burgess, L.R. 1984. *Wage and Salary Administration: Pay and Benefits.* Columbus, Ohio: Merill.

Cascio, W. 1978. *Applied Psychology in Personnel Management.* Reston, VA.: Reston Publishing.

_____. and J.W. Thacker. 1994. *Managing Human Resources.* Toronto: McGraw-Hill Ryerson.

Ceriello, V.R. 1991. *Human Resource Management Systems: Strategy, Tactics, and Techniques.* Toronto: Maxwell Macmillan.

Director, S. 1985. *Strategic Planning for Human Resources.* New York: Pergamon.

Doran, J.A., and G.M. Rampton. 1994. "Making a Business Case for a New Human Resource Management Information System." *Canadian Human Resources Systems Professionals Resource Magazine* (June): 4–8.

Downey, J., and McCamus, D. 1990. *To Be Our Best: Learning For the Future.* Montreal, P.Q.: Corporate Higher Education Forum.

Fogel, W. 1984. *The Equal Pay Equity Act: Implications for Comparable Worth.* New York: Praeger.

Hennecke, M. 1984. "The people side of strategic planning." *Training* (November): 25–34.

Kavanagh, M.J., H.G. Gueutal, and S.I. Tannenbaum. 1990. *Human Resource*

Information Systems: Development and Application. Boston, Mass.: PWS-Kent.

Kazanas, H.C. 1988. *Strategic Human Resources Planning and Management*. Englewoods Cliffs, N.J.: Prentice-Hall.

Larson, P.E., and Blue, M.W. 1991. *Training and Development 1990: Expenditures and Policies* (Report 67-91). Ottawa: The Conference Board of Canada.

Lederer, A.L. 1991. *Handbook of Human Resource Information Systems*. New York: Warren, Gorham and Lamont.

McCaffrey, R.M. 1988. *Employee Benefits Programs: A Total Compensation Perspective*. Boston, Mass.: PWS-Kent.

Miracle, M. 1993. "The Trend to Client/Server is Maturing into Acceptance." *National Underwriter Life/Health/Financial Services* 97, no. 45 (November): 2–8.

Mueller, B. 1994. "Changing Attitudes Help Shape HR Systems." *Systems Management* 22, no. 3 (March): 82–89.

Murray, L.A., and G.M. Rampton. 1986. *Human Resource Planning*. Ottawa: Directorate of Human Resources

Planning and Development Report, Canada Post Corporation.

National Committee on Pay Equity. 1987. *Pay Equity: An Issue of Race, Ethnicity, and Sex*. Washington, D.C.

Niehaus, R.J. 1987. *Strategic Human Resources Planning Applications*. New York: Plenum Press.

Rampton, G.M. 1989. "Entrenching Equity in Employment Practices." *The Equal Times: The Newsletter for Human Resource Professionals* 2, no. 3: 19–21.

_____. and J.A. Doran. 1994. *A Practitioners Model for a New Human Resources Management Information System*. Paper presented at the annual Canadian Human Resources Systems Professionals Conference. Toronto (October).

Valaskakis, K., R. Coull, and R. Clermont. 1991. *Information Technology and Human Resources: Prospects for the Decade*. A Report Prepared for the Canadian Human Resources Scanning Association. Toronto (April).

Walker, J.W. 1980. *Human Resource Planning*. New York: McGraw Hill.

3

Return on
Investment

◆ ◆ ◆

INTRODUCTION

One of the most significant challenges facing human resources managers today is justifying the cost of upgrading or purchasing a new HRMS. Yet, in today's tight economy, it is imperative that this cost justification be done if the HRMS is to receive due weight in the context of other organizational priorities.

However, the cost justification of an HRMS has always presented a challenge. Only recently, have executives and human resources practitioners turned their attention to quantifying costs and benefits of personnel systems. Compared to financial and operating information systems, HRMS cost/benefit analysis is a recent development, and still quite rare. Therefore, this chapter addresses concepts relevant to cost-justifying an HRMS.

Personnel comprises the largest part of many organizations' operating costs (Rampton and Doran, 1994). These costs can range upwards of 80 to 90 percent of total operating budgets for organizations whose primary function is to provide public services, such as universities, schools, government departments, social service agencies, or consulting firms. Proportional human resources costs are also high in the emerging high-tech/information-based industries, especially in the software development area. Even in heavy industry and the natural resources sector, human resources typically account for 50 percent or more of total operational costs.

In many respects, personnel is also an organization's most complicated and difficult resource to manage. Human resources management information and the automated systems that support them are consequently becoming important strategic tools (Berry, 1993). However, one of the most significant challenges facing human resources managers today is the justification of costs associated with the purchase and implementation of an HRMS (Gutteridge, 1988). As Stright (1993) points out:

> *HR has to earn its keep. If you can't specify exactly how you*
> *contribute to the bottom line, you'll have increasingly few*

resources available. Not only does the HRMS have to generate
a significant return, but also, customers need to understand
exactly how it's accomplishing that return (p. 70).

Many organizations already have a policy of cost-justifying new technology, but this approach has been adopted more frequently in functional areas other than Human Resources (Broderick and Boudreau, 1992).

The contributions of the human resources function are often undervalued, and not well understood by others in the organization (Cascio, 1991). Part of the explanation for this may be that human resources practitioners have failed to justify their role in a way that other managers readily understand (Foulkes and Morgan, 1980). Human resources practitioners are not used to cost-justifying what they do (Gutteridge, 1988). Many may not even believe that this can, or should, be done. It is no wonder that other functions look on Human Resources as a "necessary liability" that does not contribute to the "bottom line" in the same way as the more "relevant, hard functions," such as operations, marketing, customer service, and finance (Fitz-Enz, 1995).

Techniques for assessing the dollar value of human resources programs have existed for some time (Brogden and Taylor, 1950; Cascio, 1991; Cronbach and Gleser, 1965), but human resources practitioners have either been unaware of them or disinclined to use them. This is changing, however, and as human resources functions are able to demonstrate that their input is relevant to organizational success, they are slowly but surely gaining more credibility, influence, and input into strategic decision making (Cascio and Thacker, 1994).

The underlying principles in producing pragmatic, defensible cost-benefits analysis are similar for an HRMS of any size, although the scale of analyses may be quite different. A detailed discussion of the various methods that can be used to perform human resources cost-benefits analyses is beyond the scope of this book: the interested reader is instead referred to Cascio (1991) or Fitz-Enz (1995) for an extensive treatment of these issues. The remainder of this chapter discusses cost benefits concepts for the reader interested in justifying the cost of the first-time implementation of an HRMS, or in the replacement of one that has become obsolete, whether due to changes in the needs of the organization or to changes in technology.

◆◆◆
EXAMPLE: EMPLOYEE LISTS

The use of an HRMS to produce employee lists is a simple application, and one which is familiar to most practitioners. Let us consider how cost justification of such a simple example might be done.

In some medium to large-sized organizations (five to ten thousand employees), human resources information specialists may typically receive 10 or more requests a day to prepare address labels for a variety of purposes, such as sending pension information to recent retirees, informing selected employees about the way in which restructuring of their organizational unit could affect them, advising members and their spouses about changes in benefits programs, etc. In one real-life example, the organization had the capacity for providing address labels for its members and retirees through its HRMS. Once managers learned that Human Resources could produce address labels in much less time and at a fraction of the cost that they could be produced through other means, the demand to produce such labels grew to the extent that it began to consume about one-fifth of the time of a human resources information officer.

Rather than discourage the use of the information officer's time in producing address labels, the manager responsible decided to do a rough cost-benefits analysis of this activity. He first determined that if his employee did not produce the labels, the various people who wanted them would simply find other means of obtaining them. Since the information officer was paid about $35,000 per annum, he calculated that it was costing about $7000 (in salary-related costs alone), that is, one-fifth of $35,000, to produce the address labels.

The manager also estimated that the information officer was able to produce the address labels in about one-eighth of the total time that it would have taken others to produce them. Thus, approximately 1.6 person–years of clerical time would otherwise have been required to produce the labels (since the task occupied one-fifth of the information officer's time, and, on average, she was able to produce the labels eight times faster than those requiring them—8/5 = 1.6). Even assuming that the individuals who would otherwise have produced the address labels earned somewhat less (say $5000 less per annum) than the information officer, the total cost of producing the labels would have been in the order of $48,000 ($30,000 × 1.6). The total saving that the organization effected by having the information officer produce the labels was, therefore, $41,000 ($48,000 – $7000). This is undoubtedly an underestimate, because it assumes that other costs to produce the labels were equal no matter how the labels were produced, when, in fact, there was strong evidence that costs of supplies and wastage were less when the labels were produced by the information officer. Further, many of the individuals who might otherwise have produced the labels made as much or more, per year, as the information officer.

◆ ◆ ◆
LEGISLATIVE REQUIREMENTS

As mentioned in Chapter 2, organizations must be able to produce lists of their employees broken down in many different ways, accurately, quickly, and efficiently. This is necessary not only to develop and manage their human resources, but to meet legislative requirements for information in the area of taxation, pay equity, employment equity, and so on (Bloom, 1991). Legislative requirements often demand a general organizational response. With respect to pay equity legislation in the province of Ontario, for example, before it can be determined whether individuals in female-dominated job classes are paid less than individuals in male-dominated jobs of equal value, this information must be available in an accessible form. (Agarwal, 1988). Similarly, with respect to employment equity legislation, in most jurisdictions, to determine how individuals in any of the designated groups compare to others with respect to salary or position in the organization, this information must be available in the system in suitable form, and the system must have the capability to report it (Abella, 1984; Jain, 1989).

The penalty for not being able to meet legislative requirements can be significant—as much as $50,000 or more in the province of Ontario, in the case of pay equity. Faced with such penalties, most organizations find a way of meeting these requirements, even if it means processing the requisite information by hand. Doing so, however, is much less effective and more costly than anticipating the need for such information, having it resident in the HRMS, and being able to produce the information quickly and accurately. The principle of cost justification in such cases is exactly the same as in the previous example.

In one large Canadian organization in the educational sector, the position control module of the existing HRMS had never been activated since the system was purchased, as doing so would have required alterations costing about $35,000.

A pay equity program for administrative staff was negotiated in July 1992, two and one-half years after the implementation of pay equity legislation in Ontario. This meant that considerable amounts of retroactive salary were owed to many individuals. Further, every individual who had ever been in a female-dominated job since the pay equity implementation date on January 1, 1990, had to be tracked and, if applicable, paid for the time that they were in such positions, including those individuals who resigned, retired, or left temporarily for such reasons as maternity leave. Without the automatic tracking capability of the position control module, much of the tracking had to be done by hand, on a post-hoc basis. With more than 1200 employees, in a largely female-dominated group, this required an enormous amount of time, effort, and resources. More than five person–years of extra administrative help was necessary for the clerical aspects of the tracking process alone. This expense by itself resulted in additional personnel costs of more than $165,000. It is therefore readily apparent that not spending the $35,000 to implement the position control module in a timely fashion was a false economy. In fact, the more than $130,000 savings evident from the figures presented is an underestimate of the total savings since it ignores additional materials and other costs incurred. It also does not take into account the time and effort that had to be devoted by supervisory and management staff that could have been spent more profitably elsewhere.

◆ ◆ ◆

SALARY/BENEFITS REPORTING AND MODELLING

In one way or another, most organizations have automated their payroll information (Codega, 1991), even if they contract their payroll to an external agency. It is also likely that payroll information will be among the most accurate of the organization's automated information. However, despite the fact that salary and benefits costs comprise a substantial portion of the operating costs in many organizations, few organizations have invested in more sophisticated means of tracking trends in salary and benefits costs, or of performing "what if" analyses to help find ways of keeping costs in check.

As noted in MacPherson and Wallace (1992), until the decades of the 1950s and into the 1960s, benefits such as medical, dental, sick leave, long-term disability, and life insurance, accounted for a relatively small percentage of each individual's overall compensation package and were often referred to as "fringe benefits." In the 1960s, 1970s, and 1980s benefits coverage was expanded, with employers picking up more and more of the overall cost. And from the late 1980s and early 1990s, costs for such benefits as long-term disability and health, dental, and drug programs have tended to escalate much faster than the cost of inflation. In addition, governments have begun to alter social programs in directions that effectively shift more of the costs of health care and drugs on to employers. This may take the form of implementing payroll taxes to pay for health insurance costs; it may also involve reducing the range of health and drug coverage, thus forcing company-sponsored plans to pick them up.

Many organizations today are finding it necessary to provide closer control over salary and benefits costs (Cascio and Thacker, 1994). The only feasible way of doing this is by means of an effective HRMS, which contains accurate salary and benefits information and has the flexible analysis and reporting capability required to produce "what if" models on demand.

For payroll purposes, for example, this means being able to examine the results of various salary increase options, whether in the form of across-the-board percentage increases, flat dollar increases, or some combination of the two. The ability to produce such analyses during labour negotiations can lead to settlements that are not only more economical in and of themselves, but that can also be instrumental in avoiding costly work stoppages.

It is also important that an HRMS be able to provide analyses of various benefits options. In the past, organizations tended to negotiate salary and benefits as separate issues. Increasingly, however, organizations are negotiating the total cost of salary and benefits, so that tradeoffs are possible within the various options as long as overall costs remains within a total dollar "envelope." Accurate and relevant automated salary and benefits data, along with an effective analysis and reporting capability, are mandatory. Huge cost savings then become possible, in that even a small percentage saving in a salary and benefits settlement can lead to large dollar amounts, given that, as we have seen, human resources costs form such a large part of the operating budgets of many organizations.

◆ ◆ ◆
EXAMPLES

In one set of difficult labour negotiations having ready access to such a reporting capability by management negotiations led to a significant savings. The negotiations were with a bargaining unit consisting of about 1200 predominately white-collar administrative, technical, and laboratory staff, with a total salary and benefits package of about $50,000,000. The labour climate in the organization had been strained for several years and there was little trust between the two parties. Strikes had been involved in previous contract settlements, and it seemed that these negotiations were headed in that direction.

Some degree of trust was established by using the HRMS to produce a clear and accurate picture of the organization's financial situation. This allowed management to demonstrate that the $250,000 required for the additional .5 percent in benefits costs that were requested by the union would result in the loss of at least 10 jobs. This demonstration would not have been as timely or convincing without access to the HRMS, and it led to acceptance of the lower management offer by the union. In terms of HRMS cost justification, it is important to note that the $250,000 was an annualized cost saving. Total costs would grow in a compounded manner each year. Harder to quantify perhaps, but very important, was the fact that a potentially costly strike was avoided.

After these negotiations, a great deal of work was done to improve the labour relations climate within the organization. Part of this campaign involved using the HRMS to provide the union with more accurate and timely information. This included information that was required in the collective agreement (e.g., seniority lists), as well as information that had never previously been provided (e.g., statistics on the use of casual and relief help). The campaign was successful in reducing the number of grievances and leading to a more healthy labour relations climate overall. The savings that resulted due to fewer grievances and the increased productivity arising from the improvement in labour relations would be difficult to quantify, but it is certainly safe to say that the HRMS played a significant role in achieving them. The example described above demonstrates how HRMS information can be used to limit benefits costs through labour negotiations. Benefits costs can also be controlled by:

1. negotiating better deals with insurance carriers; or

2. managing the costs of benefits programs by more efficient administration, so that benefits can be maintained or even improved at the same or lower cost (or, at least, with minimum cost increases).

In organizations with more than 200 employees, these tasks again, require access to accurate automated benefits data, as well as an effective analysis capability.

The pension and benefits staff in one organization, of a little less than 10,000 employees used the HRMS to track benefits costs over a five-year period, and then used this information to project future cost trends. The analyses indicated increasing cost trends in the order of 38 percent per annum. Because of these unacceptably high increases, it was decided to implement a program of cost containment while maintaining the overall quality and level of the benefits provided. Needless to say, the HRMS was critical in supporting the development, implementation, and monitoring of the cost-control measurers.

Some of the highlights of this cost-control program were as follows:

1. *Coordination of benefits.* The coordination of benefits coverage with spousal coverage was implemented, resulting in savings in unnecessary payments in health and dental claims with an overall savings in excess of $40,000.

2. *Long-term disability.* Tighter monitoring and control of who was on long-term disability, for how long, and for what reasons, together with a worker accommodation program, led to annual savings of more than $50,000.

3. *Workers' compensation.* Implementation of a more effective occupational health and safety program, a workers' accommodation program, and other measures led to a lower WCB category and avoidance of penalties, resulting in annual savings in excess of $100,000.

4. *Self-administration.* Using the HRMS to do analyses and produce reports previously done by consultants resulted in an annual saving in excess of $35,000.

5. *Pension administration system.* Internal demographic studies conducted using the HRMS indicated that retirements would accelerate over the next decade to the point where staff would not be able to cope using

current technology. Handling the workload would take at least three additional staff members, although it was doubtful that the existing data system could handle the extra volume even with the additional staff. Therefore, it was decided to implement a new pension administration system for an overall cost of about $250,000.

Even discounting the payoff from the greatly increased efficiency, accuracy, and service of the new system, the $250,000 cost involved in acquiring it would soon be more than amortized by the $120,000 annual salary savings.

It is easy to see from the above examples how the cost of an HRMS may be justified by its use in identifying and implementing salary and benefits cost control measures.

◆ ◆ ◆

HUMAN RESOURCES PLANNING, DEVELOPMENT, RESEARCH, AND RELATED ISSUES

In the early 1970s, researchers and information systems staff at the Canadian Forces Personnel Applied Research Unit began work on an HRMS that was designed to contain recruiting, selection, aptitude tests, training, performance appraisal, and status information on everyone who applied for and joined the Canadian Forces from July 1968 onwards. This is undoubtedly one of the earliest examples of an effective, large-scale HRMS in Canada, and its history and contribution to its parent organization merits some discussion. While some of the requirements of an HRMS in an organization like the Canadian Forces may differ from those facing many of the readers of this book, others will be recognized as highly similar.

The system described is resident at the Canadian Forces Personnel Applied Research Unit (CFPARU), and by now it contains millions of records on hundreds of thousands of individuals. This system serves partially as a data storage and reporting facility for authorities requiring information for human resources management purposes. A more important function, however, and in fact, the reason for its conceptualization and development was its use as an applied research tool (Rampton, 1978). Therefore, in addition to the longitudinal information mentioned above, that is collected regularly on each individual, a great deal of additional information is collected, usually in survey form, and maintained in cross-sectional files.

The Canadian Forces is a large and costly federal government organization and regularly comes under the close scrutiny of such financial watchdogs as the Auditor General, to ensure responsibility to the public purse. As a consequence, great care is taken to ensure that all important personnel decisions are thoroughly costed and based on sound research and analysis. Over the years the CFPARU HRMS has been an important tool in many of these research programs (Rampton, 1979). Included have been studies:

1. to develop and implement aptitude tests and associated procedures to select the several thousand individuals entering the Forces as officers and in trades training;

2. to develop and implement assessment centres for officer training plans, including aircrew, combat arms, and naval officers;

3. to develop and validate leadership assessment instruments used in officer training plans;

4. to support human resources scanning and demographic analyses, including applicant demand and supply forecasts;

5. to examine the relationship of individual and organizational variables on attrition;

6. to develop new performance appraisal systems for all Canadian Forces personnel;

7. to implement quality of working life and organizational development procedures;

8. to examine the factors that facilitate or hinder the movement of military personnel into the civilian labour force; and

9. to provide an action research base for trials to integrate women in to all environments and roles in the Canadian Forces.

This information system evolved from rather humble beginnings over a period of more than 25 years. The initial version prototype of the HRMS was developed in-house, and brought on-line for a capital investment of $5800. Since then, many times this amount has been invested on upgrades to allow the system to become a state-of-the-art data management and research tool.

The total amount invested over the years, however, is much less than the return from the system. For example, on average, it costs more than one million dollars to train each pilot to operational standard. If research supported by this HRMS has led to even a 5 percent savings in training costs, spread over the thousands of pilots who have been selected and trained by the Canadian Forces over the years, the savings would amount to several millions of dollars.

Although the per training cost of most other trades and officer classifications is less than that for pilots, the total number selected and trained over the past 25 or so years amounts to hundreds of thousands of individuals. The total savings realized through more effective selection and trade/occupational classification and training, made possible by research supported by this HRMS, has been much greater.

We have looked at only one of the many applied research areas that have been supported by the CFPARU HRMS; the Canadian Forces have benefited from many others which have contributed to the more effective planning for, accession, development, and utilization of its personnel. It is true that the same sorts of research studies would have been required whether or not this particular system had ever been developed. However, it is also true that because of the volume of data and the complexity of the analyses involved, some system would undoubtedly have been required, or only a fraction of the research would have been accomplished, and that research would have been supported by less accurate data.

An HRMS can only be as good as its data. The needs analysis stage of HRMS development is therefore particularly critical. The CFPARU HRMS benefited from some fortunate early decisions about the information that it was to contain. As the software and hardware of this system evolved, the nature of the core data contained in the system remained intact. This has allowed personnel applied research in the Canadian Forces to reflect a longitudinal or long-term perspective in which individuals can be tracked over their entire careers, if necessary, to assess the long-term effects of implementing new personnel programs. This has allowed for a more thorough validation of new research initiatives than has previously been available to most organizations (Cronshaw, 1986).

With technology evolving so quickly, and information requirements apparently doing the same, it is easy to fall into the trap of designing a system for its "here and now," short-term payoff, with the assumption that in a few years it will probably be obsolete. While technology may become obsolete quickly, the same is not necessarily true for relevant and accurate personnel data. In fact, such information should be recognized and fostered by all organizations as a valuable part of their asset base.

It is important then, that the needs analysis of such systems be done so that the data may be maintained, with updates and refinements, as the software and hardware evolves around it. The longitudinal perspective which this allows means that the cost benefit perspectives of such systems are generally much greater than those of more temporary ones, which must go through several costly needs analysis, systems development, data gathering/transformation, and systems implementation cycles as the organization decides that old systems have to be replaced.

When a system like an HRMS has been in existence for some time, uses are generally found for it that were not intended when the system was being developed. Being able to capitalize on these new applications enhances the cost benefit of the system. Although it may not be possible to anticipate these in the initial systems planning and development stages, they can and should be used to justify the cost of systems upgrades and enhancements. Often these "opportunity applications" take the form of solutions to problems that line management, or those responsible for other functions in the organization, cannot resolve, or cannot resolve as effectively or efficiently as a human resources practitioner with the aid of the HRMS would. Being able and willing to help out in this way is often highly visible, and can do much to enhance the status of human resources practitioners and of the human resources function.

The following example, again involving the CFPARU, demonstrates the way in which new applications can arise.

QUALITY CONTROL OF CANADIAN FORCES RECRUITING AND SELECTION

The Canadian Forces operates a very effective aptitude testing program (Cronshaw, 1986). In the 1970s, item analyses and validation studies to upgrade aptitude tests for both officer and trades training plans were undertaken. All Canadian Forces Recruiting and Selection Centres were asked to send all of their completed test answer sheets to CFPARU, where the item responses on them could be automated by being physically key-punched. In addition to being used in the item analyses, automation of the items on each sheet allowed a computer program to be written to score each aptitude test and compare the result with that contained on the individual's file. Even though such reports and returns were cross-checked at least once, a significant number of the aptitude test scores contained one or more errors, whether in the recording of the scores, or in the purely clerical job of documenting them or any other information that was required on each candidate's selection documentation. Any errors in test scores, however caused, were very important to control because they could eliminate individuals from being considered for programs for which they might otherwise be eligible.

A quality control exercise was implemented with the cooperation of the 16 Recruiting and Selection Centres across Canada. As part of this exercise, CFPARU began sending reports back to all Centres providing a statistical summary of the errors that each had made the previous month. All reports with errors were sent back to the Centre concerned so that it could review the errors, and determine how they occurred and how they might be corrected. After a few months of this process, "error rate" averages in all 16 Centres dropped from a range of 5 to 10 percent, to the point where one or more errors on fewer than 1 percent of the forms were being made. Many individual Centres would go months without making even a single error on thousands of documents generated.

Although it started as a rather simple attempt to help the Recruiting and Selection Centres improve their documentation, this service was considered important enough to help CFPARU justify the purchase of optical scanning equipment to facilitate automation of the answer sheet marking. The optical scanning equipment, in turn, allowed CFPARU to develop a much more effective survey capability, since it allowed thousands of survey forms to be gathered and marked automatically.

When combined with the data analysis capability and data already contained on the CFPARU HRMS, this survey capability was used effectively to support a number of research projects that contributed to important and high profile personnel decisions. Decisions on the issues in question would have been made whether or not the CFPARU HRMS and its capability to support survey research existed. However, with more complete information, better decisions were undoubtedly made than might otherwise have been possible. In any event, being able to contribute in a significant way to the decision-making process certainly enhanced the status and future influence of CFPARU and its staff. A review of the studies presented in Wiskoff and Rampton (1989) indicates that these Canadian examples are paralleled in the research efforts of other western military forces.

◆ ◆ ◆

SUMMARY

Human resources practitioners have not generally been very good at cost-justifying what they do. This has put them at a disadvantage with other functions more experienced at demonstrating their worth in operational and/or economic terms.

One of the most significant challenges facing human resources practitioners today is the justification of costs associated with the purchase and implementation of an HRMS. Most organizations already have a policy of cost-justifying new technology, and today's tight economy dictates that this be done for every new investment of this nature. This chapter has discussed various ways in which the cost of acquiring an HRMS may be justified, using actual examples.

EXERCISES

1. Traditionally, the chief executive officers of Canada's major corporations were drawn from the ranks of people with backgrounds in operations or marketing. Increasingly, however, corporate heads are being drawn from more diverse backgrounds, such as engineering, law, or finance. It can be argued that individuals with human resources backgrounds are underrepresented as chief executives. Why do you think this might be so? Do you feel that it is justified?

2. Many organizations claim that their "employees are their most important resource." Certainly, for many organizations, costs related to human resources constitute their largest single budget issue. Human resources personnel generally maintain and operate the organization's HRMS. On the basis that "information is power," then, one might have assumed that human resources would be in an advantageous position to make their mark in the corporate boardroom. Suppose that you are the manager of a progressive human resources function in an organization of about 1500 employees. Develop a strategy to use your natural

advantages to acquire greater influence on strategic planning and decision making in the organization. Start by defining what these advantages are. Then define where you would like to see your function at the end of two years. Develop an action plan for achieving your goal. How central is the role of the HRMS in this plan?

3. It was suggested in this chapter that one of the reasons that human resources personnel have not been more successful in communicating the importance of what they do to others in the organization is because they have tended not to explain what they do in economic terms. Do you agree with this statement? Are there some human resources roles or responsibilities that should not be evaluated in dollars and cents terms? Please give examples, and explain your reasoning. Are there better criteria for evaluating them? Please explain.

4. As a human resources manager, how might you go about developing the practice of measuring what you do in economic terms? What might be the advantages and disadvantages of doing so? Do you think it would be easy to get others in Human Resources to go along with you? What arguments might you use to convince them?

References

Abella, R.S. 1984. *Equality and Employment: A Royal Commission Report*. Ottawa: Ministry of Supply and Services.

Agarwal, N. 1988. "Pay Equity in Context." In *Human Resources Management in Canada*. Scarborough, Ont.: Prentice-Hall.

Berry, W.E. 1993. "New Role for HR Requires a New Vision for Management Systems." *HR Focus* 70, no. 3 (March): 22.

Bloom, N.L. 1991. "Corporate Needs for HR Information." In A.L. Lederer (ed.), *Handbook of Human Resources Information Systems*. New York: Warren, Gorham and Lamont.

Broderick, R., and J.W. Boudreau. 1992. "Human Resource Management, Information Technology, and the Competitive Edge." *The Executive* 5, no. 2 (May): 7–17.

Brogden, H.E., and E.K. Taylor. 1950. "The Dollar Criterion—Applying the Cost Accounting Concept to Criterion

Construction." *Personnel Psychology* 3: 133–54.

Cascio, W.F. 1991. *Costing Human Resources: The Financial Impact of Behaviour in Organizations,* 3rd ed. Boston, Mass.: PWS-Kent.

_____. and J.W. Thacker. 1994. *Managing Human Resources.* Toronto: McGraw-Hill Ryerson.

Codega, K. 1991. "Compensation Applications." In A.L. Lederer (ed.), *Handbook of Human Resources Information Systems.* New York: Warren, Gorham and Lamont.

Cronbach, L.J., and G. Gleser. 1965. *Psychological Tests and Personnel Decisions.* Chicago, Ill.: University of Illinois Press.

Cronshaw, S. 1986. "The Status of Employment Testing in Canada: a Review and Evaluation of Theory and Professional Practice." *Canadian Psychology* 27: 183–95.

Fitz-Enz, J. 1980. "Quantifying the Human Resources Function." *Personnel* 57, no. 3: 41–52.

Foulkes, F.K., and H.M. Morgan. 1980. "Organizing and Staffing the Personnel Function." *Harvard Business Review* 45: 107–13.

Gutteridge, T.G. 1988. "The HRPD Profession: a Vision of Tomorrow." *Human Resource Planning* 11, no. 2: 109–24.

Hunter, D.R. 1989. "Aviator Selection." In Martin F. Wiskoff and Glenn M. Rampton, eds., *Military Personnel Measurement.* New York: Praeger.

Jain, H.C. 1989. "Human Rights: Issues in Employment." In *Human Resources Management in Canada.* Scarborough, Ont.: Prentice-Hall.

MacPherson, D.L., and J.T. Wallace. 1992. "Employee Benefits Plans." In *Human Resources Management in Canada.* Scarborough, Ont.: Prentice-Hall.

Rampton, G.M. 1978. "The Role and Function of the Personnel Applied Research Unit: Past, Present, and Future." Paper presented at APA 19 Symposium: "Research Programmes for the Canadian Forces," American Psychological Association Annual Convention Toronto (28 August–1 September).

_____. 1979. *Canadian Forces Personnel Applied Research Unit: Bi-Annual work report.* Fall report for fiscal year 1979/80. Toronto: Canadian Forces Personnel Applied Research Unit (October).

_____. and J.A. Doran. 1994. "A Practitioners Model for a New Human Resources Management Information System." Paper presented at the annual Canadian Human Resources Systems Professionals' Conference. Toronto (October).

Stright, J.F. 1993. "Strategic Goals Guide
HRMS Development." *Personnel Journal*
(September): 68–78.

Wiskoff, M.F., and Rampton, G.M. 1989.
Military Personnel Measurement. New
York: Praeger.

4

Planning a
New HRMS

INTRODUCTION

S ound planning at the beginning of any HRMS project is critical. Yet this step is often overlooked or given little attention in the rush to upgrade an existing system or to develop a new one. Too often, such projects have been initiated and are well underway before there is a realization by those involved that key issues have been overlooked, whether through the lack of an adequate needs analysis to identify systems requirements, the need to gain the commitment of key stakeholders, or in limitations in hardware or software.

This chapter discusses important considerations in planning an HRMS project including:

◆ Planning process

◆ Elements of project management

◆ Steering committee

◆ Project team

◆ Planning communications strategy

◆ Identifying and building in critical success factors

◆ Planning for the management of change

◆ Options: repair and refine, build, or buy

◆ Implementing the plan

◆ Training and documentation

◆ ◆ ◆

PLANNING

The authors have found it useful to conceptualize planning for an HRMS in three distinct phases:

◆ Design and development

◆ Implementation

◆ Maintenance

Although they are related, the planning for each of these phases differs somewhat and must be coordinated carefully. Design and development planning, for example, involves defining requirements, investigating and deciding upon options, and then developing the action plan by which the project will be made a reality. Implementation planning involves deciding how the action plan will be carried out, including who will be responsible for each step in the plan, where each step will be carried out, and what resources will be needed. Maintenance planning involves developing a strategy for ensuring that the system remains dynamic in terms of being continually updated in response to changes in user requirements and evolving technology.

These plans must include provision for users and systems maintenance personnel to have access to up-to-date and user friendly documentation and training (see the discussion on documentation and training later in this chapter), so that they may use and maintain the system to best effect, and are able to make recommendations for improvements. Detailed planning of each phase of an HRMS project will not guarantee success, but it will make success much more likely.

Project plans are established to meet strategic, tactical, and operational goals. The objectives on which a plan is based define the scope of the project, which in turn defines the project specifications. Plans can be too broad, or too detailed. Overplanning, or taking too much time to plan, can doom a project as can jumping into developing a system without a plan. Kerzner (1989) reports that project managers suggest that 10 hours per week is a reasonable amount of time to plan and replan.

Planning is a pragmatic process, with the aim of developing plans that are effective and efficient, but not all-inclusive or perfect. Plans, like their financial counterparts, budgets, represent the planner's best estimate at a specific point in time. If they are to be successful, plans should be flexible. It is the realization of the plan, through sound management, including adjusting for intangibles and reacting to resource changes, which yields success (Kerzner, 1989).

THE PLANNING PROCESS

Planning is not a new activity. Twenty-five hundred years ago, Sun Tzu, General for the King of Wu, wrote:

The general who wins a battle makes many calculations in his temple before the battle is fought. The general who loses a battle makes but few calculations beforehand. Thus do many calculations lead to victory, and few calculations to defeat; how much more no calculation at all! It is by attention to this point that I can foresee who is likely to win or lose (Clavell, 1983, 12).

The detailed steps of a planning process will of necessity vary by organization. However, most of the common steps, in a rough time order, are outlined in Figure 4-1.

The major steps illustrated are as follows:

1. Recognition of one or more needs for better human resources management (HRM) information.
2. If there is an existing system in place, determine whether it can be modified to produce the information at a reasonable cost.
3. If no system currently exists, or if the cost of modifying an existing system is not reasonable, conduct an analysis of whether buying a system or building one is preferred.
4. Prepare a detailed needs analysis.
5. Prepare a Request for Information (RFI) or Request for Proposal (RFP) and send it to selected vendors.
6. Analyze the results, reducing the short-list until only one or two options remain, and select finalist product and vendor.
7. Negotiate price and conditions, while conducting final vendor references, and financial review.
8. Receive "GO" decision and select project team to implement.

◆ ◆ ◆
PROJECT MANAGEMENT

Project management combines planning with a controlled use of resources to develop and implement specific end results, or projects, such as designing and implementing a new HRMS (Kerzner, 1989).

FIGURE 4.1 Steps in HRMS Planning

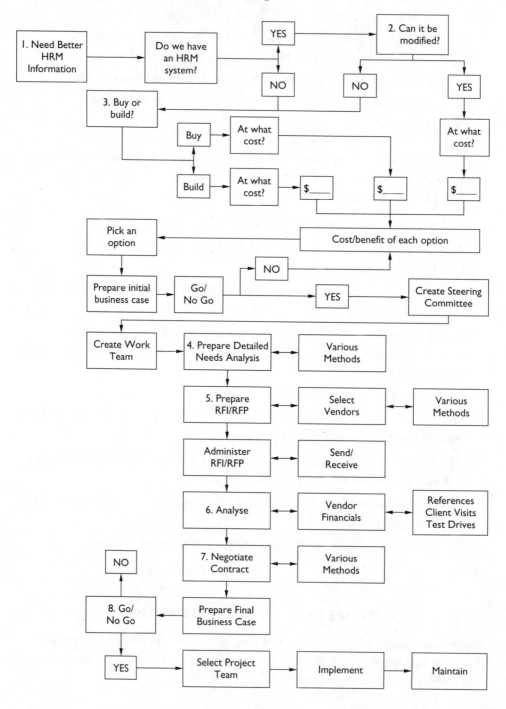

The techniques used in project management are not new. Most are applicable to and have been applied in management in general. Some authors, in fact, have argued that the primary distinction between project management and other kinds of management is the duration of the task. This distinction has met with some resistance, since it challenges traditional organizational management structures, which tend to be vertical, with multiple organization levels rather than the few which are more typically found in project management. In project management, work is generally accomplished by flatter organizational teams led by a "functional leader" who may or may not have the formal designation of manager (Kerzner, 1989).

Every unique task—like every project—has at least one specific objective as well as resource limits and specifications:

- Time (start/end dates)
- People (identification, specific skills they bring to project, availability, cost)
- Tools (equipment, software)
- Money (budget)

Project management adds in a familiar general management issue—performance appraisal—by monitoring progress against the plan, analyzing the gap and impact thereof, and adjusting the plan accordingly. Building or changing large and complex systems lend themselves to the project management process, in part because of the complexity, but also because of the sheer volume of activities that must occur, and occur in a particular sequence.

Project management adopts a planning and scheduling methodology that includes both conceptual framework and techniques to manage and track each component. It is the ongoing tracking and recording of activities and results that most distinguishes the project management approach from general management (Kerzner, 1989).

Various software tools exist that help document each step, balance and price resources, offer analysis models, and produce reports. Users may find some specific tools more useful than others, but all of the current project planning software known to the authors have limitations. Many of the more popular packages provide so much detail that overmanagement of the project becomes a potential problem. Constantly updating the plan does not equate to managing the project.

These software tools support project activities by offering such features as:

1. *Tasks definition.* Each unique activity in the project must be clearly defined.

2. *Project scheduling.* Every task/activity is integrated into the project schedule by listing an estimate of its start and end dates.

3. *Milestones.* These are events that signify some specific and significant progress or an important time.

4. *Resource assignment.* Every person and piece of equipment, together with the cost of each, must be assigned to specific accomplishment of tasks. Downtime or, in Finance terms, indirect labour (e.g., vacation, union business, maintenance) is included where it is predictable.

5. *Costs and budgets.* Resource costs are calculated and amalgamated over the expenses estimated to be required to accomplish each task.

6. *Visual representations.* There are between 30 and 40 different visual methods for the representation of activities (Kerzner, 1989). Each one provides a different way of looking at project data, and different methods provide different levels of information. There are entire books on these techniques, and those interested should consult the literature (see References at the end of this and other chapters). Some of the more common techniques are:

   a. GANTT Chart—a bar chart that graphically displays the status of a task based on time or money (see Figure 4.2).

   b. PERT (Program Evaluation and Review Technique)—PERT charts illustrate the relationships and dependencies between different activities.

   c. CPM (Critical Path Method)—CPM was developed around the same time as PERT, and performs the same function.

These tools combined with project management software, such as Microsoft Project or Harvard Project Manager, can facilitate the management and communication of the project. They assist the project manager in defining, tracking, and communicating tremendous numbers of project details. Scheduling the multiplicity of activities and tasks can be a nightmare, but a system that tracks dependencies, highlights staff availability, and allows for adjustments as required, makes the job easier and the results more profes-

FIGURE 4.2 Gantt Chart

ID	WBS	Task Name	Duration	Start	4th Quarter			
					September	October	November	December
1	1	REVIEW STRATEGIC DIRECTION	20d	Fri 95-09-22				
2	2	PROJECT TEAM	24d	Tue 95-09-0				
3	2.1	Select Team	5d	Tue 95-09-0				
4	2.2	Select Project Manager	3d	Fri 95-09-08				
5	2.3	Train	5d	Mon 95-10-				
6	3	REVIEW CURRENT PROCESSES	23d	Fri 95-10-2				
7	3.1	Human Resources	15d	Fri 95-10-20				
8	3.2	Payroll	15d	Wed 95-11-				
9	3.3	Operations	7d	Tue 95-11-0				
10	4	REDESIGN PROCESSES	23d	Tue 95-11-1				
11	4.1	Human Resources	15d	Tue 95-11-1				
12	4.2	Payroll	15d	Fri 95-11-24				
13	4.3	Operations	7d	Wed 95-11-				
14	5	DEVELOP SUPPORT SYSTEMS	30d	Mon 95-12-				
15	5.1	HRMS Management Processes	5d	Wed 96-01-				

sional (Plantamura, 1990). Whether or not a project planning tool is utilized, each step in the project should be planned.

> *The most important responsibilities of a project manager are planning, integrating, and executing plans. Almost all projects, because of their relatively short duration and often prioritized control of resources, require formal detailed planning (Kerzner, 1989, 37).*

To that list of responsibilities may be added communicating.

◆ ◆ ◆
THE COMMUNICATIONS PROCESS

The communication of plans and project status, both within a project team and throughout the organization, requires an inordinate amount of project time. Communication is not just telling; it is listening too. Peters (1987) suggests that managers and team members listening to one another, formally and informally, is one of the critical components of successful management. The project manager in particular, should be a strong communicator—speaking,

FIGURE 4.3 Five Rs of Reception

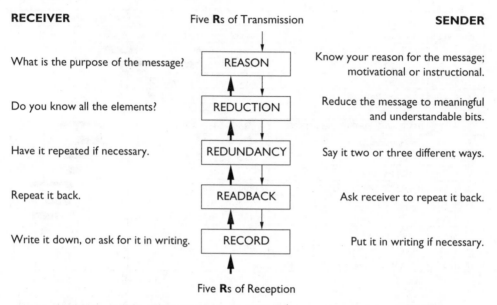

RECEIVER	Five **R**s of Transmission	SENDER
What is the purpose of the message?	REASON	Know your reason for the message; motivational or instructional.
Do you know all the elements?	REDUCTION	Reduce the message to meaningful and understandable bits.
Have it repeated if necessary.	REDUNDANCY	Say it two or three different ways.
Repeat it back.	READBACK	Ask receiver to repeat it back.
Write it down, or ask for it in writing.	RECORD	Put it in writing if necessary.

Five **R**s of Reception

Source: Adapted from D. Slevin, *The Whole Manager*. New York: American Management Association, 1989.

listening, and writing effectively. These skills are critical to the project's success. One model for communication is presented in Figure 4.3 above.

Planning encompasses both strategic and operational decisions, and requires the involvement of all groups concerned with the implementation. The involvement of all concerned—project manager, project team, primary client, and senior management—is a key component of success. Not all need to be equally involved, but the commitment that comes from participation and being part of the communication process is invaluable and irreplaceable.

This communication process encompasses the project team, the steering team, and the organization as a whole. Each must understand the project and have a sense of how the results will be integrated into the organization's business processes.

Kanter (1989) suggests that, in most projects, too little time is spent in selling ideas, keeping all participants up-to-date, and ensuring that each understands how the project fits with regard to his or her interests and responsibilities. Time spent ensuring that participation is offered and occurs is time well spent.

Kerzner (1989) points out that successful project managers are heavily dependent on the line managers who supply the human resources to a project, and on project employees who must operate in a matrix organization structure, reporting to their line managers even as they work on the project. Knutson and Blitz (1991) suggest some guidelines for developing effective team members:

1. *involve key members of the project team in developing a communication plan.*
2. *work with each team member to define how and when communication will take place and how the team will work together to solve problems that might arise on the project.*
3. *devise a strategy with each team member to help ensure that information does not get lost, and to prevent ruffled feathers that often occur when messages are mis-communicated or omitted.*
4. *begin developing a communication plan as soon as new project is undertaken, and update it as needed. Players often change in the project universe. Develop new communication strategies when this happens. Newcomers or replacement project team members are often left out and cannot fully contribute unless one takes time to involve them (p. 24).*

◆ ◆ ◆
CRITICAL SUCCESS FACTORS

A number of factors can be critical in producing success or failure for a project. The management of each factor reduces the risk of negative events and their effect on the project. The critical factors are described below:

1. *The organization's financial health.* The degree of financial health is less important than a realistic appreciation of it. However, an organization in a serious financial crisis will rarely fund an HRMS (or any) project properly, cutting corners in a rash attempt to achieve results.

2. *The organization's structure.* An organization's structure and recent or proposed changes to it, such as restructuring and downsizing, can affect the organization's climate.

3. *The organization's culture.* Projects should be accepted as formal activities well supported by the organization. If this is not the case, it will be difficult to recruit, keep, and return project staff to the organization successfully. An organization that does not have many projects or that may have problems integrating this different type of activity should carefully consider how to ensure a climate for success.

4. *The existence of a "mission champion"* (Peters, 1987). Even if the business need for an HRMS is clearly understood, the project will stand a much better chance of success if there is an identifiable champion prepared to advocate it. The better the champion(s) is/are regarded within the organization, the smoother the project's road to approvals and success is likely to be.

5. *The status and involvement of the project manager.* Is the project this person's sole responsibility? Many organizations make the mistake of giving a competent but already busy person the job of project manager, in addition to his or her regular responsibilities, and find their project failing as a result. The size of project is an important factor, but generally speaking, a project manager should be detached from ongoing operational responsibilities that fall outside of project scope.

Project management requires many different areas of expertise. Competence as a manager in human resources, payroll, or systems is not a guarantee of success. Because an HRMS should be an organization-wide system, the project manager should be seen as unbiased, favouring no particular group, but working towards a functional system for all stakeholders.

Project champions and project managers are not always the same person. In fact, as noted below, the qualities requisite for each may be quite different. Some of these differences are summarized in Table 4-1.

6. *The existence of project and steering committees.* At some early point in the process of planning for a new HRMS, the organization should establish a project team and consider the establishment of a steering committee as well.

A steering committee is often used as a strategic body for guiding the overall process by setting the scope and goals of the project. If estab-

TABLE 4.1 PROJECT MANAGER VS. PROJECT CHAMPIONS

PROJECT MANAGERS	PROJECT CHAMPIONS
• Prefer to work in groups	• Prefer working individually
• Committed to managerial & technical responsibilities	• Committed to the technology
• Committed to the organization	• Committed to the profession
• Seek to achieve the objective	• Seek to exceed the objective
• Are willing to take risks	• Are unwilling to take risks; try to test everything
• Seek what is possible	• Seek perfection
• Think in terms of short time spans	• Think in terms of long time spans
• Manage people	• Manage things
• Are committed to & pursue material values	• Are committed to & pursue intellectual values

Source: Adapted from H. Kerzner, 1989. *Project Management—A Systems Approach to Planning, Scheduling, and Controlling,* 3rd ed. New York: Van Nostrand Reinhold.

lished, it should be comprised of senior policy makers representing key organizational areas: human resources, finance, systems, and operations, and should champion the project when funding and approvals are sought. Steering committees normally meet periodically throughout the project to receive status reports from the project team and to make policy decisions as required.

A project team is also normally comprised of representatives of key organizational areas: human resources, finance, systems, and operations. The project team is the working group responsible for performing the day-to-day tasks of defining requirements, assessing current systems, determining whether to repair and refine a current system, or build or buy a new HRMS, and all other activities. Project team members are normally responsible for implementing the final system. They may also have ongoing responsibility for the subsequent management and maintenance of the system.

7. *Whether clearly defined business needs have been identified.* The requirement for the HR/Payroll system must be understood at senior management levels.

8. *Whether a formal documented plan has been developed.* HRMS projects cross functional boundaries, making great demands on all operational

departments. The complexity of the task demands that a detailed documented plan exist and be used.

9. *Whether planning has been coordinated across departments.* Each department should have a strategic plan that exists as part of a larger organization plan. If not, it will be difficult to link project decisions to the global strategic and operational plans that it must support.

10. *The extent and quality of systems support.* The quality and extent of support provided by management information specialists directly affect the project, be it technical or functional in nature. If the department expresses a preference to build the system or to buy one already programmed (neither choice is inherently better than the other), the HRMS project should be consistent with the preferred approach, or the departure must be clearly resolved in advance.

11. *The age of and satisfaction with the current system.* In today's technological volcano where change is incremental, a system of five + years is approaching obsolescence. An older system that works well is nevertheless in danger of holding the organization back if it does not offer the same degree of functional or technical flexibility as do other, newer systems. It can be harder to replace a system that is meeting current needs, but must be replaced to meet rapidly evolving requirements.

12. *Business process integration.* Implementation of a new computer system such as an HRMS provides an opportunity to re-examine the organization's human resources practices, processes, and systems, and to ensure that these are integrated with other organizational systems and processes. A number of authors have pointed out that, in order to compete effectively in today's rapidly changing world, most organizations need to fundamentally "reengineer their processes and systems" (Tomasko, 1993). Doing this, and then ensuring that the result is reflected in the design and implementation of a new HRMS, will lead to the most effective and efficient system.

13. *Realistic project budget.* Many organizations that embark on a systems project allocate as much as 90 percent or even 100 percent of the budget to software acquisition, leaving insufficient funds for many of the critical areas mentioned above. The actual requirement varies widely, but a good rule of thumb would be that a maximum of 25 percent should be allocated for system acquisition alone.

Whether or not a factor is critical will, to some extent, depend on circumstances in the organization.

◆ ◆ ◆
DEALING WITH CHANGE

The implementation of a new computer system, while presenting challenges, also provides a wonderful opportunity for the organization to introduce larger measures of change than it might otherwise be possible to do. Organizations have different tolerance levels with respect to change. Most companies in the computer industry, service industries, and in aerospace are thought to have a high tolerance for change. Other organizations—perhaps those which reside in Beck's (1992) "old economy"—are less likely to have a climate in which change is a constant.

No matter what the nature of organization, it is important to remember that employees are individuals, individuals whose capacity for change varies enormously, and even fluctuates considerably within one person over time as various life events intrude. Change occasions emotional responses that cannot be overcome by the logic of an engineered business process or detailed project plan.

These processes of change and communication imply an understanding individual and group interests and power structures; anticipating their concerns and objections; and involving them in exploring "what's in it for them."

EXAMPLE

Prior to the implementation of a new HRMS in one organization, employees wishing to change personal information such as mailing address, contact, or emergency phone numbers in their automated human resources files were required to complete a personal information change form and have it approved by their supervisor, who would then forward it to Payroll, who would enter the information in the payroll system, photocopy the originating document for their files, and send the original on to HR for entry in the HR system and filing in HR files.

Only Payroll and HR could enter the data into their systems due to the rigorous security for each. A new integrated HRMS with enhanced security permitted individual employees to directly input their changes into the system. Not only were the nonvalue-added supervisory activities stopped, but so were the duplicate data entry and filing activities.

Process re-engineering, and related concepts are, of course, not unique to human resources processes, or to HRMSs. Re-engineering business processes have wide application for organizations that wish to remain competitive in today's rapidly changing world (see the discussion of business process re-engineering in the next chapter for more detail). To illustrate this, another real-life example is provided below, demonstrating how concepts useful in human resources can have wider application.

EXAMPLE

A large mine suffered through a strike that left the nearby town ravaged. With many of its residents on strike, retail activity dropped below subsistence levels and the entire region was in peril.

Management and union alike realized that significant changes had to be made if the emotion generated by 18 months of hardship were to be overcome. The change they came up with was considered radical for the mining industry.

Previously, mechanics had to fill out a work order listing parts they required to complete repairs. Once approved by their supervisor, these paper requests would be forwarded to supply to be filled. Now, mechanics would be allowed to use computers to order directly from supply. Elimination of paper and time delays were two benefits, but by far the largest was the sense of trust that the new process engendered. In addition, supervisors, freed from their nonvalue-added paper approvals, were able to concentrate on further process improvements. Union, employees, management, and the town all became aware of and agreed on the success of this initiative.

Many organizations today are trying to "empower" their employees to assume responsibility and to act on their own in the best interests of the organization, often utilizing special training and cultural change programs, while ignoring the opportunities offered by making fundamental changes in day-to-day business processes. But organizations often understate the degree of change that a new system makes possible, and overstate the readiness of their employees to embrace that change, as the following example illustrates.

The nature of the system being implemented, and how different it is from that which existed previously will dictate how significant the change will seem to be by most stakeholders, including those responsible for using and maintaining it. Clearly a choice of technology that is new to the organization will impose more change than the continuation of current technology would. Similarly, a decision to substantially alter the underlying business

EXAMPLE

A HR department had two secretaries, both of whom typed 100 words a minute with almost no errors. At their request, the supervisor acquired new word processing equipment which would allow them to perform various time-saving activities. Training was delivered and the two secretaries willingly went to work on their new machines. But within the week both were staying late "to catch up" on their old machines, and then used the new equipment less and less. When questioned by their supervisor, they reluctantly admitted that they were not as productive on the new equipment, being neither as fast, nor as error free. Their dedication to getting the work done and their own self-images about their speed and skill with the old equipment made continued use of the old equipment more appealing.

processes through such techniques as process re-engineering activities could result in significant change. Senior management may, in fact, use the need to implement a new system as a strategic opportunity to make radical change, modifying organization culture, eliminating processes and/or positions, or excising entire departments.

Fossum (1989) states:

> There are many different models for different aspects of change. It does not matter at what level change is occurring, there is a series of stages, or phases, that will be encountered in implementing the change. While the length of time spent in each stage may vary, each will occur while coping with change. The stages are: denial, resistance, adaptation, and involvement (pp. 63–66).

Thus, individuals may respond differently to the decision to develop a new HRMS. Examples might be as follows:

Denial: "We don't need a new system; the old one works just fine."

Resistance: "We aren't going to share in its advantages, why should we cooperate? ... besides it'll cost too much."

> Adaptation: *"Well, if we're going to get a new HRMS we should...."*
>
> Involvement: *"Let's get on the project team and make sure that...."*

Each model of change is useful and applies to certain components of project management. The project must be planned in such a way as to deal with the organization's stages of change.

◆ ◆ ◆
PLANNING IMPLEMENTATION

The scope and schedule of each step must be coordinated to ensure a timely process. A common mistake is to work blindly backwards from management's desired implementation date, making the plan fit the expected end-date. Of course, it is necessary to respect management's priorities and operational requirements for information and the systems designed to gather, maintain, analyze, and provide it. The plan must, however, be realistic, not merely designed to fit the time that has been allotted for it. Acceding to an unrealistic timetable may result in a plan that easily gains management acceptance, but is difficult or even impossible to manage.

The integration of a well-developed system into the organization will dictate how the organization reacts to the system, and its ultimate usefulness. A complete, documented plan is key to the successful implementation of any information system.

◆ ◆ ◆
TRAINING AND DOCUMENTATION

Deadlines and cost constraints are given higher priority over user comprehension in the planning, development, and implementation of many HRMS applications. In planning for the development and implementation of a new HRMS, the two related functions of documentation and training are often overlooked or given insufficient priority (Demarco, 1987; MacAdam, 1991). Overriding concern for getting the system "up and running," often leads to putting documentation and training off to another time when there "will be more time and resources to devote to them." Unfortunately this means that, for many systems, these important functions are never dealt with effectively.

For reasons discussed below, the critical need to plan for systems training and documentation should be identified early in the planning process for any HRMS.

The project team responsible for planning a new HRMS may produce a state-of-the-art product tailored to the needs of the organization. Whether it will be used effectively within the organization, and therefore be successful, will depend on how well users understand and accept it. This, in turn, may depend on the effectiveness of how users are introduced to the system and are trained to use it (Fay, 1988; Martin, 1987, 1988). Some of the requirements of effective systems documentation and training are outlined below.

PURPOSE OF DOCUMENTATION AND TRAINING

There are various levels of documentation and training required depending on whether the individual will be primarily concerned about procedural or technical aspects of the system (MacAdam, 1991). Different levels of documentation and training may be required for managers with access to the system, specialist users such as human resources personnel, and management information specialists (MIS) responsible for maintaining technical aspects of the system.

The purpose of systems documentation is to ensure that there is a complete and up-to-date record of the system's technical details, and how it operates (Eason & Eason, 1988; Horsfield, 1987). Training for MIS personnel is most often aimed at imparting an understanding of the technical details of the system, while the training for other users is aimed at teaching why and how the system operates. Therefore, training must be tailored to the requirements of the particular target group. It is unlikely that one course will satisfy the needs of all groups requiring training (Gueutal et al., 1988; MacAdam, 1991).

Systems documentation involves making a complete and accurate record of both the technical underpinnings of the system, as well as how the system may be used. Such documentation forms the basis of technical and operational reference material for both users and maintenance personnel (Easton & Easton, 1988; Horsfield, 1987).

Documentation is generally done in both technical and users manuals. Training needs analysis is used to determine which content in the manuals needs to be taught, how, to whom, using what teaching methods. Teaching has traditionally involved classroom presentations with practical hands-on laboratory demonstrations and the opportunity to practise specific applications, perhaps supplemented with audio-visual presentations. More recently, other methods, including self-paced, video-disc based, and computer-assisted applications have gained prominence (MacAdam, 1991; Martin, 1988).

TRAINING PHASES

Well-developed training programs fall into the following phases (Belcourt & Wright, 1995; Birnbrauer, 1988; Goldstein, 1974).

1. *Training needs analysis.* In this phase the task to be performed, the standard of performance required, and the skills needed to perform at this level are identified. In gathering this information, one may use such data-gathering strategies as:
   - Focus groups
   - Structured interviews
   - Questionnaires/surveys
   - Direct observations
   - Analysis of documents such as technical manuals or job descriptions

2. *Identification of training media and methods of training.* In this phase the project team training specialist determines the most appropriate training media and method of training for imparting the required knowledge and skills, to the given standard. Training media may include standard manuals, video-tape, video-disc, or various kinds of computer aides. Method of training might include standard classroom presentations, laboratory experiential learning, self-paced computerized adaptive teaching, or combinations of these.

3. *Training program development.* In this phase the training program is developed using the media and method(s) selected.

4. *Training conduct.* This phase involves the scheduling and conduct of training.

5. *Training evaluation.* This critical phase is often overlooked or given short shrift. It links back to the needs analysis phase, and involves ensuring that the training program actually does what it was designed to do. The purpose is to identify and implement improvements.

6. *Skill maintenance.* This is another phase that is often overlooked. It involves developing and implementing the means of maintaining the required knowledge and skills on the system as time goes on. Ongoing training and development may be needed to get new people started on the system, raise individuals to higher levels of expertise, and refresh skills.

7. *Continued support for post-implementation documentation and training.* As time goes on, after the system is up and running, amendments will be required, whether as a consequence of up-grades provided by the vendor, or changing in-house requirements. It is important that allowance for both of these be planned for.

IN-HOUSE OR OFF-THE-SHELF SYSTEMS

If the system is being developed in-house, all aspects of systems documentation and training must be developed from scratch. In such cases it is advisable to have a training specialist on the project team from the start. Systems purchased off-the-shelf, from external suppliers, as sets of pre-developed modules, usually come with documentation and training packages.

In fact, the adequacy of these documentation and training programs should be included as an important set of criteria to be considered when deciding to purchase HRMS systems off-the-shelf. Among the criteria to be considered are:

◆ Comprehensiveness, relevance, and "user-friendliness"

◆ Any additional costs

◆ Number of people to be trained and what level of training is required

◆ Any differentiation in training depending on the needs of the various "users"

TIMELINESS OF DOCUMENTATION

Those responsible for planning and developing the system have unique insights into its capabilities, limitations, and peculiarities (MacAdam, 1991). Once they get away from it, they will progressively lose touch with specific details. It is very difficult for anyone else to learn the system sufficiently to do an effective job of documentation later. Whether the system is developed in-house or purchased off-the-shelf, therefore, planning for systems documentation and training must begin when the HRMS needs analysis is initiated and must carry on through all phases of the project. Every system has subtle changes or modifications arising from unforeseen problems. Accurate and timely documentation ensures that one can maintain a clear picture as to whether the system ends up doing what it was intended to do, and the rationale and potential impact of any changes.

As time goes on after systems implementation, modifications will be necessary to keep up with user requirements, including those resulting from technological advances and legislative changes (Martin, 1987). If system documentation is not complete and up-to-date, the progressive overlay of these modifications can render system maintenance very complicated and time-consuming.

The distinction between documentation and training has become less pronounced with the advent of such innovations as:

1. User friendly database management information systems that do not require much technical sophistication to program and maintain data menus, input screen, and reports;

2. User instruction documentation and tutorials built into the system to guide database modification, and data input and retrieval; and

3. Graphical user interface (GUI), which on the one hand makes the purpose and use of various functions more evident and, on the other, has readily available help facilities to provide assistance when problems arise or clarification is needed.

Some systems utilizing combinations of these innovations have evolved to the point that a user with some familiarity with data management information systems, human resources systems, and graphical user interface can begin to use the system with little or no formal training by following the on-line aids and instructions provided. Formal training programs are still required with such systems, but should be co-ordinated with the built-in documentation and aides.

Written technical manuals for MIS professionals, and procedures manuals for such users as line managers and human resources professionals are still required. Each of these manuals must have a table of contents, a comprehensive index, and a method for updating. All must be clearly written. The managers' manual, in particular, should explain how the system can enhance the individual's role as a manager, in simple terms. These manuals should be consistent and integrated with tutorials, aids, and explanatory information resident in the system.

◆◆◆
TIMELINESS OF TRAINING

Training should be timely so that the individual can apply what was learned as soon as possible after the training was provided (MacAdam, 1991). Too often, for economic or other reasons, individuals are scheduled for training when the course is available, rather than when it is needed. This means that individuals may be given a course, but have no need to use it for some considerable length of time later. In the meantime, the individual's knowledge and motivation to apply what was learned wanes. Other individuals may be given training months after they begin working on the particular application in question. In such cases the individual must "learn by doing." Although many people have done very well under such circumstances, this process can be wasteful. Individuals are forced to flounder, learning things by "trial and error." Sometimes training is provided that is no longer required. Those responsible for using and maintaining the system become demotivated and give up when they could have succeeded with appropriate and timely training and development.

Readers are referred to Belcourt and Wright (1995), Goldstein (1974), and Birnbrauer (1988) for more detailed overviews of the technical aspects of training needs analysis and course development.

◆◆◆
SUMMARY

The cross-functional nature of an HRMS makes it one of the more complex and sensitive projects to manage. Project management is a discipline of its own and is not easily done by the inexperienced. Plans should not be made for their own sake, nor should they become all consuming, but plans and other project management tools are essential to manage the complex and detailed processes of an HRMS. Just as planning and project management are key success factors, so too is a complete communication plan and an honest assessment of the organization as measured against the critical success factors.

This chapter provided an overview of the training and documentation issues that need to be considered when planning for a new HRMS. Conducting an effective needs analysis, and then successfully developing and implementing the requisite training programs calls for a considerable degree of skill and experience. For this reason, it is generally advisable to have training specialists included as integral members of the HRMS project planning, development, and implementation team(s), or at least to have ready access to them.

EXERCISES

1. This chapter has outlined a number of factors that are critical to the success of an HRMS project. Can you assign a priority to these factors? Explain your reasoning.

2. Project management is different from the management of a department on a day-to-day basis. Explain the similarities and differences.

3. Contemporary HRMS projects are generally organization-wide in scope, including at least four major functional areas: Human Resources, Payroll, Systems, and Operations. Think about projects in other functional areas, such as Finance or Operations. Should these projects also cross functional boundaries. Why, or why not?

4. Do small organizations of 50 to 100 employees need to establish a project team? Is a dedicated project manager realistic for such an organization? Is a steering group required? What are the similarities and differences in the requirements for such committees and their leadership between small, medium, and large organizations?

5. The strategic planning department of a Canadian organization with about 7000 employees had a database specialist with a flair for producing ad hoc databases and reporting programs. He could produce very quick practical solutions to a broad variety of problems. Users came to rely on these solutions rather than bother with the longer time frames and "bureaucracy" (including documentation) that they encountered from MIS. This administrative convenience and quick turnaround was not without a cost, however, in that very little documentation on these ad hoc solutions existed, except in the head of the programmer. What future problems do you foresee for this organization? How might these problems be avoided?

6. Do you think that there may sometimes be grounds for trade-offs between too much and too little documentation? What variables might lead you to move toward more or less documentation in any particular example?

7. Given that training on how to use a new HRMS will generally be provided when the system has been implemented, why is it important to have training specialists on the systems development and implementation team throughout?

References

Beck, N. 1992. *Shifting Gears—Thriving in the New Economy.* Toronto: HarperCollins Publishers Ltd.

Belcourt, M., and P. Wright. *Managing Performance Through Training and Development.* Toronto: Nelson Canada, 1996.

Birnbrauer, H., ed. 1988. *ASTD Handbook for Technical and Skills Training* (2 vols.). Alexandria, Va.: American Society for Training and Development.

Clavell, J. 1983. *Sun Tzu's The Art Of War.* New York: Doubleday Dell Publishing Group, Inc.

DeMarco, T. 1979. *Structured Analysis and Systems Specification.* Englewood Cliffs, N.J.: Prentice-Hall.

Easton, T.S., and E.D. Easton. 1988. "HRIS Documentation: a Road Map to Application and Maintenance." *Computers in Personnel* (Fall): 38–40.

Fay, C.H. 1988. "Educating Old and New HR Managers." *Computers in Personnel* (Summer): 20–25.

Fossum, L. 1989. *Understanding Organizational Change–Converting Theory to Practice.* Los Altos, Cal.: CRISP Publications, Inc.

Goldstein, B.L. 1974. *Training: Program Development and Evaluation.* Monterey, Cal.: Brooks Cole.

Gueutal, H.G., S.I. Tannenbaum, and M.J. Kavanagh. 1988. "Where to go for an HRIS Education." *Computers in Education,* 22–25.

Horsfield, D. 1987. "Home-grown Documentation." *Computers in Personnel* (Summer): 51.

Kanter, R.M. 1989. *When Giants Learn To Dance.* New York: Simon and Schuster.

Kerzner, H. 1989. *Project Management— A Systems Approach to Planning, Scheduling, and Controlling,* 3rd ed. New York: Van Nostrand Reinhold.

Knutson, J., and I. Bitz. 1991. *Project Management—How to Plan and Manage Successful Projects.* New York: American Management Association.

MacAdam, M. 1991. "Training HRIS Users." In A.L. Lederer, ed., *Handbook of Human Resource Information Systems*. New York: Warren, Gorham and Lamont.

Martin, M.P. 1987. "The Human Connection in System Design: Part VI. Designing Systems for Change." *Journal of Systems Management* (July): 14–18.

_____. 1988. "The Human Connection in System Design: Part VII. Prototypes for User Training." *Journal of Systems Management* (July): 19–22.

Peters, T. 1987. *Thriving On Chaos*. New York: Alfred A. Knopf.

Plantamura, L.M. 1990. "Automated Project Management." *The Review Human Resource Systems Professionals* (October/November): 19–21.

Schein, E.H. 1978. *Human Resource Planning and Development: a Total System*. Boston, Mass.: MIT, Sloan School of Management.

Tomasko, R.M. 1993. *Rethinking the Corporation—The Architecture of Change*. New York: AMACOM.

5

Designing and Developing a New HRMS

◆ ◆ ◆

INTRODUCTION

This chapter discusses concepts that are relevant to designing and developing a new HRMS. Some of the questions addressed include: What are the components of an HRMS, and what steps are needed to develop one? What is the best way to acquire a new HRMS—to develop one internally or to buy one from an external software supplier?

Information technology has changed considerably over the last four decades. We have gone from carbon paper and Gestetner machines to scanners and high speed colour photocopiers; from cutting and pasting with scissors and glue to cutting and pasting digitalized images on a computer (Forrer & Leibowitz, 1991).

Computer systems design has also undergone considerable change. Many organizations that formerly built information systems now build information management structures instead. Into these structures they insert the appropriate software applications, to communicate through networks of electrical, telephone, and various kinds of cable connections (Weizer et al., 1991).

Whether the decision is made to build an HRMS internally, or to acquire an already developed system from a software supplier, the design of the system can facilitate or restrict the uses to which it is put. Many systems both facilitate and restrict, depending on the functional area or application involved.

◆ ◆ ◆

GENERAL DESIGN CONSIDERATIONS

The design of any software package requires both functional and technical decisions, and it should be predicated on the uses to which the system will be put. A computer software company determines the components of the HRMS it is building by developing its own concept of what an HRMS should be, and by taking into account market conditions, that is, what potential clients want and what competitors offer.

◆ ◆ ◆
APPLICATIONS: BREADTH AND DEPTH

The degree to which an HRMS is useful to potential clients can be measured by what are termed its "breadth" and "depth." The breadth of a system indicates how many different applications or functions are covered by the software. Some of the most common HRMS functions or applications were outlined in Chapters 1 and 2; they include human resources planning and development, staffing, training, occupational health and safety, compensation and payroll, benefits, and pension. The depth of a system may vary by functional or application area. A system that provides a lot of detail in one functional area (benefits administration, for example), may provide less detailed coverage in another area, such as health and safety. Another system will offer a different breadth and/or depth. These differences in software packages provide users with options by which to evaluate packages depending on their specific requirements.

The payroll function, for example, has one common purpose across all organizations, that is, to pay people accurately and on time. However, a comparison of different payroll systems will show a surprising number of differences in how the functions are performed, and many ancillary payroll functions (such as retroactive payments or mass updates) may exist in some systems and not in others.

The manner by which systems offer breadth and depth will also vary. Some systems are totally integrated, while others offer a core, or main, module along with a number of other optional modules. In these cases, the core module often has limited capability in every area, with the additional modules offering much more depth in specific areas. Thus, the buyer can pick and choose both the breadth and depth of system depending on the needs, or finances, of the organization.

Most systems offer at least some capability in all areas, but the manner in which they appear may vary considerably. They may be contained within a core module, a secondary module, or both, to varying degrees.

Table 5-1 and Figure 5-1 illustrate the relationships between HRMS core and application modules design. Table 5-1 shows how the applications modules relate to the core HRMS/payroll module, while Figure 5-1

TABLE 5.1 COMPARISON OF CORE AND SECONDARY TRAINING MODULE

Core System—Training Section
- Individual employee education/training history, referencing:
  - Table of training classes
  - Table of degrees
  - Table of licences
  - Table of colleges/universities

Secondary Training Module
- Full Administrative Model with:
  - Session & class scheduling
  - Room assignments
  - Expenses per class
  - Materials requirements
  - Audiovisual and other equipment booking
  - Salary cost of student participation
  - Student expenses

FIGURE 5.1 Modular Design

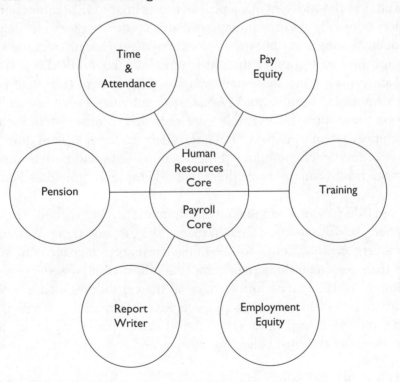

Source: Ross Systems Inc., 1995

demonstrates the relationship between a training module and the counterpart segment on the core module.

Normally the core modules can operate independently of the secondary modules, but are required for the secondary modules to work. Systems designers usually have extremely detailed flow diagrams of their systems. These data diagrams act as maps to the system which can be used by functional and technical users alike. A data dictionary accompanies the data diagram and lists every data element (e.g., "surname") together with its definition and characteristics. Characteristics include the nature of the field (alpha, numeric, or both), the size of the field (28 characters), and sometimes, the screens on which that particular data element appears. Data diagrams and dictionaries are key parts of system design documentation and can be of great help to prospective purchasers in understanding the conceptual framework of the system.

Tracking the movement of people is a primary HRMS function. This function is usually spread among several sections or modules. Beginning with documenting an application for employment (usually recorded in the applicant tracking section of the staffing module), most HRMSs will record hiring an employee and subsequent employee movement (transfers, promotions, demotions, termination). Associated activities—such as additional salary on promotion, for example—are recorded in other modules, in this case, compensation and payroll. These salary changes will in turn effect changes in the benefits module, the pension module, and perhaps even the training or health and safety modules (cost of employee time based on salary cost).

An HRMS should be designed to inform management about employees and other workforce participants (Walker, 1993). As noted in previous chapters, modern organizations require human resources management systems rather than personnel or human resources information systems (Broderick and Bourdeau, 1992). The former have all the capabilities of the latter, but in addition, provide managers at all levels with information reporting, analysis, and modelling capabilities for the effective management of human resources, rather than just collecting, storing, and reporting human resources information.

Thus, HRMSs are not merely buckets into which data is poured and retrieved, but tools to manipulate data into usable information. A theme throughout this text is that HRMSs are no longer restricted to "employees," whatever that term may imply; rather, a modern HRMS is a critical tool in the strategic and operational management of the total workforce of the organization. Whereas systems of five years ago referred to "employee databases" and contained information on employees only, those being designed today include contractors, consultants, and all significant others.

Huva (1995) points out some of the shortfalls in the design of current HRMS programs measured against Walker's (1993) principle of total workforce inclusion:

> *Very few HR systems can track membership in teams. We have a hard enough time tracking the department to allocate payroll costs, let alone something as ephemeral as teams. We cannot track the historical relationships between people to discover if our team members had worked together within the last three years. We cannot track the outcome of work such as the 18% profit margin on the last project. We cannot track the competencies that our people have gained through the work experience. Even if we could track contractors, which very few HR systems can do effectively, we know even less about a contractors competencies than we do our employees (pp. 29–30).*

◆ ◆ ◆

LANGUAGE REQUIREMENTS

Organizations building or buying an HRMS should begin by examining what current and *future* requirements the HRMS should be satisfying for the organization. To do this effectively it might be necessary to analyze, in turn, the effectiveness of the human resources processes that the system is being designed and developed to support. In Canada an additional and highly significant design feature is whether or not the system will be bilingual (English/French), unilingual (just one or the other), or whether two unilingual systems (one each of English and French) are desired. The issue of language has long been recognized in European software, and it is currently gaining prominence in the design of systems in the United States due to the increasing Spanish influence in that country.

Another issue that is gaining prominence is that of multiple currencies. Very few software packages on the market as this text is being written provide for a "home country currency" and other currencies. Turnbull (1994) uses the example of an organization based in the United States with employees in the United Kingdom and other countries which is faced with keeping a record in U.S. dollars or U.K. pounds, but not both. Either choice places severe restrictions on management's ability to use the system effectively.

◆ ◆ ◆
SECURITY

Data security is a very important aspect in the design of any HRMS (*Personnel Journal*, 1994). The system's security features should permit the organization to group individual users by various and multiple criteria such as job function, organization structure, level within an organization, union (of both user and employees accessed), and geographic location. Ideally, security profiles, which should be date effective (start and end dates) would be defined by position (e.g., Director HR vs. Director Finance), and the employee movement portion of the system would then link the position's security profile to the user identification (i.d.) of the current incumbent(s) of that position. Linking security profiles to position level rather than to individual users makes the day-to-day administrative elements of the system as simple as possible; employee movement in and out of positions does not require extensive administrative intervention.

Flexible security structures within a system usually indicate that the system will satisfy concerns regarding system control and privacy. System control is often offered through audit trails that allow users to analyze system usage and to review processes for a variety of purposes. Audit records after the fact can be used to analyze system activity by type of transaction, or by user. The proper use of audit trails and system security can replace various traditional control mechanisms, such as the requirement of multiple authorization signatures before an action can be taken.

In most states and provinces (to varying degrees) privacy is a legislated right of anyone whose personal data resides within an HRMS. Privacy rules usually address the "need to know," and require that access to data that is considered to be of a particularly personal nature (racial characteristics and medical information for example) be restricted to those who require it as part of their job (Campion and Campion, 1995). Thus a supervisor may be permitted access to an employee's home phone number in order to call that person to return to work, but denied access to that same employee's employment equity declaration.

Other systems operations issues include the existence of date effectivity. Date effectivity allows a system to have multiple versions of a table or event, with each occurrence having a start date and an end date. Thus, for example, a system can hold many copies of a salary structure, each coming into effect within its own time parameters. The question of standard reports and an ad hoc report writer should also be considered. Most software packages come with some predefined or "standard" reports, but for a system to be truly usable, it must have an easy-to-use report writer to generate new reports as required.

Technical issues include the type of hardware on which the HRMS will run, the type of database used, whether the system is accessed through dumb terminals, work stations, PCs (IBM standard), Macs (Apple standard), or some combination. Just as functional requirements will vary by organization, so too will technical requirements.

◆ ◆ ◆
ANALYSIS OF BUSINESS PROCESSES

Too often in the past, new systems have been developed based on existing organizational requirements (Rampton and Doran, 1994). This has greatly limited the lifespan of such systems. Some were obsolete even before being implemented.

Acquiring/developing and implementing new computer software without considering how it can best be applied to achieve organizational goals is likely to be, at best, a costly exercise, and at worst a complete waste of resources. The automation of inefficient work flows will simply produce the wrong result more quickly. Even more important, automation of current processes can mean that totally unnecessary activities are being codified.

It is important to ensure that the human resources processes being automated are effective. The following paragraphs outline a number of concepts that have recently gained prominence as a means of analyzing and improving "business processes," including "human resources processes" (Hammer and Champy, 1993).

In their landmark work, *Re-engineering the Corporation*, Hammer and Champy (1993) argued that American corporations had to radically change the way they did business, or go out of business. The arrival of this work coincided with an extended economic downturn throughout the Western world, a downturn that had managers at every level and in every industry worrying about the future of their businesses and their careers. Industry and nonprofit organizations alike searched for ways to improve productivity and financial performance. Nurtured by other concepts, such as customer service (Albrecht and Zemke, 1985), total quality management (Farquhar and Johnston, 1990), and continuous improvement (Johnston and Daniel, 1991), organizations examined the value of every employee and every task with a new intensity.

The concepts of re-engineering and "restructuring" were wholeheartedly embraced by business, although the emphasis has been on evolution rather than revolution as encouraged by Hammer and Champy (1993).

The term "re-engineering" implies that business processes in the corporation have already been engineered or designed, but that is rarely the case. Organizations have evolved over time, one step at a time. New tasks are identified as necessary, and new employees are added to perform them. Davenport (1993) considers the term "re-engineering" to be too narrow in scope for the techniques that have come to be included in this general area, and prefers "process innovation" as the more inclusive and descriptive term. A more accurate term, might even be "business process engineering."

Whatever descriptor is chosen, the common theme is "if it ain't broke, break it" in a stark contrast to the catchphrase of just years before "if it ain't broke, don't fix it." In fact, Burrus and Gittines (1993) suggest that one of the shifts we have seen in business is the understanding that breaks may exist even if they cannot be seen.

The core steps in business process re-engineering are:

ANALYSIS PHASE

1. Identify WHAT tasks are being done.
2. Determine WHY those tasks are being done.
3. Analyze HOW they are being done.
4. Identify WHO is doing them.

PROBLEM-SOLVING PHASE

1. Identify what tasks should be done, along with why they should be done.

2. Determine how the tasks should be done.

3. Determine who should do the tasks, along with where and when the tasks should be done.

In conducting these steps,

1. Develop a strategy and scope for the re-engineering plan.

2. Ensure that management at all levels are convinced of the value of project, and committed to supporting it.

3. Chart process flows and analyze current high or low level tasks.

4. Consider what supporting application software will be required.

5. Conduct value for money audits to ensure that you can justify your project in terms of dollars and cents (see Chapter 3).

6. Develop benchmarks for the projects to be used as standards to be met (or exceeded) by the project.

7. Develop new effective and efficient tasks and processes.

8. Prepare an implementation plan (see Chapter 6).

9. Implement the plan.

10. Develop a plan for maintaining the system.

The degree of change to effect this restructuring may vary—within the human resources department, between departments, across the entire organization, and even between organizations—on a continuum ranging from dramatic radical innovation to small incremental change. Both strategic and operational goals can be addressed as part of business process re-engineering.

It should be noted that business process re-engineering and related concepts are not without their critics. Tomasko (1993), for example, has characterized business process re-engineering as "another useful but narrow and potentially static path to organization improvement (p. 13)."

Using tools improperly, or depending on any one tool or set of tools to provide "the answer" has never been successful. Nor is jumping on a new solution or "fad" (Lasden, 1985). But properly implemented, business process engineering can pay big dividends (Champy, 1995).

Once it has been decided that the human resources processes in the organization are the "right ones to automate" attention can then be turned to designing the HRMS to automate the processes in the "right way."

Ceriello (1991) outlines the steps to be followed in designing an HRMS:

1. Design a database with the capacity to handle the relevant populations.

2. Label each field and each data element to create a complete data dictionary.

3. Create tables of values that can be drawn on by data fields as appropriate.

4. Establish data relationships, including all algorithms and routines, to optimize editing and validation of fields.

5. Create menus and screens to assist users in navigating through the HRMS.

6. Create operator messages that specify action options.

7. Build in error-checking routines.

8. Build in data security, including audit trails.

9. Define standard reports.

10. Include a tutorial module to assist new users (p. 142).

◆ ◆ ◆
TOOLS TO ASSIST IN HRMS DESIGN AND DEVELOPMENT

FLOW CHARTS

The graphic depiction of the activities and sequence of business processes can be useful in designing and developing an HRMS. Additional data, such as the amount of time per process, can be added to charts or to supplementary text. Flow charts highlight duplication, roadblocks, and process gaps and make the job of designing new processes easier. Existing processes should be mapped to determine the strategic principles you want to ensure will exist in the new ones.

The level at which flow charting is done can be a factor. Extremely high level processes will not provide enough detail to make significant changes in the day-to-day processes, but too low a level can create mountains of detail that obscure rather than enlighten.

BOX 5.1 SOFTWARE ATTRIBUTES FOR HAPPY USERS

- Easy to establish contact with software (sign-on process; security)
- Uses icons, menus, or both to guide user choices (no need to use code or learn mnemonics)
- Software easy to learn and use (windows, scrolling, and other features)
- Users are guided through various processes; help to correct mistakes is easily available
- Error messages are fully explanatory

- Data dictionary is available on-line
- Software has edit checks to verify syntax, semantics, and overall data integrity (i.e., The Canadian Social Insurance Number has nine digits; the software should require nine before data entry continuation is permitted)
- Downloads/uploads to/from PC products such as word processors, spreadsheets
- Effective use of graphics

Whether charting large and/or complex processes, or getting ready to assess current or future software, a data dictionary with a set of standard terms and definitions could be useful. Information systems professionals may already have developed flow diagrams and/or data models with data dictionaries, which should be made available to you.

As with any tool, flow charts have their limitations. Harrington (1991) states that: "Many business people have used flowcharting techniques with enviable results. Others, however, have been less successful. Generally this happens because they view their flowcharts as the end of, rather than the means to, what they are seeking (p. 9)."

Several new systems use a concept known as "work flow." Work flow is a method and tool that allows the user to map out and to integrate the entire business process with the computer support system.

Traditional HRMS have used the technique of sequencing a number of screens to simulate the flow of paper in a process. Systems with work flow take this concept a step farther by automating much of the paper flow. This is accomplished by linking the HRMS to other application tools such as spreadsheets, word processors, e-mail systems, and schedulers.

Thus, for example, the need to do a performance appraisal, is triggered by a flag in the HRMS and the responsible supervisor is reminded automatically by e-mail. The supervisor does the evaluation, and then he or she and the employee put notes together on an electronic form and complete the "paperwork" by e-mailing the form back to Human Resources where it becomes part of the HRMS.

BENCHMARKING

Even as organizations are flowcharting, analyzing, and engineering processes, many are casting glances both internally and at other organizations to determine if there are any standards or benchmarks with which to compare or aim for.

Benchmarking is a process for continuously measuring and comparing an organization's business processes against the processes of business leaders elsewhere in the world to help the organization improve its performance (Belcourt et al., 1996).

As noted in Chapter 3, contrary to popular belief it is possible to quantify the value of human resource management. Fitz-Enz (1995) writes:

> *A mythology has developed around personnel work. It has to do with the nature and purpose of the work. More important, it deals with the outcomes or results of the labour. The fundamental belief was that the true and full value of personnel's work could only be judged by those who perform it. There was a belief that business-type measures could not be applied to this function (p. 7).*

Fitz-Enz (1995) then offers some principles in performance measurement:

> *The productivity and effectiveness of any function can be measured by some combination of cost, time, quantity, or quality indices:*
>
> 1. *A measurement system promotes productivity by focusing attention on the important issues, tasks, and objectives.*
> 2. *Professional and knowledge workers are best measured as a group.*

3. *Managers can be measured by the efficiency and effectiveness of the units they manage.*

4. *The ultimate measurement is not efficiency, but effectiveness (pp. 261–63).*

◆ ◆ ◆
TO BUILD OR BUY

Should an organization design and build its own HRMS, or acquire one that has already been developed by an external supplier? The answer to this question can perhaps be sought in the importance the organization attaches to human resources in achieving organizational goals. Donovan (1991), for example, states that strategic applications should not be purchased "off the shelf" from external suppliers, since strategic applications must be designed to reflect internal re-engineered business processes.

Are human resources management systems strategic? Donovan defines an information system as strategic when: "it enables an organization to meet its highest goals, giving that organization a competitive advantage, be it survival, profit, or increased business (p. 3)." In today's business and political environment, with downsizing and right-sizing occurring in almost every organization, it seems clear that human resources, and the systems that manage them, do fit that definition.

So, does this imply that all organizations should build their own HRMSs from scratch? No. We do not believe that this is necessarily the case. The rate of change for most organizations has increased to the point where commercial developers of HRMS software produce new versions of their software annually or even more frequently. Donovan (1991) points out that the goals and environment of organizations change, and that taking years to build strategic applications will produce outdated systems.

Organizations must understand that the strategic advantage of good information systems comes not from building some unique tool, but by ensuring that the tool has all of the capabilities that the organization requires, and by using these capabilities well. Selecting the correct system, installing it properly, ensuring that converted data is accurate and complete, designing complimentary and efficient business processes, and then using the combination of processes and software efficiently and effectively are all important.

If analysis of the organization's needs compared to systems available on the market indicates that no system will meet them, then building a system internally may be necessary. If there is a close match between needs and a system off the shelf, from an external supplier, buying the system and amending it to meet the requirements of the organization may be the better option.

The amount of fit that is desirable before a buying decision is made is a matter of debate. Ceriello (1991) suggests that a 75 percent fit is sufficient for the buying decision, while others suggest as much as 95 percent. The less fit there is between user requirements and a software package, the greater the change that will be required. This may be a combination of changing business processes, and therefore user requirements, and modifying or customizing the system. Modern systems offer tools to make many changes, ranging from screen colour to the addition/deletion/re-sizing of data elements. However, the more a system is modified or customized the more difficult it may be to maintain, especially when updates must be made frequently or when new versions have to be loaded.

Building a custom HRMS has operating implications as well. Most external software suppliers offer training and maintenance services to compliment their products (Ceriello, 1991). As outlined in Chapter 1, legislation has considerable impact on both the human resources and payroll elements of an HRMS. Program developers regularly update their software to meet legislative requirements. These updates are released at least annually, and sometimes quarterly. An organization that undertakes to build some or all of an HRMS must determine how it will meet these legislative imperatives.

◆ ◆ ◆
SCREENING AND SELECTING SOFTWARE

Comparing different HRMSs can be difficult, since they may have been developed with different organizational assumptions and requirements in mind. The traditional approach to software selection involves the following steps:

1. Definition of user requirements.
2. Development of a request for information (RFI) or request for proposal (RFP), which is then sent to appropriate software suppliers. These list

functional and technical requirements and ask suppliers to compare their systems against that list.

3. Assessment of supplier responses, screening out systems or suppliers that do not match sufficient criteria.

4. Demonstrations of short-listed products to get the "look and feel" and to confirm that stated capability does exist.

5. Assessment of vendor and software reliability.

DEFINITION OF REQUIREMENTS

The definition of an organization's requirements can be simple or detailed and complex, depending, again, on the organization's requirements.

Requirements are generally defined according to three categories: functional, system operations, and technical requirements. Functional requirements include determining the depth and breadth of each functional area necessary to successful operation. Organizations use various methods for establishing functional requirements.

Systems operations issues include such matters as how the user moves around within the system and ease of use of the system. Ceriello (1991) lists some attributes of "user-friendly" systems:

◆ Easy to establish contact with software (sign-on process; security)

◆ Icons, menus, or both are used to guide user choices (no need to use code or learn mnemonics)

◆ Software is easy to learn and use (windows, scrolling, and other features)

◆ Users are guided through various processes; help to correct mistakes is easily available

◆ All error messages are fully explanatory

◆ The data dictionary is available on-line

◆ Software has edit checks to verify syntax, semantics, and overall data integrity

◆ Downloads/uploads to/from PC products such as word processors, spreadsheets

◆ Demonstrates an effective use of graphics

DEVELOPMENT OF AN RFI/RFP

A request for information (RFI) or request for proposal (RFP) can contain very similar information. The primary distinction is considered to be that a software supplier's response to a RFI is not binding, whereas a response to a RFP forms part of the information that the parties may use as the basis of a subsequent contractual arrangement (Turnbull, 1996).

Determining the criteria for selecting and comparing suppliers and products is a critical step in the process. There are tools available to reduce the work required in the selection process. For instance, the HR_Matrix (Heinen, 1994) compares information on many HRMSs in a grid. What applications are included, their capabilities, options and/or modules, and various other information are laid out in a large checklist for buyers to assess products. This comparison of vendor-supplied data against the organization's needs can help to narrow the number of systems/suppliers to be contacted. Their responses should consequently be of higher quality, and the time required to assess them may therefore be used more effectively.

Unfortunately, the detail available in a matrix such as is produced by this software is somewhat limited. The same terminology used by two different software suppliers may imply system capabilities that are considerably different in breadth and depth. This may not be possible to determine these differences from information in the matrix. In addition the warning of *caveat emptor* (buyer beware) should be heeded. No buyer should rely on this kind of tool alone to make a "buy/no buy" decision.

Developing an RFI/RFP is a complex task. The RFI/RFP should be designed in a way that will facilitate comparative analysis of several software supplier's responses. Open-ended questions invite open-ended answers which are very hard to compare. To the extent possible, questions should be specific. One method of achieving this is to offer multiple choice responses followed by a "comments" section for the software supplier to elaborate as required, thus providing comparative data and allowing for an explanation of variances (Turnbull, 1996).

ASSESSMENT OF VENDOR RESPONSES

Where the RFI/RFP has been designed well, the analysis of results should be easy, if often time-consuming. The purpose of the analysis is to weed out unsuitable systems or suppliers, leaving only the best options for further review.

DEMONSTRATIONS

Potential suppliers should be asked to provide demonstrations of their products. Demonstrations of software can be as short as one hour, or as long as a week or more. Many software selection processes include at least two phases: a short (one to three hours), general, initial demonstration, followed by a more detailed and focused demonstration.

Organizations may ask suppliers to help them work through a detailed set of scenarios meant to simulate various functional and/or technical issues that are critical to the organization's success. These detailed "test runs" can be both complex and time-consuming, but they are well worth it. Time and money spent at this stage will help to ensure that the final decision and implementation have the maximum opportunity for success.

As an example, a forestry company in western Canada was concerned about the performance characteristics of a particular software product. The software vendor provided software and hardware and was present to assist in a multi-site simulation over a five-day period. The test results provided the company with new ideas about the most desirable hardware and communications network configuration, and confirmed their business process design concepts.

SUPPLIER AND PRODUCT RELIABILITY

Buying a software package, particularly an HRMS, should mean that you are buying not just the current software version, but future versions as well. This investment in a product and its supplier can be a marriage of five, ten, or even more years. It should only be made if the buyer is sure that the supplier and the product are reliable, that is, that both are a good investment.

The research should be much more rigorous than a simple reference check. Many suppliers have made arrangements with current clients to allow prospective buyers to visit. These visits can include watching the system in operation, and question and answer sessions regarding everything from the implementation process and training to ongoing maintenance.

Supplier reliability analysis can include a review of the supplier's products and its development plans (both HRMS and other product lines), financial stability, problem hot-line, maintenance costs and approaches, and software upgrade policy.

◆ ◆ ◆
BUILDING AN HRMS OR
CONTRACTING OUT

If the decision has been made to develop the HRMS in-house, the first question that must be asked is what the breadth and depth of the system will be? Perhaps more fundamentally: Will the HRMS contain a payroll module as well as other human resources management modules? As Figure 5-1 suggests, the core human resources and payroll functions can exist separately.

Today, the decision to build an HRMS is most often based on the assessment that existing commercial HRMS software does not have all of the HRMS capabilities that the organization requires. There is another option, however. Rather than relying on external suppliers for HRMS software products, some of the services typically provided by an HRMS can be contracted out (Sloftsra, 1994).

CONTRACTING OUT EXAMPLE: PAYROLL
SERVICES

There are several components to the pay process (Turnbull, 1996):

- ◆ Determining employee entitlements (as derived from union and/or individual employee contracts and policy)

- ◆ Basic pay

- ◆ Secondary pay (overtime, shift differential)

- ◆ Calculating employee deductions (statutory, mandatory, company policy)

- ◆ Tracking time worked/not worked

- ◆ Making gross to net calculation of pay

- ◆ Generating cheque/electronic deposit

- ◆ Generating/delivering pay slip to employee

- ◆ Generating annual report calculations (T4, PAs, etc.)

A payroll service usually performs only the last four functions, based on data drawn from the organization regarding the other components—entitlements, deductions, and time worked/not worked. This is a significant portion of the work, but it does not relieve an organization of its legislative responsibilities. Too few payroll systems include or are linked to automated systems for capturing employee schedules, time worked (direct labour) or not worked (indirect labour costs). The steps generally performed by payroll service bureaus (the last four mentioned above) are those that are most heavily reliant on computers.

Many payroll professionals who use a third party service argue that the use of a service ensures employees are paid on time. This presumably reflects past use of internal systems that were so unreliable as to be "crashing, or going down" at some crucial point in the payroll process on a regular basis. Regardless of the relative perfection of a third party's processing, the responsibility for paying employees correctly and on time continues to reside with the organization's payroll staff.

The payroll application software and the computers available today would seem to make this kind of problem highly unlikely. However, if an organization's internal computer resources are sufficiently unreliable, payroll service bureaus are an option well worth considering. The primary advantage to this process is that no in-house system expertise is necessary. But there are risks. Sookman (1994) warns that contracting out may lead to rigid costing structures, licensing and security problems, and a loss of control over key organization data. Some payroll service bureaus, for example, control the generation of management reports and charge for each line of each report (a particularly nonservice-oriented approach). The cost of other payroll service bureaus is based on the number of employees being processed, with secondary pricing for a number of variables, including generation of reports.

Since the initial cost of contracting out is much lower than purchasing and implementing an internal payroll system, it is often considered a cheaper solution. Over the longer term, however, contracting out payroll services may not be as cost effective, particularly for larger organizations. Those thinking of using a payroll service bureau should analyze all costs over a period of at least three years before making a decision.

Some organizations have multiple payroll software applications and many other applications—often available to only one person—such as PC-based statistical packages for compensation. These applications can range from an internal payroll system or a payroll service system to a complete HRMS. In between these options lie various mainframe programs that were written in response to specific requirements, or PC software purchased to meet a functional requirement.

◆ ◆ ◆
SUMMARY

This chapter has pointed out the need for those undertaking to design and develop a new HRMS to begin by answering the following questions:

1. *Are there new and/or different business requirements that require a change in functionality?* The current system may be fine for today's needs, but inadequate for those of tomorrow.

2. *Are new or different legislative requirements expected?* If a software supplier has a good track record with respect to keeping pace with legislative change one can be reasonably assured about the future—although it must always be remembered that the host organization, not the software supplier, has the legal responsibility to ensure compliance with legislation in the day-to-day operation of the HRMS.

Existing HR, payroll, and time and attendance computer systems (whether mainframe, mini, or PC-based; integrated or stand-alone) should be assessed to determine which functions should be retained or replaced, and how to interface/integrate any of these systems that remain with the HRMS.

Designing an HRMS, whether the design be for the internal development of a system, or the preparation to buy and install a system, is a complex task. Functional and technical issues must be dealt with, and occasionally compromises must be accepted.

The effective contribution of human resources management to an organization's success is directly related to the effectiveness of underlying human resources management systems. Organizations that spend time considering all aspects—including supporting technology—of the work they do will surely perform better then those which do not.

Every computer system works in support of a set of business processes. Engineering or re-engineering those processes is an important piece of the system design and development puzzle.

EXERCISES

1. Suppose you were given the responsibility for designing and developing a new HRMS in a financial institution with 15,000 employees headquartered

in Winnipeg, Manitoba, but with branches across Canada. What are some of the global (high level) design issues that you feel should be considered? Should some issues take precedence over others? Discuss.

2. Chapter 1 lists several human resources functions (the following chapters greatly expand on that list) that are often included in an HRMS. Some HRMSs do not include components for such functions as time and attendance and occupational health and safety. Why might this be? Are there ways in which the HRMS might communicate and work with such modules, even though they may exist in departments within the organization? Are there other important modules with which the HRMS should network, for example, finance, operations or corporate planning? How might this be done?

3. This chapter reinforces statements made in earlier chapters which outline the difference between personnel and payroll systems, human resources information systems (HRISs), and human resources management system (HRMSs). How might these distinctions show themselves when considering HRMS design?

4. What is a RFP? How does it differ from a RFI, and to what purpose(s) can each be put?

5. List three methods by which an organization can verify vendor claims about an HRMS product. Which are most important, and why?

6. Why is it important to examine the human resources business processes being automated when designing and developing a new HRMS? Given that the "powers that be" agree to conduct a business process re-engineering (or engineering, if preferred) study of the organization's human resources function, who do you think should be involved in such a study? Who should lead it? Should it contain representatives from outside of Human Resources? What role should management information specialists play?

References

Albrecht, K., and R. Zemke. 1985. *Service America: Doing Business in the New Economy.* Homewood, Ill.: Dow Jones-Irwin.

Belcourt, M., A.W. Sherman, G.W. Bohlander, and S.A. Snell. 1996. *Managing Human Resources*, Toronto: Nelson Canada.

Broderick, R., and J.W. Boudreau. 1992. "Human Resource Management, Information Technology, and the Competitive Edge." *The Executive* 5, no. 2 (May): 7–17.

Burrus, D., and R. Gittines. 1993. *Technotrends—How to Use Technology to Go Beyond Your Competition.* New York: Harper Business.

Campion, M.A., and L.L. Campion. 1995. "A Practical Checklist for Content and Organization." *HR Focus* 72, no. 1 (January): 12–13.

Ceriello, V.R. 1991. *Human Resource Management Systems: Strategy, Factors, and Techniques.* Toronto: Maxwell Macmillan.

Champy, M. 1995. *Re-engineering Management: the Mandate for New Leadership.* Toronto: HarperBusiness.

Davenport, T.H. 1993. *Process Innovation—Re-engineering Work through Information Technology.* Boston, Mass.: Harvard Business School Press.

Donovan, J.J. 1996. *Opportunities in Technology.* Cambridge, Mass.: Cambridge Technology Group.

Farquhar, C.R., and C.G. Johnston. 1990. *Total Quality Management: A Competitive Imperative* Report. 60–90. Ottawa: The Conference Board of Canada.

Fitz-Enz. J. 1993. *Benchmarking Staff Performance.* San Francisco, C.A: Jossey-Bass.

_____. 1995. *How To Measure Human Resources Management,* 2nd ed. New York: McGraw-Hill.

Forrer, S.E., and Z.B. Leibowitz. 1991. *Using Computers in Human Resources.* San Francisco, C.A.: Jossey-Bass.

Hammer, M., and J. Champy. 1993. *Re-engineering The Corporation: A Manifesto for Business Revolution.* New York: HarperCollins.

Harrington, H.J. 1991. *Business Process Improvement.* New York: McGraw-Hill.

Heinen, J.C. 1994. "Automating the Process for HRIS Selection." *Employment Relations Today* 21, no. 4 (Winter): 371–80.

Huva, W. 1995. "Globalization and the HRMS." *RESOURCE* 4, no. 3 (September): 29–30.

Johnston, C.G., and M.J. Daniel. 1991. *Customer Satisfaction Through Quality: An International Perspective.* Report 74-91-E. Ottawa: The Conference Board of Canada.

Lasden, M. 1985. "Fad in fad out." *Computer Decisions* (May): 74–88.

"Privacy and Security Measures in Computing." 1994. *Personnel Journal* (November): 9–10.

Rampton, G.M., and J.A. Doran. 1994. *A Practitioners Guide for a New HRIS.* Paper presented at the 9th Annual CHRSP Conference (October): 4–7.

Slofstra, M. 1994. "A Positive New Image in the Works." *Computing Canada* 20, no. 16 (August): 27.

Sookman, B. 1994. "The Legal Issues Abound." *Computing Canada* 20, no. 16 (August): 29.

Turnbull, I.J. 1994. *Let the great world spin*. London, England: The Interactive Group Softworld Report and Directory, "Alphabet Soup—RFIs, RFPs, etc. ..." Paper presented to the Greater Toronto Chapter of IHRIM, March 7, Toronto.

Tomasko, R.M. 1993. *Rethinking the Corporation—The Architecture of Change.* New York: AMACOM.

Walker, A.J. 1993. *Handbook of Human Resource Information Systems.* New York: McGraw-Hill.

Weizer, N., G. Gartner III, S. Lipoff, M.F. Roetter, and F.G. Withington. 1991. *The Arthur D. Little Forecast on Information Technology and Productivity.* New York: John Wiley and Sons.

6

Implementation

◆ ◆ ◆
INTRODUCTION

This chapter deals with the most complex and potentially the most expensive phase of an HRMS project (Johnston, 1995): implementation. At this point the customer takes the HRMS from the design state to an operational state (Ceriello, 1991). Where the organization has purchased a pre-programmed HRMS, this could be described as taking the product out of its shrink-wrap and making it work.

Implementing an HRMS can take from one to two years, or even longer, depending upon a number of factors (Ceriello, 1991). For a smaller organization, installing a PC- or LAN-based HRMS, this time frame may be much shorter, particularly if the requirements of the HRMS are limited and well defined. But even for a small organization with simple needs, the impact of implementation can be significant. In the case of a large organization implementing an HRMS using a mainframe or a client/server network, the cost of implementation can be three to five times that of the original software purchased from the software supplier (Eckhert, 1996a). Realizing this from the start of the project, and planning accordingly, will increase the chances of successful implementation (Doran, 1996).

◆ ◆ ◆
CHANGE

One of the more significant challenges facing an organization implementing a new HRMS is the resistance that many people have to change (Kavanagh et al., 1990). In most situations, the implementation of the new system will necessarily mean change for many people. Some potential examples are described below.

1. *Technology.* Moving, for example, from a mainframe to a client/server environment could affect:
   - ◆ technical personnel having to learn to use new tools;

- ◆ traditional users of the system having to familiarize themselves with new tools and new procedures; and
- ◆ additional users who may be given access to the new system because of its increased capabilities (Drechsel, 1995).

2. *Business.* Implementing an HRMS could affect:
- ◆ the way information is captured and used in terms of:
   a. a move to decentralized data capture;
   b. users now being responsible for the quality and timeliness of data;
   c. the elimination of procedures through the use of modern business processes such as process re-engineering; and
   d. the provision of management information to users, including ready access to flexible, and easy-to-use reporting tools.

To determine the extent of the changes that may be involved, we need only go back to the basic reasons for moving to a new HRMS. These may include a change in computer technology that may or may not be a result of an overall organizational change. Such technological change will not necessarily have a significant impact on the HRMS or those that depend on it. If an organization is reasonably comfortable with its existing HRMS but wants, for example, to standardize its computer technology, it may be possible to buy a version of the current HRMS that will work on the new computer technology. If this is the case *and if* the organization is satisfied with existing procedures, the technological change may only affect those involved with the transition to the alternate software programs.

More than likely, however, a change in technology will be associated with some degree of "re-engineering" of work processes (Tapscott, 1993). For example, the move away from large mainframes to client/server or LAN-based systems generally results in a degree of decentralization of information gathering and use, as well as increased accountability for the entering, accuracy and use of information by the users of that information (Iorfida, 1996).

One of the most common reasons for implementing a new HRMS is the need to increase HRMS capabilities. If the old HRMS was essentially a centralized recordkeeping system, one that only met the most basic HR information requirements of the organization, the push for a new system may have been linked to the need to have the new HRMS take on more strategic human resources management functions (see Chapter 1). This may or may not be coupled with a move to new technology. Whatever the circumstances, and regardless of the extent of change involved, planning how to manage that change is an integral part of HRMS implementation (Ceriello, 1991).

PITFALLS IN HRMS IMPLEMENTATION

A number of problems have been identified as leading to failures in HRMS implementation (Kavanagh et al., 1990). Some of these include:

1. lack of management commitment, leading to inadequate resources and personnel;
2. failure to assign a project team for the duration of the project (it is imperative that the core project team members stay with the project from inception to implementation);
3. political intrigue, conflict, hidden agendas;
4. poorly written, incomplete needs analysis reports, leading to incorrect decisions and a costly system that does not meet the needs of the organization;
5. failure to include key personnel on the project team—this can exacerbate political problems and reduce perceived ownership to a small group; and
6. failure to survey/interview key groups in the organization (Small, 1995).

IMPLEMENTATION PHASES

A successful HRMS implementation requires that many people in various parts of the organization cooperate effectively with the shared goal of implementing the HRMS successfully. Good communication and project management are crucial to each stage of project implementation.

During an HRMS implementation a number of overlapping processes occur:

- Implementation planning
- Input of the steering committee
- Policy and procedure development
- Project team training

- Installation
- Fit analysis
- Modification
- Interfaces
- Conversion
- User training
- Unit and integrated testing
- Parallel testing

◆ ◆ ◆
IMPLEMENTATION PLANNING

When the software program has been chosen and finally arrives on-site, a great deal of time must be devoted to planning the HRMS implementation. Before beginning the planning process, a number of things must be known, including the scope and goals of the project. If the needs analysis was thorough and the successful software vendor represented the capabilities of its product realistically, this task will be simpler. The team entrusted with the implementation must have very good project management skills, as well as some knowledge of the HRMS product and the technology base to be used. If the latter two are new to the project manager and to team members, some training may be in order before a proper plan can be developed (Doran, 1993; 1996).

An effective project plan will include:

- Project Goals
- Timetables
- Responsibilities
- Resources
- Monitoring and Reporting Mechanisms (Doran et al., 1994).

Some project management tools that the project manager may find useful include Gantt Charts, CPM, PERT, and Project Management Software. (See Chapter 4 for details.)

PRIORITIES

During the development of the overall implementation plan, key resources from Human Resources and from the Information Technology area must work together to ensure that all of the expectations of both areas are met. If, in fact, users are going to be greatly affected (through new duties, responsibilities, re-engineering) they too should be involved in the initial planning. In all cases, the priorities of Human Resources, Information Technology, and the user area must be addressed. Quite often an outside consultant or neutral third party expert is used to facilitate the development of the implementation plan and to ensure the needs of all areas are addressed (Doran et al., 1994).

Items for consideration during the development of the implementation plan include the following:

1. technical environment: what equipment or technology must be purchased;
2. priority assigned to individual HR modules; whether to implement all at once, or in a specific sequence;
3. expectations of new users, such as moving to a decentralized system;
4. availability of resources, including whether Human Resources or Information Technology expertise will be provided by internal resources, contract resources, or external consultants; and
5. availability of training for project team.

IMPLEMENTATION SCHEDULES

Once priorities have been reviewed and a consensus reached, the HRMS project manager must work with the team leaders to schedule each task in the plan. This is a critical component of success and the only way to control costs and resources effectively (Ceriello, 1991).

The implementation schedule must include estimated completion dates, as well as the elapsed time or duration of each task. Again, it is very important to obtain input from everyone with a significant interest in the effective implementation and use of the HRMS. The time estimated to complete each task will be based on experience in this area as well as the planned availability of key resources to complete the work. This will include knowledge gained during the selection of the software program(s), including knowledge of the supplier's ability to provide support in key areas. If consultants are going to be used on the project team, they must have input into this planning process and be able to clearly communicate their knowledge and abilities in related areas, as well as the availability of resources in the time frames being discussed.

Once the implementation plan has reached the draft stage, it must be circulated to all members of the HRMS project team, the steering committee, the software vendor, and consultants (if applicable). All of the individuals involved in the project should have input into the development of the schedule. Many projects have found it wise to give a thorough presentation of the project schedule to all affected individuals, to explain what the plan means, and point out areas on which each individual may want to concentrate before final input is reviewed. A follow-up presentation to explain the final plan will go a long way toward building a solid project team, whose members understand that this is their plan.

◆ ◆ ◆
THE HRMS PROJECT IMPLEMENTATION TEAM

During the earlier stages of the HRMS project, the key people involved have been functional experts from Human Resources, Information Technology, line management, a consultant (if applicable), and the project manager (often from Human Resources). Quite often many of these people have already worked as a team in the ongoing maintenance of the HRMS to be replaced. During the implementation phase, the number of people involved frequently increases. In some cases, almost the entire Human Resources department becomes involved, particularly if important new applications will be included, or if work processes are being re-engineered. Certainly, anyone in Human Resources who will eventually be using the new system should have some role to play in the implementation.

Quite often, Information Technology resources are also expanded at this time. If a stable HRMS has been in place, a few knowledgeable individuals will have been maintaining the application. During the upcoming implementation phase, additional ones are often required. Several specialists may be added, depending upon the scope of the project. These may include additional application programmer/analysts; DBAs (Data Base Analysts);

technical support: communications experts, software experts, and security specialists; a project manager (for project or information technology staff); or documentation specialists.

Other members on the implementation team may include:

1. *Implementation specialists.* Quite often an external consultant who is an expert in the implementation of HR systems, and in particular of the specific software purchased by the organization, is hired to provide important technical and planning guidance.

2. *Internal or information systems auditor.* This individual would be responsible for reviewing the new HRMS from the point of view of its acceptability on behalf of the corporation, ensuring that it meets all of the expectations of such a system. The effective auditor monitors progress on the project and provides sound advice on how to avoid potential pitfalls. Ultimately, the auditor must ensure that the system is accurately performing all calculations, deductions, and payments correctly.

3. *Training coordinator/adviser.* Training on an HRMS project takes place at various intervals, including up-front technical training by the software vendor. Sometimes it is advisable and more cost effective for the software vendor to train only the key people and allow them to train the remainder of the team. The training coordinator may actually deliver some of that training, but at the minimum required to ensure that those who will be training others in their turn have the support they need to deliver it correctly. Once the system is nearing readiness for testing, the training coordinator may assist in the training of the end-users who are currently using the system, and/or new users who may be using the system, so that they will know how to perform their work using the new system during the test phase. During final implementation, the coordinator will be involved in training the user community who may or may not be taking on new or different responsibilities. The actual training is often given by members of the user community, but with guidance from the training coordinator.

4. *User representatives.* If the new HRMS is going to be extended to a variety of users, line management, etc., representatives from these groups must be on the project team. If this is a new area of responsibility for particular groups, the representative/s of these group(s) must be chosen even more carefully. An important role of these representatives is to

provide input into the implementation of the new HRMS. At least as important is their role in serving as a focal point of communication between the project team and the functional area that they represent.

◆ ◆ ◆
THE HRMS MANAGER

Quite often the overall HRMS project manager is in fact the HRMS manager from Human Resources, if such exists. Even if this is not the case, it is the HRMS manager who effectively takes over the new system once it is implemented. Where the HRMS being implemented is the first such system acquired by the organization, the HRMS project manager may, in fact, become the HRMS manager once the system is in place. This is not always the case; the interests and skills of the project manager may lean towards project planning and to working as a systems administrator. Nonetheless, the HRMS manager is a key player in the implementation phase of an HRMS and needs effective skills in three main areas:

◆ Strong knowledge of main functional areas of human resources

◆ Automated systems

◆ Organization management (Ceriello, 1991)

◆ ◆ ◆
POLICY AND PROCEDURE ISSUES

The implementation of a new HRMS generally has a significant impact on the policies and procedures of functional and technical aspects of human resources information management. To implement the new system effectively, and to integrate the new procedures into the organization, close attention must be paid to any impact on these policies and procedures (Walker, 1993). Quite often, it will have been made clear during the initial stages of an HRMS project that one of the reasons for implementing a new system is to make way for change, to make things easier, more effective. Throughout the implementation process, new and different problems/opportunities will be encountered that must be addressed.

During the implementation of a new HRMS, an organization, will usually take the time to revisit its policies, procedures, work flow, and goals, and to re-engineer the business. If this is done in advance of the HRMS implementation, that implementation will be delayed; an organization will therefore sometimes undertake to do this work in parallel, or it will wait until the implementation is completed before trying to effect any significant change. There are many arguments for doing this re-engineering work first, but quite often, once a decision on a new HRMS is made, it must be implemented and as quickly as possible. In these cases, the re-engineering work generally comes later (Kurcharsky, 1995; Kurcharsky and Turnbull, 1996).

An organization might review its policies and procedures for any of the reasons outlined below:

1. *Work flow.* Using evolving business process re-engineering tools, organizations determine whether current processes can be eliminated, replaced, or made easier.

2. *Regulatory requirements.* If the new HRMS cannot meet all of the regulatory requirements imposed on it, alternatives must be reviewed. Usually, the new HRMS will enable the organization to more easily address those requirements, but in some cases the old system was modified to handle unique requirements. Will the new system be similarly modified?

3. *Data capture.* Will the organization move the responsibility for data capture out to line management? Will new technology be used to capture information closer to the source?

4. *Business cycle.* Will the organization change any of its deadlines (e.g., payroll cut off dates), or the way that it processes information, in order to take advantage of the new system's capabilities?

5. *Security.* If a variety of users are given direct access to the system (e.g., through their office PCs), what data will they be able to add, to see, to change?

6. *New technology:* New tools, such as the Internet (or Intranet for companies considering internal web sites) raise many questions about security, accountability, and training (Huntington 1995, 1996).

◆ ◆ ◆

THE ROLE OF THE STEERING COMMITTEE

Ostensibly, dealing with policy and procedure issues is the role of the HRMS steering committee. A steering committee may or may not have been set up to guide the requirements definition and software vendor selection phases, but in most cases, it will have been established just prior to the implementation phase.

◆ ◆ ◆
CORPORATE/EXECUTIVE SPONSOR

The HRMS steering committee will generally be made up of a minimum of the following:

♦ Chair (corporate/executive sponsor (see below) or other senior executive)

♦ Vice-president or director of Human Resources

♦ Vice-president or director of Information Technology

♦ Executive level representative(s) from line management

A steering committee will sometimes include:

♦ Vice-president or director of Finance

♦ Change agent (senior person responsible for business process re-engineering)

♦ Representative from the board of directors

♦ Director of Internal Audit

The following individuals are generally not included on the steering committee:

♦ HRMS project manager

♦ HRMS manager

♦ Information Technology manager

♦ Other HRMS project team members.

The HRMS Project Manager and HRMS and Information Technology managers report to the steering committee.

Generally speaking, every project of any magnitude will have corporate or executive sponsor. This will be the person who takes the case to the CEO and/or board of directors of the organization to obtain approval and funding for the project. It is usually this person to whom the HRMS steering committee will report. In some cases, this individual, will be chair of the steering committee.

◆ ◆ ◆
PROJECT TEAM TRAINING

The best HRMS in the world will only work if users know how to use it effectively. Human Resources can foster that knowledge by providing explicit training and ongoing support as part of the HRMS (Ceriello, 1991).

Training is one of the keys to a successful HRMS implementation. At one time, many organizations ran their business systems on one main computer system. And although upgrades were made from time to time, the basic hardware and software technology did not change nearly as quickly as it does now. In most cases today, however, technology is changing so fast that with each new implementation, new skills must be developed. Table 6-1 shows some of the changes that have been made to implement a new HRMS at one large Canadian organization.

TABLE 6.1 TECHNICAL AND OTHER CHANGES IN HRMS

Technology	Old HRMS	New HRMS
Software	Integral HRIS	People Soft HRMS
Computer	IBM 3090	DEC Alpha
Database	CICS/VSAM	Oracle 7
Environment	MVS	Open VMS
Tape Drives	IBM	Various
Disk Drives	IBM	Various
User Work Stations	IBM 286 or 3270	DEC Pentium
User Connections	Modem or hard wired	Ethernet, TCP/IP
Security Interface	Local	Open Horizons/Oracle
Scheduling	Operations run	Process Scheduler
Bank Interface	Tape by taxi	EFT to bank
Carrier Interface	Tape by courier	Disk by courier
Reporting	ASAP & SAS	Crystal, SQR

Traditional HRMS implementations have had to address the way in which the system will be used during the project, and how key users and others will use the system after its implementation. Today, an HRMS implementation may require an extensive training program because of the large changes in technology and user-requirements. In some cases it will be necessary to hire new resources and/or consultants to assist during the implementation (Winter, 1996).

THE TRAINING PLAN

The HRMS project manager will work with the training coordinator and team leaders to develop a training plan that will address all areas of training related to the project. The time taken to plan, develop, and deliver the training must be built into the project plan. An effective training plan will include:

1. identification of the actual kinds of users requiring training;
2. identification of the type of training needed;
3. an estimate of the number of individuals to be trained on each topic;
4. an inventory of specific information and skills each group requires;
5. decisions on training media;
6. identification of the trainers;
7. a schedule for the training; and
8. a development plan for the training materials (Doran et al., 1994)

If the organization is adopting a whole new area of technology and if it also plans to extend access to a broader variety of users, many levels of training will be required. These will include:

1. technical training on the new technology;
2. computer equipment, databases, programming tools, communications tools, and security;
3. key user training on the HRMS software;
4. technical training for Information Systems personnel; and
5. specific user training for Human Resources personnel, including benefits, payroll, reporting, and staffing applications.

Every person on the project and every person who will eventually be a user will require some level of training. The HRMS Project Plan should allocate time and staff to address training issues, both to deliver the training and to receive it.

TECHNICAL TEAM TRAINING

Technical training must take place early, especially if the organization is changing technology. In particular, the HRMS project team, the nucleus of the project, must receive thorough training on all aspects of the new product to assist others on the project with its use. This training must be delivered at an early stage in the project or the team will waste a great deal of time trying to figure out things that would have been clear if proper training had been received.

Most software vendors offer training in the streams mentioned above: technical, human resources, benefits, payroll, and reporting. As this training is usually expensive, careful thought must be given as to who will receive the training, and when. When training resources are scarce, (and they usually are), it is advisable to prioritize training so that key personnel get it first (they may then share what they know on return), and when it is needed (Winter, 1996).

In the case of other users, it is often beneficial to provide some hands on experience with the application, and time to review the user manuals, before official training is provided. Taking the training course and then waiting two months for the application to become available on the work stations is a waste of time and money.

EXTENDED TEAM TRAINING

Once the project is well underway and the core project team is well trained, time should be set aside to train the extended members of the team, including for example, the employees in Human Resources, Payroll, and Benefits who will be using the system as soon as it is ready. This training can generally be done in-house by members of the core project team, usually from Human Resources. Training addressed during these sessions will relate to the way in which the new system works and any new procedures that may have evolved during the early phases of the implementation (Doran, 1994).

The training coordinator will be of great use in setting up formal training for those who require it. Just because these employees are busy and already know most of the business side of the application, their training should not be glossed over. Training should be formal; it must be provided in a proper training environment, where the correct tools are available.

TRAINING OF OTHER USERS

During the early phases of the project, the project team will have identified who in the organization should be trained on the new HRMS. This may extend from the current users in Human Resources to a new group of users in the general community (e.g., line management). During the various phases of the project, this user community would have received regular updates informing it that this training was coming, and why. Again, this training should be formal, and given in a proper setting, using professional equipment. The staff providing it should be the experts in the area, generally Human Resources employees who work with the data on a regular basis. Before this training takes place, the new user group should be surveyed to determine if any additional technological training is needed and to determine access requirements. Once trained, this group should have access to a Help Desk support group that can not only assist them with the basics of the technology, but more importantly, provide information about the functional aspects of the system being used.

◆ ◆ ◆

INSTALLATION

The installation of new HRMS software involves much more than just removing the shrink-wrap from the packages and loading the software. In many cases a new system means new technology. By the time the software is ready to be loaded and run on real data, in a test mode, the project team should have done a great deal of groundwork. In addition to the steps outlined above, this will mean ensuring that the old system and the new one may run in parallel until the new system is running smoothly. Sizing and evaluating different computer options or testing new communications technology may be necessary.

Generally speaking, the support team responsible for running the new system along with the old one does not have to meet on a regular basis for any length of time with the HRMS project team; however, it will require clear direction as to what equipment and peripherals to set up. Once that environment has been established and stabilized, the new software can be loaded and testing can begin.

After the software is loaded, the technical support group and the information technology application staff work in parallel to test out various aspects of the software. It is accepted practice to set up one or more test environments with all of the software loaded and accessible to the project team. Once it is clear that the software has been loaded successfully, access can be extended to the remainder of the project team for future project work. This stage generally involves becoming acquainted with the software. If timed correctly, the users on the project will already have received their manuals, and will have some time to play with the system before taking their initial training.

◆ ◆ ◆
FIT ANALYSIS

Once the software has been installed and users have been trained, fit analysis can begin. During the earlier phases of the project, when needs were being identified and analyzed, good documentation was developed to enable the fit analysis to be conducted. Sometimes called gap analysis, a fit analysis is basically the determination of the differences between the delivered system and what the client wants to do with it (Doran, 1996).

It is often said that the amount of time spent early on a project saves 10 times this amount later on: this is most true of fit analysis. If the team has done a thorough job of recording the details of requirements, this phase will be significantly easier to complete (Hughes, 1995).

At the beginning of a fit analysis, the project team divides up the various requirements to be tested. Generally a two- to three-person team works on each task, each of which is modelled or trialed on one of the test databases. Often, several hundred examples of real data or data that have been created to have the characteristics of real data are loaded into the test database for the project team to work with. Each task to be evaluated is reviewed fully, with notes taken on any gaps. A simple example of a task to be reviewed would be to simulate the hiring of a new part time casual worker. All of the steps involved will have been well documented. Using this information as a guide, a team member could try and create a "new hire" on the new system: any difficulties or anomalies experienced would be documented in the fit analysis notes. If the new system would not enable the team to follow through with HRMS requirements or support the test case to their satisfaction, the deficiencies are reviewed with the project team. In some cases the software vendor may have to be contacted to help fix the anomaly, or to offer an alternate solution to the problem. If the new system will not handle a requirement, the team is faced with either modifying the system, changing corporate procedures, or a combination of the two (Eizen, 1996).

Once the project team has come up with a recommendation on how to handle the problem, it is usually documented and submitted to the HRMS steering committee for approval. If the recommendation is a modification to the delivered system, a cost estimate of the fix and the benefit it will deliver if completed must be included. If the recommendation is to leave the system as is and change some corporate procedures, the impact of this change must be fully documented as well. Once all the gaps have been identified and fully documented, the project plan can be modified to reflect the additional work (Eizen, 1996).

◆ ◆ ◆
MODIFYING THE SYSTEM

Making modifications to the system after it is delivered can have very significant long-term costs. Traditionally, such modifications meant that with each subsequent official software release from the supplier, the modification had to be redone or carried over. This is changing, with modular systems and new tools designed to track these modifications. Software vendors today try and deliver systems where the changes made to the original version can be tracked and accounted for relatively easily with vendor supplied updates (releases). If a modification is made to a system that is not easily tracked, the cost of maintaining that modification over the life cycle of the system can be considered. For example, if it is estimated that the modification will cost 20 person–days to make, and 10 person–days with each subsequent release, the total estimated cost over five years (and four more releases) will be 60 person–days. If there are 20 modifications of this type, the estimate will be 1200 person–days to perpetuate the maintenance of the modifications over five years. This gives pause to approving modifications that do not absolutely have to be made.

Fortunately, many new systems being developed today permit some modifications that are not labour intensive over time. Where this is not the case, the cost of the modification over time must be weighed against the savings to the organization from having a system more responsive to its needs. Once all of the modifications have been documented, costed, and approved, they must be added into the project schedule. Generally these modifications can be made during unit testing of the system (Eizen, 1996).

♦ ♦ ♦
UNIT TESTING

To some extent, the system has already been heavily tested. During the fit analysis, every possible requirement should have been tried. Shortcomings will have been noted and corrections made or fine-tuning of the system completed. By now, the system should be running almost as it will when it is fully implemented. But to ensure that all components are working properly, unit testing of each function within the system is required.

Unit testing involves a review of every major process planned for the system and the testing of outputs. Hiring a hypothetical employee to ensure all deductions can be set up properly; terminating a hypothetical employee to ensure all the final calculations are correct; or calculating pay for a hypothetical employee and comparing it to an actual pay are examples of simulations that might be set up as part of unit testing.

This testing will reveal any obvious problems or "bugs" in the system. Any problems detected are discussed with the project team and corrective action planned. When the correction is made, the system is tested again. Once the system is working well, the team will move on to testing more of its integrated features, such as a full payroll simulation using the test database (Doran, 1994, 1996; Thompson, 1995).

Another method of testing is to attempt to enter incorrect data into the system to ensure the edits are working correctly. Testing of the system is a "user-driven" activity, with all of the project team working together and coming up with test cases. Each function within Human Resources (including Payroll) must come up with a test for every conceivable item to be tested. Apart from validating the system, this accomplishes several objectives. First, users have an opportunity to practice what they have learned in training and thus become more familiar with the system. Second, the test reassures users that the HRMS functions correctly (Ceriello, 1991).

◆ ◆ ◆
CONVERSION

Often underestimated in project planning, conversion is a very important phase in the project, and one that is potentially very time-consuming. Seldom is enough time set aside for converting information from the old system to the new one. In most cases, there will be data to be converted, unless the HRMS implementation takes place in a very new company without any history (Doran, 1996).

In many cases, the information currently in the existing HRMS is an accumulation of a succession of HR systems which have in turn been converted. Why is conversion so difficult and time-consuming? In most cases, design of the new HRMS will be significantly different from that of the old one, and data elements will not translate to the new HRMS exactly as they appeared in the old system. As well, each successive software package may handle data a little bit differently. Older, character-based systems retained information in longitudinal files, while modern systems use relational database technology and virtually all data is stored in tables (see Chapter 1). To this end, data from the old HRMS may have to be split up to be stored in the newer system.

During the "requirements definitions" phase, the organization will have documented all details sufficiently to know how much data from the old system must be converted. During the fit analysis, just how the new system would handle that data would have been determined. Where changes are necessary, decisions will have to be made on how to effect that change. In some cases, an organization may simply choose to key in the data in the new format manually. But in most cases, an algorithm (program) may be written to convert the data from its old format to the new. After each data element is converted and transferred to the new system, one of the most common ways to check the new information is to run reports displaying the information, and checking these manually. Another test is to run calculations or cross tabulations on the data and compare the results to the current system.

Once the conversion process, and as much checking as possible, have been completed, it is time to conduct parallel tests of the new system (Ceriello, 1991).

◆ ◆ ◆
PARALLEL TESTING

When all of the steps described above have been completed, a significant amount of testing has been done on the new system. During the fit analysis and unit testing, however, test data (not real data) may have been used. Once real data from the existing HRMS has been converted and copied over to the new system, it is time to test the system using real data.

Following the final conversion of all the data from the current system, the project team may decide to run a test based on the last few months of activity. For example, if the conversion is completed at the end of October, the system may be tested by actually running a test of payroll processing for September and October. This kind of testing provides an immediate and realistic indication of potential problems. In this example, if the payroll is run for each of September and October, and the results are the same as from the existing system, there is every indication that the system is working properly. In most cases there will be some differences, and fine-tuning of the new system may be required. Each new system calculates things a bit differently and often small differences occur as the result of the way in which the systems round fractions/decimals. These are generally easy to fix (Doran, 1996).

Once the system has been stabilized with all the new data on it, the project plan will call for a parallel test that may vary from one to several months. During this time period, corporate information will be entered into both systems and the results compared. Generally the old system will be used to actually pay employees, but the new system will be handled exactly as it would during full live production. The results from the payroll runs, reports, and other activities will be carefully compared during the parallel trial period and adjustments made to the new system, if necessary.

During the parallel period, not only will input be duplicated on both systems, but both systems will be used to:

1. produce cheques;
2. print pay advances

3. print payroll distribution;

4. calculate and print regular reports;

5. generate pay transactions for bank deposit, which may then be tested with the bank;

6. generate carrier transactions for insurance providers, which may be cross-checked live with the carriers;

7. generate interfaces to other systems, including:
   a. the general ledger; and
   b. other sub-HR subsystems.

During the parallel testing, Human Resources should monitor the system very carefully. Once HR has determined that the system is operating to its full satisfaction, the project team will work out an actual cut-over date, where the old system will be shut down and the new system will be used in full live production (Ceriello, 1991; Doran, 1996).

◆ ◆ ◆
SUMMARY

Implementing a new HRMS can be complicated and time-consuming. As HRMSs become more important in the strategic management of critical organizational resources, and a broader range of users access the HRMS from their offices, individuals at all levels in the organization are finding that they have a stake in the effective implementation of such systems.

This chapter has described the steps required for the successful implementation of a new HRMS, as well as the pitfalls to avoid. The *who, what,* and *when* of each step has been explored, along with various governance issues, such relationships between executive sponsors, steering committees, project committees, project members, and user representatives. The importance of training was documented, as was the need for systematic testing at each stage of implementation.

EXERCISES

1. List the types of people you would like to have on your HRMS project steering committee, and describe why it's important to have people with various backgrounds.

2. Describe the role of the HRMS project manager. Outline the skill set required for this job.

3. Describe some of the options available with respect to re-engineering work processes around the HRMS project.

4. How might one go about assessing whether a training program has been successful? Do you think such "training validation" is important? Why? Whose responsibility should it be?

5. Suppose you are responsible for determining who should attend the first course to "learn how to use the new HRMS." The course has proven to be very popular. You have 200 applicants for only 20 training billets. What criteria might be used to decide who should get the training?

6. Are there differences in the content and manner of delivery of the courses given to individuals learning how to use the HRMS for the first time, and those given as refresher courses or for upgrading? Describe the similarities and differences you think are important for each.

7. Outline the various types of testing that are normally done in a project. Develop a list of test cases.

References

Ceriello, V.R. 1991. *Human Resource Management Systems: Strategy, Tactics, and Techniques.* Toronto: Maxwell Macmillan.

Doran, J.A. (1996). "Human Resources on the Internet." Unpublished paper presented at the Annual HR Technology Conference, Canadian Institute. Toronto (March).

_____. 1996. "Implementing HRMS Client/Server at York University." Unpublished paper presented at the

Annual HR Technology Conference, Canadian Institute. Toronto (March).

_____. L. Magagna, and S. Busse. 1994. "HR Applications Plan. A Project Document for York University." Toronto (June).

_____. L. Magagna, N.L. Rankin, and D. Willamson. 1994. "Training Project Plan. A Project Document for York University." Toronto (June).

Drechsel, D. 1995. "Principles for Client/Server Success: the Difference between Winners and Losers." *The Association of Human Resource Systems Professionals Review Magazine* (September): 26–29.

Eckhert, G. 1996. "How to Define Needs and Requirements for an HRMS." Unpublished paper presented at the International Association for Human Resource Information Management Conference. Toronto (February).

Eizen, M. 1996. "Business Modelling: a Technique for Implementing Your PeopleSoft HRIS." Unpublished paper presented to The PeopleSoft Eastern Canada Regional Users Group Toronto (March).

Hughes, P. 1995. "Marrying Technology to the Business of Human Resources." Unpublished paper presented at the annual Canadian Human Resources Systems Professionals Conference. Vancouver (October).

Huntington, G. 1995. "Electronic Survival Guide for Human Resource Managers: Using the Information Highway." Seminar workbook used at the 1995 Annual Human Resource Systems Professionals Conference. Reno Nev. (June).

_____. 1995. "The Internet for *HR—To be or not to be?*" *The Association of Human Resource Systems Professionals Review Magazine* (September): 36–42.

_____. 1996. "Less than a Second: Using the Internet to Revolutionize the Way You Work." Unpublished manuscript.

Iorfida, R. 1996. "Implementation and Change Issues: HR System Challenges, the Vendor's Experience." Unpublished paper presented at the Annual HR Technology Conference, Canadian Institute. Toronto (February).

Johnston, J. 1995. "Coming to a Company Near You: Purchasing and Installing an HRIS is a Complex Process. To be Successful it must be Well Planned." *The Canadian Association of Human Resource Systems Professionals Resource Magazine* (March): 18–19.

Kavanagh, M.J., H.G. Gueutal, and S.I. Tannenbaum. 1990. *Human Resource Information Systems: Development and Application.* Boston, Mass.: PWS-Kent.

Kucharsky, P. 1995. "Re-Engineering the Personnel Action Form." Unpublished paper presented at the annual Canadian Human Resources Systems Professionals Conference. Vancouver (October).

_____. and I.J. Turnbull. 1996. "Human Resources and Technology at York University." Unpublished paper presented at the Annual HR Technology Conference, Canadian Institute. Toronto (February).

Small, D. (1995). "Why it Didn't Work ... HRIS Projects that Fail." *The Canadian Association of Human Resources Systems Professionals Resource Magazine* (December): 14–15.

Tapscott, D.C. 1993. *Art Paradigm Shift: The New Promise of Information Technology*. Toronto: McGraw-Hill.

Thompson, C. 1995. "HRMS Implementation—Approach and Process." Unpublished paper presented at the annual Canadian Human Resources Systems Professionals Conference. Vancouver (October).

Walker, A.J. 1993. *Handbook of Human Resource Information Systems*. New York: McGraw-Hill, Inc.

Winter, Robert W. 1996. "HRMS Project Management: The Basics are Essential to Success." Unpublished paper presented at the '96 Greater Toronto Chapter Vendor Show, International Association for Human Resource Information Management. Toronto (March).

7

Maintaining the HRMS

♦♦♦

INTRODUCTION

The reasons for investing in an HRMS should never be overlooked. As outlined in various ways in Chapters 1 through 4, an HRMS provides information about the organization's most important resource—its human resources—so that they and thereby the whole organization can be managed more successfully. An HRMS is not merely a place where information is collected and stored.

Successful implementation of a new HRMS is often regarded as the conclusion of a project and, indeed, it is. But it is not the end of the larger issue of managing human resources data, or of ensuring that the system remains up-to-date and effective. Implementation marks the beginning of an ongoing and continuous maintenance process.

Once an organization has implemented an HRMS, focus must turn to the day-to-day use of the system in support of human resources management processes and organizational goals. No matter how good the hardware and software contained within an HRMS are, or how well the project team has completed its responsibilities, problems and issues will arise. Maintenance issues include continually monitoring the effectiveness of the system, and upgrading or replacing hardware, software, communications (networks), and business processes.

The entire system is dynamic: new users emerge and others cease to use it. Usage patterns may shift within a day, or over a week; processes change as user needs change (or as organizations reorganize/downsize); and files vary in length and in complexity. Unlike many software systems, HRMS products are often updated quarterly to accommodate legislative changes. Each new update, or "release" as they are commonly known, brings the potential for problems.

Compounding these problems is the fact that most HRMSs are being used continuously, so that it may be difficult or impossible to shut the system down for any length of time during the process of upgrading. Therefore, issues/problems are generally tried out in a test environment before they are implemented in the actual HRMS. Further, the project team dedicated to the implementation probably no longer exists; its members have either moved on to other projects or returned to whatever job they held prior to the commencement of the project.

◆ ◆ ◆
HARDWARE AND COMMUNICATIONS MAINTENANCE

Hardware and communications network(s)—the physical body and neural links of the HRMS—require maintenance like any other electrical or mechanical device. They suffer from wear and tear, and must be maintained regularly or they lose their effectiveness. In addition, it is a rare organization indeed that requires neither expansion nor change of the hardware or the network. The mere moving about of furniture in a single office can require the computer connections to be moved. Wholesale reorganizations can place heavy demands on those who maintain the physical network.

◆ ◆ ◆
SOFTWARE MAINTENANCE

Lientz and Swansen (1980) categorize software maintenance into three types:

◆ Corrective (60%)

◆ Adaptive (25%)

◆ Perfective (15%)

Corrective maintenance is defined by the authors as fixing problems that prevent the system from working as intended. These are not just "bugs" (programming errors), but also include poor definition of requirements, design flaws, coding flaws (true bugs), and various other problems. Adaptive maintenance refers to modifications to the HRMS made in response to changes in technology, government regulations, or external forces (see Ceriello, 1991). Perfective maintenance is the term used to describe modifications to the system in response to user and/or technicians' requests.

This last area can consume considerable time and expense. Organizations tend to want to make extensive changes to software products to make them "fit" better. These fit issues may be minor changes to the name of a data element—"Surname" to "Last Name," or the colour of a screen, for example. But they may also involve major restructuring of several screens, addition of data elements, or changing the properties of existing elements.

◆ ◆ ◆
BUSINESS PROCESS MAINTENANCE

"Managing for excellence requires process thinking ... A process can only lead to excellent results when it is managed as a series of flexible, repeatable tasks that are continuously improved, and the variety removed" (Brimson and Antos, 1994, 45). Just as software must be maintained, so must the business processes of an organization. In North America today people see themselves as customers and expect a high level of service from every supplier, be it government or pizza delivery. To become and remain competitive, organizations must constantly enhance service, improve productivity, and control (if not reduce) costs.

The target of excellence is not static or absolute. Brimson (1991) defines excellence as the cost-effective integration of activities within all units of an organization to continuously improve the delivery of products and services that satisfy the customer. This trend is confirmed by Spencer and Spencer (1993) whose book, *Competence at Work—Models for Superior Performance* underlines the need for individual competence in order to achieve excellence.

The last few decades have seen many management improvement philosophies come into favour: Quality Management Systems (QMS), Total Quality Management (TQM), Continuous Improvement (CI), Business Process Engineering/Re-engineering/Improvement (BPE, BPR, BPI), ISO9000, and Activity-Based Costing among them. These philosophies have significantly affected the way that many organizations conduct business. It is wise for HRMS personnel to have a strong understanding of these concepts because those individuals will often be called on to assume critical leadership roles in the implementation of these new philosophies in their organizations. (See the discussion in Chapter 4 on business process re-engineering.)

Total Quality Management (TQM) is the single management philosophy having the most longstanding impact worldwide. TQM's avowed focus, "to delight the customer," is achieved through continuous process improvement. To find the source of the continuous improvement process, Martin

(1995) directs us to the Japanese management philosophy of "kaizen." Kaizen, which, roughly translated means everybody improving everything all the time, can be seen in Deming's and Juran's work during and after World War II.

TQM's prominence has recently receded—as is typical of many such popularized management concepts over time (Lasden, 1985); probably because it has either lost favour or organizations have absorbed the concept into their culture and daily life. Less than successful TQM programs have been reported and publicized. The reasons for such failures have many causes, including a lack of top management leadership and/or commitment, unrealistic expectations of quick (or easy) results, lack of true employee empowerment, failure to recognize the need for cultural change, too restricted a scope, or emphasis on internal customers at the expense of the paying, external customer (Martin, 1995).

Each new "management philosophy" offers its own perspectives on business processes and how to improve them, but students of these philoso-phies will realize that few are mutually exclusive. The message is generally consistent. Change, however radical or slight, is normal, not exceptional. And in our modern era of rapid change, no process, however recently created or blessed, should be assumed to be inviolate. This continuous change reflects a need to regularly maintain business processes.

Juran (1988) proposes that a process of "value analysis" be used to focus the desire for excellence on value-added activities which will supply func-tions needed by customers at minimal cost. Martin (1995) agrees, and suggests that "value stream"—an end-to-end set of activities that is collec-tively valuable to a internal or external customer—is a much more precise and useful term than "process."

Planning for quality, establishing an organizational framework for continuous improvement, a climate in which constant organization change is desired, encouraged, and supported is not easy. Practitioners of the tradi-tional HR functions of organizational design, development, behaviour (OD, OD, and OB) and human resources systems find themselves at the same table with accountants working with activity accounting, and management information systems staff responsible for business process engineering (BPE). Working at the detail level of modelling processes is very useful, but should never be taken as an "end unto itself." Ould (1995) stated that "many models can be drawn of a process, all will be wrong, but some will be useful

(p. 210)." The individuals responsible for maintaining an HRMS must continually work to stay up-to-date with business, human resources, and technical trends and, in fact, be prepared to act as proactive change agents in their areas of specialty.

◆ ◆ ◆
ROLES

What roles must those responsible for maintaining an HRMS play to ensure that it operates and is used effectively? To a large extent, these roles vary according to the way an organization has structured its business and computer processes, and the way it has defined the relationship between its technical and functional staff. Some organizations view the support of an HRMS as a technical function, with systems staff providing all expertise. Other organizations supplement or replace internal systems and/or functional expertise with consultants from the vendor of the system, or from a third party. Still others create a new function of HRMS specialist within the organization.

The last option (internal HRMS specialist) is growing in popularity, as evidenced by the growth in membership in HRMS specialty professional organizations, such as the International Association of Human Resources Information Management (IHRIM) which grew out of the Association of Human Resources Systems Professionals in the United States (HRSP), Canada (CHRSP), and elsewhere (IHRIM, 1996).

A 1994 survey conducted by the University of Sherbrooke and the Canadian Association of Human Resources Systems Professionals (Haines and Petit, 1994) states:

> *One of the most important findings of this study is that satisfaction levels and usage of (HRMS) systems are much higher where there is a specialized HRIS unit than where there is no such unit (p. 4).*

The formation of a specialized HRIS/HRMS unit can be quite contentious. For example, the Management Information Systems department may feel threatened by users allowed to have system-management responsibilities that had previously been handled exclusively by their department.

Also, if Human Resources and Payroll staff report through different organizations there may be turf wars, as each argues that they should be responsible for various aspects of systems maintenance.

◆ ◆ ◆
RESPONSIBILITIES

A number of responsibilities that fall to those employed to maintain an HRMS (whoever they report to in the organization) derive naturally from the requirements to keep the HRMS operating effectively. Each organization's list may vary somewhat, but the core responsibilities are described below.

FUNCTIONAL MAINTENANCE

No sooner than an HRMS is implemented changes will occur. Union agreements will be settled, court decisions will require special reports or retroactive adjustments, and so on. Modern HRMSs are constructed with tables containing "date specific" information; for example, salary compensation (ranges, steps, ...), benefit amounts, deductions and taxes, and performance criteria. Each of these tables may change annually, or more often, and will need to be updated and otherwise managed effectively, which in turn requires a degree of functional expertise.

In addition, a number of additional data management considerations must be taken into account. These considerations can be specific to a single application (e.g., payroll, human resources/strategic planning, pension and benefits, training and development, and occupational health and safety), or to many.

EXAMPLE An organization of 60,000 puts in place a three point scale for employee performance:

3	2	1
exceeds expectations	meets expectations	below expectations

Employee X is rated as "2," or average, her first year, and again in her second year. In year three the manager responsible for performance management systems changes; the new manager, determined to make her mark, recommends implementing a five-point scale:

5	4	3	2	1
greatly exceeds	exceeds	meets	almost meets	far short

EXPECTATIONS

Once again employee X is rated as average, only now the code for this rating is "3." The HRMS has a performance appraisal report that graphs an employee's performance over time for bonus participation and promotional opportunities. Unless the system administrators have taken the proper steps to adjust for the change in the rating scale, the net result could make it seem that the individual's performance has increased, when, in fact, all that has happened is that the rating scale had changed.

TECHNICAL MAINTENANCE

Computer structures are never static for long. Most organizations have several software systems using much the same sort of technology, often on the same computer. Even if a specific software package remains completely unchanged over a year, the computer that runs it, and the communications network that provides input into it and ensures that its output gets to where it is needed, may be shifting constantly.

Performance demands on the HRMS or other systems, backup, disaster recovery, the number and nature of central processing units, data storage units, and communications networks all require constant management. This is true whether the organization is using its own staff or contracting someone external to maintain the system.

FUNCTIONAL/TECHNICAL MAINTENANCE

If the HRMS in question has been purchased from an external software supplier or vendor, the vendor usually provides regular program "updates." These updates can contain not only changes in the way the system handles human resources issues, but also changes of a more technical nature. A human resources and payroll system update for example, may include changes in taxation from every applicable legislative jurisdiction. Such updates are often made available by the software vendor on a quarterly basis.

New versions (upgrades) of the software can come out annually or even more frequently. Implementing new software containing either specific updates or upgrades may not be critical. However, successive functional and technical changes will generally assume that prior releases have been implemented; without implementing them the system will rapidly become out of date.

◆ ◆ ◆
NEW FUNCTIONAL REQUIREMENTS

At some point, perhaps a week or a year after the HRMS has been implemented, new functional requirements will be added to or turned on in the system. Each of these will itself be a mini-implementation project and should be treated as such, using the sorts of procedures outlined in the previous chapter.

◆ ◆ ◆
USER SUPPORT

Ideally, as outlined in Chapter 6, an organization will have trained every user to operate the system as it is being implemented. However, the "users" of the system will change jobs, new responsibilities will appear, complex reports never before conceived will be required, and users will forget what they learned. Ongoing training and coaching on every aspect of the system will be required, as will documentation updates.

◆ ◆ ◆
COORDINATION WITH OTHER CLIENTS/USERS

INTERNAL

There is an ongoing requirement to ensure that the HRMS is operating effectively, in terms of meeting the needs of its main client groups and the organization at large. As noted in earlier chapters, access to an HRMS, formerly restricted to HR and Payroll, is increasingly organization-wide in scope. Executives, line management, and employees at all levels are being given direct access to information on the system, and to reports prepared by it, on a need-to-know basis that is defined more and more broadly over time.

Some progressive organizations have adopted a steering committee to coordinate human resources issues, including those associated with the maintenance and use of human resources information. Others recognize the interdependence of all of their major operating systems and give long-standing information systems steering committees more focus on data management and software integration, instead of the hardware and communications issues that more normally occupy their time.

USER GROUPS

If an organization has acquired an HRMS from an external software supplier, other organizations will have acquired the same software. Most software suppliers encourage their clients to join together in "user groups." User groups allow those who use the same system to network and exchange ideas about the software, its foibles and follies, its strengths and opportunities.

Active participation in such organizations—from both technical and functional perspectives—allows organizations to gain from each other's experiences and to approach the vendor with joint requests for significant modifications or customization. In addition, most vendors look to the user group to set future development priorities.

Traditionally structured along product lines, these groups usually meet at least annually to trade functional and technical war stories. The degree to which vendors direct or support their user group(s) varies widely. Some fund all meeting expenses; others offer optional user group attendance as part of maintenance contracts; others pay some support while expecting users to contribute the bulk of the cost; and some vendors have no formal user group program at all.

Elaborate multiproduct user conferences are held in various desirable travel destinations, with key note speakers and numerous functional and technical sessions on everything from minute detail to the future vision of a particular product line. At the other end of the scale, small groups of users borrow meeting rooms to discuss joint concerns. Regardless of the degree of financial or administrative support provided to user groups by vendors, the user group is a very useful tool for vendors and users alike. Users can compare notes on problems, solutions, or new desirable functionality. This later activity can be a major money-saver. Instead of each paying for unique customization, user organizations can combine their requirements and focus on convincing the vendor to make the changes or provide the new functionality within the core product at no cost. For one organization, this resulted in a saving of almost $200,000 which had been earmarked for custom programming.

Vendors, too, like the user group concept. It gives them one or more opportunities to reinforce their clients' purchase decisions. It gives them a captive audience to sell new products to, and provides an opportunity to hear and diffuse or act on complaints before they get out of control. Many vendors use the annual user group meeting to survey clients on new perceived requirements. Clients may be asked to complete a survey form or to vote on their most desired changes to the system. From the client's perspective, this should require some planning. Attendees at the conference may not represent the full range of knowledge about problems or the relative priorities for future development, and should always try to prepare "at home" before venturing forth to represent their organization in this way.

Other tools that vendors utilize to maintain communications between themselves and users, or between users and users, are electronic bulletin boards, groupware products such as Lotus Notes, and Internet e-mail and home pages. All of these tools offer opportunities for geographically separated people to exchange ideas electronically. Electronic bulletin boards are being replaced by "chat groups" on the Internet, but the concept remains unchanged. Each user can access a common file where they can read other's thoughts and add their own. File topics may be very general or very specific, and depending on the technology used, comments may be relatively private, or very public.

◆ ◆ ◆
SUMMARY

The preceding chapter discussed concepts relevant to implementing a new HRMS. This chapter extended that discussion by outlining what is required to maintain the HRMS after implementation.

An HRMS is composed of many different parts, all of which must be maintained to keep the system functional and effective. Implementation of a software package or completion of a re-engineering project does not represent an end but a beginning: the start of using the system, and continually upgrading it to accomplish management objectives. Keeping an HRMS effective and up-to-date means fostering a culture of continual improvement.

EXERCISES

1. Coming (as it does in this text) at the end of the HRMS development cycle, maintenance activities often appear to be the least valued in the planning, design and development, implementation and maintenance cycle by many organizations. Do you feel that this is warranted? What should the relative emphasis of each phase be?

2. There are several different types of maintenance issues and activities associated with an HRMS. List the primary issues and discuss their relative importance.

3. Suppose that you were the manager in charge of a newly implemented HRMS. Discuss what issues might be relevant in helping you decide how to establish a process for maintaining your HRMS, in keeping with Lientz's and Swansen's three types of software maintenance. Would the decisions facing you be different if your HRMS were, say, about four years old and meeting most of the organization's strategic and operational needs for human resources information? What if the HRMS were 10 years old and widely recognized as needing replacing?

4 Many HRMS software vendors offer some kind of opportunity for their clients, the users of their product(s), to come together and share experiences. Do you agree with this idea? Why? Is there any point at which financial support of such "networking" could constitute a "conflict of interest?"

5. Some authors have suggested that the term "business process re-engineering" may be inappropriately applied to business processes, because these processes were never "engineered" in the first place. Would it make more sense to call these tools "business process engineering," or would some other term be more appropriate? Can one engineer business processes?

6. This chapter discusses a number of ways in which an HRMS must be maintained. Would it ever make sense to contract some of these maintenance responsibilities out to external "experts?" Discuss the advantages and disadvantages of undertaking the various types of maintenance (see question 1) in-house, or contracting them out.

References

Bennett P., and Swansen, B. 1980. *Software Maintenance Management*. New York: Addison-Wesley.

Brimson, J.A. 1991. *Activity Accounting*. Toronto: John Wiley and Sons.

————. and J. Antos. 1994. *Activity-Based Management*. Toronto: John Wiley and Sons.

Ceriello, V. 1991. *Human Resource Management Systems—Strategies, Tactics and Techniques*. New York: Lexington Books.

Haines, V., and A. Petit. 1994. "Explaining HRIS Success." *RESOURCE* 4, no. 4 (September): 4.

International Association of Human Resource Information Management (IHRIM) Membership Statistics (January): Toronto, 1995.

Juran, J.M. 1988. *Planning For Quality*. Toronto: Maxwell Macmillan International.

Martin, J. 1995. *The Great Transition*. Toronto: AMACOM.

Ould, M.A. 1995. *Business Processes*. Toronto: John Wiley and Sons.

Spencer, L.M., Jr., and S.M. Spencer. 1993. *Competence At Work*. Toronto: John Wiley and Sons.

8

Human Resources Planning and Development

◆ ◆ ◆
INTRODUCTION

The general human resources model presented in Chapter 1 was designed to show the relationships between traditional human resources programs, the external and internal strategic context, and an HRMS. This chapter explores more deeply many of the concepts raised by discussing the uses of an HRMS in human resources planning and development. Using variations of the general human resources model (see Chapter 1, Figure 1-3) this (and subsequent) chapters discuss HRMS applications in support of the following core human resources functions:

◆ Human resources planning and development

◆ Staffing

◆ Training and development

◆ Compensation and payroll

◆ Pension and benefits

◆ Occupational health and safety

◆ ◆ ◆
INTERNAL AND EXTERNAL TRENDS

In Chapter 1 we pointed out that, increasingly, legislative, sociodemographic, and business trends are exerting pressures for organizational change (Soloman, 1994). Many organizations are finding it easier to make technical changes than to make human resources changes. In fact, the ability to adapt their human resources to new requirements is proving to be a limiting factor to success for many organizations (Coates, 1990; Towers Perrin, 1992). This should lead to a recognition of the importance of the human resources function in the organization's strategic boardrooms and the critical supporting role of the HRMS in support of this evolution (Rampton and Doran, 1994;

Stright, 1993). As we move into the last half of the 1990s, there are several reasons why human resources planning and development is becoming more important (Cascio and Thacker, 1994; Coates, 1990):

1. the prospect of skill shortages in key areas (e.g., systems analysts, engineers, database specialists, information/communications specialists) caused by a greater demand for information processing skills, along with a shrinking labour force (the baby bust), making it increasingly important to plan for and develop staff effectively;

2. the requirement to foster management teams capable of "accomplishing more with less," and with a more diverse workforce;

3. the challenge of containing human resources costs in the context of the trend by governments to off-load training/development, health, benefits, and other costs onto corporations;

4. the pressures of accelerating social and legislative changes (e.g., pay equity, employment equity); and

5. the challenge of making the most of staff, many of whom are, in terms of education, highly qualified but underutilized.

Corporate downsizing, restructuring, and the move to organizational levelling is leading to fewer and more widely placed rungs on the corporate ladder. This, along with more sophisticated demands in many jobs, will make the transition between levels more difficult, rendering the probability of being able to learn the skills required for successive levels by osmosis alone less likely. In addition, the available workforce will be more diversely based, increasingly composed of new Canadians, women entering or re-entering the workforce, and members of ethnic minorities (Coates, 1990). The ability to assess and keep track of skills and qualifications, as well as progress on skills refocusing and upgrading programs, will be an increasingly important HRMS function (Liker and Thomas, 1991).

Many organizations are finding that alarming numbers of secondary and post-secondary school graduates do not have the literacy, numeracy, and technical skills that they require (Coates, 1990). Some of these problems may stem from the fact that increasing numbers of employees are working in their second language, while technological and other changes are creating new demands that the educational system cannot respond to quickly enough.

With many demands on their resources, the need to plan more systematically for the people required to staff and manage organizations, now and into the future, is critical (Cascio and Thacker, 1994; Dyer and Holder, 1988; Urlich, 1986; Wagel, 1990). Such planning cannot be done effectively in organizations that have more than a few hundred employees without the support of an HRMS (Horsfield, 1991).

◆ ◆ ◆
THE IMPORTANCE OF EFFECTIVE HUMAN RESOURCES PLANNING

With the support of tools such as HRMS, human resources staff have increasingly been able to demonstrate that they have an important contribution to make to bottom-line strategic corporate decision making (Rampton and Doran, 1994; Snell et al., 1994).

Those human resources executives who can show that they have something important to contribute to the bottom-line success of the organization are consequently being welcomed to sit on senior executive committees (Dyer and Holder, 1988; Wagel, 1990).

The objective of human resources planning is to ensure that there are sufficient numbers of competent and motivated employees to meet an organization's current needs, and those of the foreseeable future (Walker, 1980).

The use of an HRMS in strategic corporate decision making can facilitate these goals by improving:

1. understanding of the human resources implications of business/operational strategies;
2. awareness of the experience, knowledge, and ability of the organization's employees;
3. productivity; and
4. the selection/development of potential replacements for key/vulnerable positions (see Horsfield, 1991).

◆ ◆ ◆
DEMAND AND SUPPLY FORECASTING

The structure of an organization's workforce, including the number of employees that may be required, with specified skills, in defined positions, should be determined from the organization's strategic/business plans through *demand forecasting* (Director, 1985; Walker, 1980). The availability of human resources to meet these demands, whether from within the organization, or from the external labour market may be determined through *supply forecasting*, as shown in Figure 1-3. The purpose of supply forecasting is to identify whether individuals exist to meet the needs of the organization. Supply forecasting is also meant to identify whether there are sufficient numbers of individuals with the potential to develop the skills that may be required for the future. If such individuals do not exist in sufficient numbers within the organization, then an attempt is made to discover whether they may be found outside of the organization (Kazanas, 1988; Stewman, 1986). A number of sources can be referred to for an overview of national labour market supply and demand information, which include: the Canadian Employment and Immigration Commission; COFOR, Canadian Occupation Forecast Program; and the Economic Council of Canada (Belcourt et al., 1996).

Human resources and succession planning are used to determine how the organization will satisfy the requirement of having the "right number of individuals, doing the right things, in the right places, at the right time" (Walker, 1980). Human resources and succession planning determine whether gaps exist in the demand and supply of human resources for the organization, and if so, how these gaps are to be dealt with. In terms of staffing, this may mean determining first whether a vacancy exists, and then whether and how it will be filled (Niehaus, 1987).

◆ ◆ ◆
HUMAN RESOURCES PLANNING

Human resources and succession planning are sometimes confused. We have found the following rule of thumb to be useful in distinguishing between the two (see also Walker, 1980):

1. *Human resources planning* is aimed at resolving gaps that may exist with respect to human resources of certain skills, whether across the organization, or in specific organizational units.

2. *Succession planning* is aimed at determining how specific key, and/or vulnerable positions are to be filled appropriately.

Thus, in operating specifically at the position or individual level, succession planning may be regarded as a subset or special application of human resources planning.

◆ ◆ ◆
HUMAN RESOURCES REPORTS

An effective HRMS will have, at minimum, modules for positions and employees. In addition, an "organization module" is often present to record how positions are structured within the organization (Horsfield, 1991). Using information contained in these modules, analyses can be done of such issues as:

1. the structure of the organization, as well as units within it, relative to defined organizational requirements;

2. the numbers of unfilled positions;

3. the qualifications and assessed performance of the workforce relative to present and future defined requirements;

4. the age distribution of the workforce across the organization, within organizational units, and within specific functions;

5. employment equity reports, including the distribution of women, individuals with disabilities, native people, and visible minorities in the workforce, relative to the distribution of such individuals in the population; and

6. turnover statistics by unit, function, qualifications, employment equity category, etc. (Snow, 1987).

Such analyses may be included in regular or ad hoc reports to executives or line management at various levels in the organization. They may also be necessary to fulfil legislative requirements such as employment equity reporting.

◆ ◆ ◆
THE USE OF AN HRMS IN HUMAN RESOURCES/SUCCESSION PLANNING

Figure 8-1 is a model showing demand forecasting, supply forecasting, employee information, and human resources succession planning processes that were implemented in a large Crown corporation (Murray and Rampton, 1986) and in a large forest industry research laboratory.

Human resources and succession planning are most effective when done by line management of the organizational areas involved (Walker, 1980), supported by human resources personnel.

FIGURE 8.1 Human Resources/Succession Planning Model

INPUTS	Demand Forecast	Supply Forecast	Employee Information
	What are the requirements of all positions in the unit?	What is the statistical overview?	How well are current staff performing? (performance review)
	What are the key jobs within the unit?	What is the vacancy forecast?	What are the development plans, areas of interest, skills, strengths?
	What human resources will be needed when, where, and with what knowledge and skills?	What resources are/will be available (using HRMS, job profiles, and career ladders)?	What are the assessment results?
	What are the change plans?		

PROCESS

MANAGERIAL REVIEW

HUMAN RESOURCES/SUCCESSION PLANS FORMULATED

IMPLEMENTATION

PROGRESS FEEDBACK

OUTPUTS

HUMAN RESOURCES PLANS

APPROVED CAREER DEVELOPMENT PLANS

SUCCESSION PLANS

Line management begins the process by asking the following questions:

1. Are there any special business/economic factors that are likely to have major effects on the organization over the next one to five years? For example, do foreseeable trends in the market and economic conditions lead one to believe that restructuring and or/downsizing may be necessary? What specific functions are likely to be affected? What strategic/business plans exist to address these external influences?

2. What will the organizational unit look like one year from now? Two years from now? Three years from now? The HRMS should provide up-to-date organization charts as a starting point in this process, as well as the capability to support "what-if" modelling so that alternate organizational structures may be produced quickly.

3. What organizational problems are being experienced? This question gives the management team involved the opportunity to discuss any troublesome reporting relationships or communication problems that need addressing.

4. What human resources problems are being experienced—performance, skill, deficiencies, recruitment? How many people will be needed? When, where, and with what experience, knowledge, and ability?

Answers to these questions should be documented in writing, as they may be used as the basis for the organization's business plans with respect to human resources.

Significant parts of the data required to answer the above questions (e.g., performance appraisal results, academic qualifications, skills inventories, applicant data, turnover data, job description and job requirements data) should be resident in the HRMS, as should an analysis capability, so that relationships may be drawn in the data and the results of these analyses reported in clear, "user-friendly" form. Knowing what is on the system, as well as how to conduct the requisite analyses and report the results, provides human resources personnel with a golden opportunity for gaining credibility with line management in an area that is crucial to the long-term health of many organizations.

The human resources practitioner should be able to use the HRMS to provide statistical overviews for the whole organization, as well as each unit involved in human resources/succession planning (Horsfield, 1991). The overview should summarize flow data, such as recruitment, separations, promotions, transfers and turnover; and personal data, such as sex, designated group for employment equity purposes, language(s), group and level, age, and years of service. A preliminary estimate of potential vacancies based on retirement projections should also be provided. More detailed assessments of these data may be conducted with line management wherein information can be added that is not formally contained on the HRMS but may be known in the work environment, such as possible transfers, promotions, resignations, and retirements.

The HRMS should contain, or at least have access to, job description information that can be related to its modules which have detailed information on the positions and organizational structure (Schneider and Konz, 1989). It should possess the capability of presenting this information quickly, in user-friendly form. The human resources practitioner should then do summary analyses which can be provided to line management in advance of any planning meetings; he or she should also be prepared to do further "what if" modelling as part of the planning process. Line management should use this information to review job descriptions/positions that will probably become vacant in the next few years and/or those that have significant operational impact. These analyses should not be too conservative, since more than the identified positions may become vacant. The job description information should be examined to help identify the major qualities of experience, knowledge, and ability that will be required in successors to the present incumbent (Schneider and Konz, 1989).

The HRMS can then be used to provide information on current employees, including the latest performance review and career development reports that have been entered on the system. Summary reports of this information prepared by human resources practitioners and supplied to line management beforehand can be used to refresh memories regarding individual strengths, areas that need improvement, career interests, and development plans.

While the human resources practitioner can help line management identify potential successors for all positions that have been identified as "key and or vulnerable," he or she can play a special role in using the HRMS to identify appropriate individuals in organizational units other than the one in question. The human resources/succession planning module of the HRMS should have pre-established screens that allow those responsible for human resources/succession planning to document the additional knowledge expe-rience, or formal training that is determined to be necessary for the identi-fied individuals to qualify as candidates when each position becomes vacant.

The organizational charting function of an HRMS should be able to show the relation of such "key or vulnerable" positions to each other, and to other positions in the organization, thus providing a graphic overview of the health of management "depth" of the organization, as well as where there might be weaknesses (Horsfield, 1991).

Figure 8-2 provides an example of the documentation for succession planning of a single position. The methodology underlying this figure was adapted from Walker (1980) and has been used successfully in a number of organizations of various sizes over the last 25 years.

Human resources/succession planning is often done by committees formed from the senior management team of the organizational unit

FIGURE 8.2 Succession Planning Chart

	Manager of XYZ	XI
3	V.P. Hebert (Incumbent)	A
4	M. Jones (Candidate 1)	B1
4	T. Smith (Candidate 2)	B2
3	C. Jette (Candidate 3)	B2

PERFORMANCE LEVEL
1 - Below Requirements
2 - Marginally Met Requirements
3 - Met Requirements
4 - Exceeded Requirements
5 - Greatly Exceeded Requirements

POTENTIAL
A - Retain at Current Level
B - Potential for Promotion One Level
  1. Ready Now
  2. T & D Needed
C - Potential for Promotion Two Levels
  1. Ready Now
  2. T & D Needed
D - Senior Management/Executive Potential
  1. Ready Now
  2. T & D Needed

POSITION STATUS

WHY - W - No Incumbent Change Expected
    X - Will Become Vacant
    Y - Position Redundant
    Z - New Position to be Created

WHEN - 1 - Within 1 Year
    2 - Between 1 & 2 Years
    3 - More Than 2 Years

concerned, with the head of the unit as chair and a human resources practitioner as a resource person. Such a committee attempts to reconcile the demand of personnel with the required skill mix and the available supply reflected in the career planning and development information and summary reports available through the HRMS. The committee examines this information in the context of what the unit requires now and in the future, both generally and for specific positions (including employment equity considerations).

The main basis for human resources/succession plans are organizational requirements (as determined by the demand/supply forecasts outlined earlier). It is generally more effective and economical to develop human resources internally. When, however, it is evident that certain requirements will not, or may not, be met through such efforts, then the human resources plan must have contingencies to ensure that appropriate individuals are recruited externally (Niehaus, 1987).

◆ ◆ ◆
CASE STUDY—APPLICATION OF AN HRMS IN HUMAN RESOURCES PLANNING

In the mid-1980s an on-line, direct access HRMS was developed for a large Crown corporation, during and after this organization made the transition from being a department of the federal government to becoming an independent Crown corporation. Development of this HRMS was initiated within the human resources planning and development function in Head Office, so that the capability to do strategic human resources planning was a critical design feature of the system. This capability has provided the organization with the means of conducting human resources planning analyses and reports as input into corporate strategic planning processes since its implementation.

The foundations of the program were summarized in a report prepared by Murray and Rampton (1986). Some of the accomplishments outlined in that report are repeated here to illustrate applications of the sorts of analyses and reports alluded to above.

1. A detailed analysis of the organization's 1985/86 business plan was conducted, with the focus on comparing estimates of natural attrition with forecasts based on past separation patterns and retirement eligibil-

ity. This study highlighted the importance of good attrition forecasts in determining person–year requirements.

2. Several analyses were conducted for line managers on specific key employee groups. These analyses focused on eligibility for retirement data, as well as predictions regarding positions that would be vacant. Analysis of the population of likely feeder groups was then completed to identify the potential for filling these positions with existing internal resources, and/or to flag future gaps in supply versus demand.

3. The groundwork was laid to ensure that the organization had the necessary data and programs in place to meet the requirements of the federal employment equity legislation.

4. Analysis of the "hidden workforce" examined the use of personnel services contracts by different departments and discussed patterns regarding the implications of replacing these contracted resources with employee person–years.

5. Monthly snapshots of front-line employee population highlighted factors such as male/female ratios, anglophone/francophone distributions, full-time/part-time ratios, as well as age distribution and eligibility for retirement. One object of these analyses was to monitor the progress of retrenchment activities underway at that time, and to provide feedback on the impact of redeployment on human resources (including staffing) policies and programs.

6. Population analyses were conducted on major functional groups (Operations and Marketing, Personnel and Labour Relations, Management Information Systems) with emphasis on factors to be considered in an accelerated attrition/downsizing program (e.g., differences in strength by division and by bargaining unit, ratio of male/female employees, eligibility for retirement and for accelerated attrition, and forecasts of the number likely to apply for accelerated attrition).

At the time of the writing of the report (1986), the organization was in the early stages of developing an effective HRMS *cum* human resources planning program. Most organizations in this situation will find, as this one did (Murray and Rampton, 1986), that, of necessity, early analysis will tend to deal more with what is, rather than what will be. Forecasting activities concentrated on predicting the eligibility for retirement and for accelerated attrition, estimating the numbers likely to apply for accelerated attrition, and extrapolating past natural attrition patterns into the future. This, of course, reflected the internal and external pressures on the organization at the time. The groundwork was, however, laid to use more sophisticated modelling/simulation techniques, among other things to prepare a proactive human resources plan.

◆ ◆ ◆
SUMMARY

Many organizations claim that their human resources are their most important asset. However, few actually devote the organizational priority and resources to fostering this asset to the extent that such a claim would seem to require. There is some evidence that this is changing, as it becomes more and more evident to the leadership in progressive organizations that the key to future success in the quickly evolving business environment will be how they plan for and develop their workforce. The volume and complexity of information required for effective human resources planning and development requires the support of an effective HRMS. This chapter has discussed the use of an HRMS in this very important application.

EXERCISES

1. Some organizations consider employment equity planning to be a special case of human resources planning, and have the two integrated within a Human Resources department. Pay equity data analysis and reporting may then also be integrated into and processed using the HRMS. Other organizations keep the pay equity office and, sometimes, pay equity data gathering and analysis processes separate from Human Resources. What might be some of the pros and cons of

each approach. Which option would you chose?

2. When managers become used to receiving regular, concise human resources reports reflecting pertinent information about their employees, they come to expect and depend on it. Suppose you were in charge of an HRMS for a medium-sized manufacturing firm. What sort of information do you think might be relevant to the managers in your organization? How might you go about defining clearly

what (and in what format) might be of most use to managers in your organization? How might you introduce these reports to your managers?

3. In many organizations, managers have ready access to computer terminals that can be linked to the HRMS. This capability can be used to provide direct access to either specific employee data, pre-programmed reports, or even to the capability of doing ad hoc reports. Confidentiality of sensitive data, or data on employees in organizational units other than the manager's, can be maintained, as can control of what, if any data the manager can update. What implications might providing managers with this capability have for the human resources function generally, or the HRMS more specifically? Do you feel the overall impact is likely to be positive or negative?

4. Human resources/succession planning sessions can provide an opportunity for human resources personnel to gain credibility with managers at all levels. Which human resources personnel should be involved in these sessions? What role should those responsible for the HRMS play?

References

Belcourt, M., A.W. Sherman, G.W. Bohlander, and S.A. Snell. 1996. *Managing Human Resources*, Canadian ed. Toronto: Nelson Canada.

Cascio, W.F., and J.W. Thacker. 1994. *Managing Human Resources*. Toronto: McGraw-Hill Ryerson.

Coates, J.F. 1990. *Change Requires Retraining: Success Depends on Workplace Skills*. Technical Report. Washington, D.C.: J.F. Coates Inc.

Director, S. 1985. *Strategic Planning for Human Resources*. Oxford: Pergamon.

Dyer, L., and G.W. Holder. 1988. "A Strategic Perspective of Human Resource Management." In L. Dyer, ed., *Human Resource Management: Evolving Roles and Responsibilities*. Washington, D.C.: Bureau of National Affairs.

Horsfield, D. 1991. "Human Resource Planning Applications." In A.L. Lederer, ed., *Handbook of Human Resource Information Systems*. New York: Warren, Gorham and Lamont.

Kazanas, H.C. 1988. *Strategic Human Resources Planning and Management*. Englewoods Cliffs, N.J.: Prentice-Hall.

Liker, J., and R.J. Thomas. 1991. "Prospects for Human Development in the Context of Technological Change: Lessons from a Major Technological Renovation." In D. Kocacglu, ed., *Handbook of Human Resource Information Systems*. New York: Warren, Gorham and Lamont.

Murray, L.A., and G.M. Rampton. 1986. *Human Resource Planning*. Ottawa: Directorate of Human Resources Planning and Development. Report, Canada Post Corporation.

Niehaus, R.J. 1987. *Strategic Human Resources Planning Applications*. New York: Plenum Press.

Rampton, G.M., and J.A. Doran. 1994. "A Practitioner's Guide for a New HRIS." Unpublished paper presented at the 9th annual CHRSP conference (October): 4–7.

Schneider, B., and A. Konz. 1989. "Strategic Job Analysis." *Human Resource Management* 28: 51–63.

Snell, S.A., P. Pedigo, and G.M. Krawiec. 1994. "Managing the Impact of Information Technology on Human Resources Management." In G.R. Ferris, S.D. Rosen, and D.T. Barnum, eds., *Handbook of Human Resources*

Management. Oxford: Blackwell Publishers.

Snow, C.C. 1987. *Strategy, Organization Design, and Human Resources Management*. Greenwich, Conn.: Jai Press.

Soloman, C.M. "Managing the H. R. Career in the '90s." *Personnel Journal* 73, no. 6 (June): 62–76.

Stewman, S. 1986. "Demographic Models of Internal Labour Markets." *Administrative Science Quarterly* 31: 212–47.

Stright, J.F. 1993. "Strategic Goals Guide HRMS Development." *Personnel Journal* (September): 68–78.

Towers, Perrin. 1992. *Priorities for a Competitive Advantage, an IBM-Towers Perrin Study*. New York: Towers Perrin.

Urlich, D. 1986. "Human Resource Planning as a Competitive Edge." *Human Resource Planning* 9, no. 2: 41–50.

Wagel, W.H. 1990. "On the Horizon: HR in the 1990s." *Personnel* 67, no. 1: 11–16.

Walker, J.W. 1980. *Human Resources Planning*. Toronto: McGraw-Hill.

9

Staffing

INTRODUCTION

I n helping to shape the organization's human resources, the staffing function plays an important role in maintaining the long-term health of the organization. Even in those organizations where employment counsellors do not make direct selection decisions, but support line management in this role, the counsellors still have great influence through file screening and specialized HR support provided to both line management and applicants.

The staffing function also has an important public relations role since employees' first impressions of an organization are often formed by contact with the staffing component of its HR function. Further, the organization's image and reputation may be significantly affected by the way that job openings are advertised and unsuccessful applicants are treated. An HRMS is an important support tool for staffing personnel to identify human resources needs and priorities, effectively and efficiently fill these needs now and in the future, and present a professional public image. This chapter discusses the use of an HRMS in support of the staffing function.

◆ ◆ ◆

STAFFING MODEL

In Figure 9-1, the human resources model is applied to staffing.

Staffing specialists often see their jobs as consisting solely of the functions outlined in the boxes at level 3 (Rampton and Doran, 1994). But, as we saw in Chapter 1, human resources personnel must adopt a broader perspective of their domain. Supported by an effective HRMS, the traditional human resources functions should be placed in the broader strategic context of the external environmental and business pressures impinging on the organization. These are then tied to traditional human resources programs through strategic planning and demand forecasting.

FIGURE 9.1 Staffing

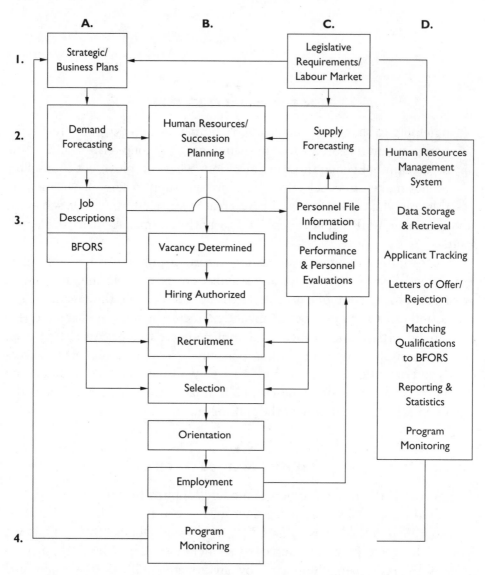

Most human resources programs are sufficiently complex that they cannot be changed overnight. The cost involved and the time required to implement change in these programs necessitates sound planning and lead time (Senge, 1990). To effectively support the organization's operations, human resources programs, including an HRMS, must be designed not only to meet current external and internal strategic requirements, but also to anticipate evolving requirements (Valaskakis et al., 1991).

Thus, staffing specialists must understand the external labour market, as well as its sociodemographic context and evolving legal requirements. Only then can effective, efficient recruitment strategies be developed, in accordance with organizational needs and legislative requirements such as pay or employment equity (Rampton, 1989).

An HRMS must be structured to contain information, perform analyses, and prepare reports that are useful in the organization's larger strategic planning processes. The nature and form of this support, information, analyses, and reports should depend on organizational requirements (Ceriello, 1991).

◆ ◆ ◆

STAFFING PROGRAMS: AN OVERVIEW

Block A-3 of the staffing model outlined in Figure 9-1 suggests that, at the individual level, the organization's human resources requirements should be reflected in job descriptions. In keeping with employment equity legislation, the minimal criteria (e.g., skill, experience, training/education, certification) required for each position are recorded on these job descriptions as "bona fide occupational requirements" (BFORS—see Belcourt et al., 1996; Cascio and Thacker, 1994; Jain, 1989). Essential job profile information on each position in the organization may be contained in the HRMS position module mentioned above. Information on employee skills, experience, qualifications, performance history, employment equity category, and biographical information will be contained in an HRMS employee module.

When a vacancy is determined and hiring is authorized, staffing specialists should check to ensure that up-to-date job descriptions/job requirements for the position are available. This information, along with documented bona fide occupational requirements, is then incorporated into a job posting. The advertising to be done will vary. In some cases it may be felt that the jobs should be advertised externally; some organizations, however, may prefer to fill a certain proportion of their vacancies through internal promotion. Such decisions may be made on the basis of information from succession planning, supported by documented performance and personnel evaluation information.

All recruiting and selection processes should be conducted objectively and fairly, based on BFORs, to ensure the most effective use of human resources, to fulfil employment equity requirements, and to ensure company morale and maintain confidence in the system. What is done must not only be fair and objective; it must be seen as fair and objective as well.

Once the individual is selected, he or she will normally pass through an orientation phase. A formal letter of offer will be accepted, and the new employee will be briefed about and signed on to benefits programs, entered on payroll, etc., prior to being employed on-the-job (Wanous, 1992).

♦ ♦ ♦
APPLICATIONS

Again, we can turn to the military for examples of effective use of an HRMS. Western military forces recruit most of their personnel at the beginning of their careers, and then provide them with the training and experience necessary to do their jobs. Many of these jobs are highly technical and demanding. Therefore, great care is taken in human resources planning, selection, training, and development (Wiskoff and Rampton, 1989), because errors cannot generally be corrected by terminating the employment of a trained serviceman and replacing that individual with an external applicant at the same level. These organizations are also very large, with recruiting being done from across the country, and training and deployment of personnel conducted not only across the parent country but in other parts of the world as well.

The processes involved in managing personnel functions such as human resources planning, staffing, induction, and training in a modern military force are complicated and interrelated, requiring extensive HRMS support (Baker and Ellis, 1989; Schratz and Ree, 1989; Kroeker, 1989). The Canadian Forces, for example, has separate headquarters directorates responsible for recruiting and selection, training, requirements control, manpower analysis, manpower utilization, career management, and second careers. All receive regular and ad hoc reports from the main personnel file, on which they rely for data and analysis relevant to their particular needs.

On the position/structure side of the organization, other directorates exist for determining military occupational structures and performing on-site manpower reviews. The Canadian Forces and other Western military forces have traditionally used extensive survey/interview-based processes for determining job requirements and organizational structures. The data thus gathered have generally been collected, stored, and analyzed using the comprehensive occupational data analysis programs (CODAP). CODAP has been widely used by a number of Western military forces, as well as such civilian corporations as Ontario Hydro (Rampton, 1980).

HRMSs are used to conduct human resources modelling to project the need for human resources in the various military occupational classifications (MOCs), or military occupational specialities (MOSs), as they are known in the American military forces (Wiskoff and Rampton, 1989). Recruiting and selection quotas are then established and assigned to recruiting and selection units across the county. The timing of specific job openings is also coordinated, through the use of HRMS programs, with the availability of training slots for basic military and trades skills. The scheduling of these training programs is based in large part on the human resources modelling made possible by an HRMS (Kroeker, 1989).

Recruits are generally sworn in as members of the military service concerned at the recruiting and selection unit, where relevant information, including biographical, selection (aptitude test scores, results of selection interviews), and other relevant information are entered into the HRMS, and the automated personnel file for each individual begins (Baker and Ellis, 1989). Recruiting and selection information on individuals who apply for positions, but for whom suitable openings do not exist, is maintained on special "applicant tracking files." It is important to be able to track applicants from one competition to another since applicants passed over in one competition may be a good match for another, with significant potential cost-savings.

The Canadian Forces and allied Western military forces' use of an HRMS in support of staffing demonstrates the utility of such systems in very large and complex organizations. The same general concepts, however, apply in much smaller applications—although in these cases more informal techniques may be used in some areas.

For example, in the late 1980s similar procedures were implemented at the Pulp and Paper Research Institute of Canada (PAPRICAN), a research and education organization consisting of about 400 personnel, mainly scientists, engineers, and technicians. This prominent research centre plays an important role in keeping one of Canada's most important industries at the forefront of technology in its sector (Sankey, 1976). Scientists and engineers are recruited from around the world. Human resources planning, staffing, and other human resources programs are very important to attracting and keeping the best possible personnel in research and research support roles (Miller, 1986). PAPRICAN's HRMS had virtually all of the capabilities discussed in the previous example. If anything, because of the nature of the personnel involved, more information was required on each individual in the primary HRMS modules, as well as in applicant tracking, although the numbers of individuals involved was many times less.

A well-designed and effective HRMS, when integrated with technological innovations such as the Internet and "intelligent" optical scanning, has the potential for revolutionizing the staffing function (MacCallum, 1996).

A number of organizations are using Internet HR home pages for recruitment purposes. Other organization have adopted the same technology as a kind of "intranet." This allows internal or external candidates to log on to the personnel home pages to review job listings or apply for jobs. In Hewlett-Packard, for example, this facility has been integrated with the automated HR file. Employees can update information on-line, such as qualifications or résumés, so that their data is complete should a suitable employment opportunity arise. This has greatly reduced paperwork and facilitated communication for Hewlett-Packard's HR staff.

Canadian Tire also uses the Internet to handle some of the 50,000 résumés that it receives annually. Others are received via FAX or mail. The résumés are optically scanned so that they may be managed in automated form. Like Canadian Tire, Canadian Imperial Bank of Commerce uses optical scanning technology to automate résumé information. In this case, an "intelligent résumé input system" automatically indexes information in the résumé via key words and organizes it into a database for HR personnel use.

The Globe and Mail has developed a web site that enables their advertising clients to post jobs that can be seen by Internet worldwide. These jobs descriptions appear exactly the same as in the daily paper, and while an ad in the paper may cost up to $15,000, the Internet posting is scheduled for only an additional $100. Employers can pay a special fee to post their résumés on the same web, having *The Globe and Mail* code special key words (skills and experience) so that the whole database can be searched for potential candidates.

Using their web site and additional technology, the paper is planning to extend their services to scan in hard copies of résumés, accept fax input, receive résumés via e-mail, and codify them all, which will create an applicant database for the client—without the company touching one piece of paper.

Helen Ziegler and Associates, leaders in the business of placing medical staff worldwide, is a Toronto-based firm. When the World-Wide Web became available, Helen Ziegler and Associates developed job and applicant information management software to make it easier for their clients to post jobs worldwide and to have applicants apply for openings.

This software makes it possible for the employer to match the applicants with the job on-line and to rank the applicants according to "best-fit" on skills and experience. The employer can then have Ziegler call the suitable applicants to see if they are interested in setting up appointments.

This software has the capability of allowing an organization to quickly and efficiently handle internal or intranet job postings. A template has been developed that enables an authorized user to create a posting that includes job title, applicable information on department, job level, salary, job description, and qualifications necessary for the job. No technical training is required to do this as the template is delivered intact.

Once the requisite information has been entered on the system, the job immediately becomes visible on the local home page. Potential applicants in the organization (e.g., members of a bargaining unit) can check these job listings and apply on-line for an opening. A personal identification number (PIN) ensures that only authorized employees can apply. The employee fills out a shadow template recording their skills and experiences.

At the end of the posting period, the hiring department or human resources specialist can simply press one button on the computer to get a list of all the candidates in order of their scores, and thus, make a decision on which applicants to interview. The hiring department has a variety of reports they can run, which include a brief résumé of each applicant showing narrative form skills and experiences, a list of qualification, or a combination of both. A report can also be run to show the applicants where they fall short of qualifications relative to the pre-established criteria. After a final selection is made, an additional report can be run to show all the candidates who were successful.

One of the features of this system is a security precaution that allows only employees within the organization to actually change information on the server. The organization may decide not to let just anyone see the job listings, but only those authorized would be able to change the job requirements and run the reports.

◆ ◆ ◆
PROGRAM MONITORING FOR STAFFING

Staffing is a very dynamic area in many organizations, and although attempts are made to objectify it, many aspects, including those associated with applicant assessment and selection decisions remain fundamentally subjective, based on the judgment of the person(s) responsible for the selection decisions (Wanous, 1992; Webster, 1982; Weisner and Cronshaw, 1988). It is a well-established principle that the quality of such decisions is improved when individuals have access to feedback as to the consequences of their decisions, in this case, the performance in training or on the job of the employees that they assessed or selected (Cascio, 1991). Other important aspects of the staffing process should also be monitored and correction or improvements made as the need arises.

In Chapter 3 the role of the HRMS in quality control of the Canadian Forces recruiting and selection administrative procedures was used to demonstrate the return on investment that can result from implementing such a program. This is an important example of the HRMS-assisted program monitoring that can be done in the staffing domain. Far more important, however, is monitoring the success rate of individuals actually making selection decisions, and feeding any trends back to them and to the individuals responsible for managing the recruiting and selection functions, so that appropriate adjustments can be made. This is done routinely in most Western military forces. Similar HRMS staffing program review and monitoring procedures were implemented at a large Canadian university that experienced huge staff turnover and recruitment pressures during the economic boom of the mid- to late 1980s. The procedures established provided feedback that helped the university to respond not only to these pressures, but also to make the adjustments required during the subsequent economic recession and resulting retrenchment program.

◆◆◆
SUMMARY

This chapter has discussed information requirements in support of staffing, as well as the use of an HRMS in related applications. Staffing specialists have typically seen their role as administering recruiting and selection procedures on request from managers in other functions. In the future, these individuals will require an appreciation of how larger strategic and business requirements interrelate with and affect staffing. In support of this goal staffing specialists will also have to accept an HRMS as a fundamental staffing tool, and acquire a comprehensive working knowledge of those features of the HRMS that relate to the staffing function.

EXERCISES

1. In today's business environment, to be effective, staffing specialists must be aware of the organization's strategic and business plans, as well as pressures and trends in the external labour market. In what ways do these demands differ from those of the past? Will these demands require different knowledge, background and skills in staffing specialists? How might the staffing specialist prepare for these changes? How important will familiarity with and skill in using an HRMS be?

2. If those responsible for the staffing function are to keep abreast of human resources trends in the organization, they will probably require regular reports from the HRMS. What sort of information should these reports contain?

3. The most important aspect of any staffing program is establishing the objectives, or requirements, of the program. Since the advent of employment equity, the requirements related to each job have come to be known as bona fide occupational requirements. With the need for more accuracy and accountability in the definition and use of BFORs for each job, do you think that more reliance will be placed on an HRMS? What other ways can the HRMS be used to help with the implementation and administration of employment equity in the staffing process?

4. It is generally contrary to the employment equity legislation in most jurisdictions to collect information on designated equity classification (age, sex, race, religion, disability, sexual preference) and maintain it in such a

way that it could influence selection or other administrative decisions. Yet the organization must collect and store such information to prepare and implement employment equity plans in accordance with the legislation. How can this apparent contradiction be resolved?

5. Why are effective staffing program monitoring procedures important? What information should be included in such a program? Who should this information go to, and how should it be used?

References

Baker, G.B., and R.T. Ellis. 1989. "Computerized Vocational Guidance Systems." In M.F. Wiskoff and G.M. Rampton, eds., *Military Personnel Measurement: Testing, Assignment, Evaluation*. New York: Praeger.

Belcourt, M., A.W. Sherman, G.W. Bohlander, and S.A. Snell. 1996. *Managing Human Resources*, Canadian ed. Toronto: Nelson Canada.

Cascio, W.F. 1991. *Applied Psychology in Personnel Management*, 4th ed. Englewood Cliffs, N.J.: Prentice-Hall.

_____. and J.W. Thacker. 1994. *Managing Human Resources*. Toronto: McGraw-Hill Ryerson.

Ceriello, V.R. 1991. *Human Resource Management Systems: Strategy, Tactics, and Techniques*. Toronto: Maxwell Macmillan.

Kroeker, L.P. 1989. "Personnel Classification/Assignment Models." In M.F. Wiskoff and G.M. Rampton, eds., *Military Personnel Measurement: Testing, Assignment, Evaluation*. New York: Praeger.

McCallum, T. 1996. "Embracing the chip: State-of-the-art technology propels HR into strategy's front lines." *Human Resources Professional* (April): 13–16.

Miller, D.B. 1986. *Managing Professionals in Research and Development*. San Francisco, Cal.: Jossey-Bass.

Rampton, G.M. 1989. "Entrenching equity in employment practices." *The Equal Times: The Newsletter for Human Resource Professionals*. Toronto: Bedford House 2(3): 19–21.

_____. and J.A. Doran. 1994. *A practitioner's guide for a new HRIS*. Paper presented at the 9th Annual CHRSP Conference (October): 4–7.

_____. ed. 1980. *Proceedings of the 22nd annual conference of the Military Testing Association*. Toronto: Canadian Forces Personnel Applied Research Unit (October): 27–31.

Sankey, C.A. 1976. *PAPRICAN: The First Fifty Years*. Pointe Claire, Que.: Pulp and Paper Research Institute of Canada.

Schratz, M.K., and M.J. Ree. 1989. "Enlisted Selection and Classification: Advances in Testing." In M.F. Wiskoff and G.M. Rampton, eds., *Military Personnel Measurement: Testing, Assignment, Evaluation*. New York: Praeger.

Senge, P.M. 1990. *The Fifth Discipline*. New York: Doubleday.

Wanous, J.P. 1992. *Organizational Entry: Recruitment, Selection, Orientation, and Socialization of Newcomers*, 2nd ed. Reading, Mass.: Addison-Wesley.

Webster, E.C. 1982. *The Employment Interview: A Social Judgement Process*. Schomberg, Ont.: S.I.P. Publications.

Wiesner, W.H., and S.F. Cronshaw. 1988. "A Meta-Analytic Investigation of the Impact of Interview Format and the Degree of Structure on the Validity of the Employment Interview." *Journal of Occupational Psychology* 61: 275–90.

Valaskakis, K., R. Coull, and R. Clermont. 1991. *Information technology and human resources: Prospects for the decade*. A report prepared for the Canadian Human Resources Scanning Association, Toronto, Ont. (April).

Wiskoff, M.F., and G.M. Rampton. 1989. *Military Personnel Measurement: Testing, Assignment, Evaluation*. New York: Praeger.

10

Training and Development

INTRODUCTION

Futurists, demographers, and labour market specialists are predicting skill shortages as the technological requirements of the information age become more pressing, and the "baby boomers" reach retirement age (Coates, 1990; DeSouza, 1990; Canadian Labour Market and Productivity Centre, 1990). Many organizations have already experienced these pressures and are responding by increasing the priority that they attach to employee training and development (Senge, 1990; McIntyre, 1994). This in turn has been reflected in more resources being applied to training and development (Larson and Blue, 1991; McIntyre, 1994), including the expertise required to determine the need for, develop, implement and manage the organization's training and development programs.

◆◆◆
STRATEGIC CONTEXT

In Canada, the appreciation of the importance of training and development to corporate success has been a recent development (Downey and McCamus, 1990; Larson and Blue, 1991). As the secretary of the Treasury Board of Canada pointed out in an address to the Ottawa Branch of the North American Society for Corporate Planning (Manion, 1985):

> *Canadians have not, traditionally, been good human resources planners and managers, either in the overall labour market, or in individual enterprises. We have tended to expect qualified people to be available when we need them, either from the domestic labour market or from the immigration flow. We have done far too little training and development for our own staff. We have tended to discard our workers when their*

skills became obsolete or redundant, rather than planning for their retraining, or redeployment.

By 1991, however, on the basis of a training survey, the Conference Board of Canada was able to report:

> *The results of this survey indicate clearly that leading Canadian firms understand the strategic imperative of creating a competitive advantage through the training and development of their workforce (Larson and Blue, 1991, 21).*

◆ ◆ ◆
TRAINING AND DEVELOPMENT: AN HR MODEL

Figure 10-1 depicts the relationship among training and development processes, from strategic planning through human resources/succession planning and training development programs to program review and monitoring.

Bernard and Ingols (1988) outline a number of characteristics shared by effective training and development programs. Foremost among these is basing programs on a strategic vision related to the corporate goals and objectives of the organizations, including human resources philosophies and programs (block A1 of Figure 10-1).

Training specialists who understand the interrelationships between strategic planning and human resources training and development, and who can work comfortably in both domains, are gaining more influence and prominence in many progressive organizations (McIntyre, 1992). As in the case of staffing specialists, discussed in the previous chapter, training and development specialists must understand the business of the organization, including its strategic context and the implications that this has for human resources. Thus, they must be experienced trainers—but much more as well. They must possess good analytic skills; understand the larger corporate perspective; have a clear vision of what human resources planning and development is, and should be, in their organization; and be able to explain this vision to others. Very importantly, training and development specialists must be change agents (Cascio and Thacker, 1994; Geis, 1991).

FIGURE 10.1 Training and Development

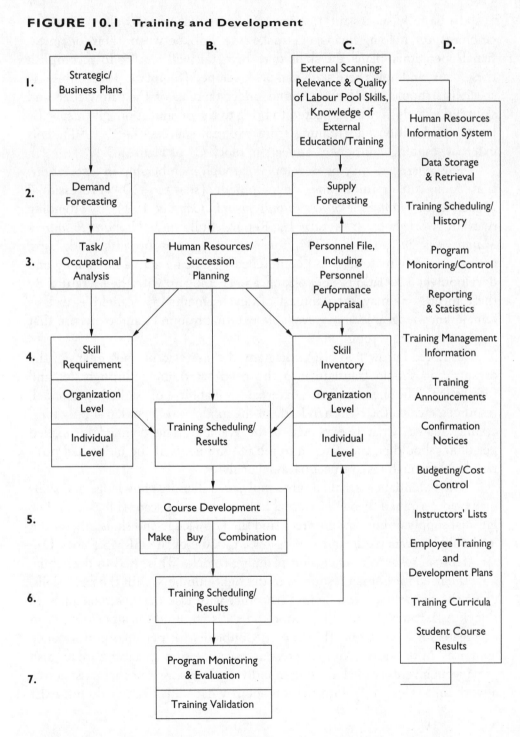

To be fully successful, training specialists will have to place increased emphasis on helping managers make the link between their organizational/operational plans, the skills that their staff will require to accomplish these plans, and how these skills can be developed (McIntyre, 1992). Training specialists should also have a sound understanding of the knowledge and skills individuals may be expected to bring to the organization, given specific levels of education and training from external sources (Geis, 1991). This external scanning component appears in block C1 of Figure 10-1.

This awareness may be developed through membership in associations that focus on training and development (see tab 10, "Professional Associations," *Human Resources Management in Canada*, 1994), by attending relevant workshops (see tab 1, "Report Bulletins," *Human Resources Management in Canada*, 1994, for regular updates on HR workshops, courses, training materials, and conferences) by being active in training and development associations, networking, and keeping up with the literature. By these means one may keep abreast of developments in the field as well as remain knowledgeable about available external resources and expertise that can be drawn on as required.

As noted in row two of the diagram, the strategic/business plans of the organization should translate into the need for training through demand forecasting. The internal and external availability of skilled personnel, resources, etc., on the right hand side of the model is reflected in supply forecasting; that is, what is expected to be available. The demand for skilled personnel should be translated into job requirements at the individual position level through task or occupational analyses.

The potential external labour supply, as well as its knowledge and skills may be determined through external human resources scans (block C1). The internal supply of human resources, and the knowledge and skills inherent in it, should be available from the employee module of the HRMS (block D).

Human resources/succession planning (block B3) is used to determine how the need for human resources in the right numbers, with the right skills, doing the right things, will be met. Together with task/occupational analyses (block A3), it may be used to define the skills required for a position, or in aggregate, for a work unit (block A4). Coupled with personal/performance appraisal information, human resources/succession planning may also provide an inventory of skills that an individual possesses, or that exist across a work unit (block C4). Information about what skills exist or do not exist among employees may be used with training surveys of various kinds in training needs analysis to determine whether training and development is required (block B4).

Training needs analysis, in turn, may serve as the basis for decisions about what training and development might best meet the need (block B5) (Belcourt and Wright, 1996). This may be formal courses provided in-house, external courses, or on-job training. Even with in-house courses, decisions must be made about whether to develop the training package in-house, to buy a ready-made package externally, or combine the two (e.g., buy a basic package and modify it to suit the specific needs of the organization).

Once training and development programs have been developed and implemented, procedures are required to schedule courses and attendees, to manage logistics issues, and to gather and store the results of training (block B6). A description of each course should be included, along with trainee results and evaluations of each course by trainees, instructors, and supervisors of the trainees (Belcourt and Wright, 1996).

The cost-effectiveness of training and development for the organization should be monitored continuously by program monitoring and evaluation procedures commonly referred to as "training validation" (block B7). Such program monitoring should include, but not be restricted to, the course reporting and evaluation procedures mentioned above (Smith and Braendeburg, 1991).

◆ ◆ ◆

TRAINING MANAGEMENT INFORMATION

The management of training and development in many organizations can be complex. As a consequence, training and development departments in some organizations develop independent training management systems. This situation may arise where training and development staff require automated assistance to help them manage their training and development information, but do not have access to an effective central HRMS; or want direct control of the collection and use of training information.

Training and development modules are included as integral parts of most comprehensive HRMSs. Nowadays, of course, seemingly independent training and development modules may be linked to other HRMS modules to form coordinated networks (see the discussion on HRMS modules in Chapter 5).

The data elements documented in Figures 10-2 to 10-4 are representative of data screens that currently exist in training modules of HRMS operating in a number of organizations, across such diverse sectors as the government, post-secondary education, resource industries, Crown corporations, and social services.

The first of these screens, Figure 10-2, illustrates typical training and development information that may be gathered on each individual. The next, Figure 10-3, shows typical data gathered for course management purposes. The last screen, Figure 10-4, depicts useful data on each individual relative to courses taken by that individual.

FIGURE 10.2 Employee Screen from a Hypothetical HRMS Training Module

EMPLOYEE SCREEN

Employee Name _____

Employee Number _____

Position Number _____

Organization Number _____

Address

      Work _____

      Home _____

Training and Development Required:

_____

_____

Data Requested _____

Priority _____

Data Scheduled _____

Date Completed _____

Cost _____

FIGURE 10.3 **Sample Course Detail Screen for a Training Module of a Hypothetical HRMS**

TRAINING MANAGEMENT SCREENS

COURSE SCREEN

Course Title _____

Course Code _____

Course Description _____

Course Location _____

Tuition (if any) _____

Other Costs _____

Prerequisites (if any) _____

Instructor _____

Method of Instruction _____

Equipment/Materials _____

Start Date _____ End Date _____

Minimum Enrollees _____ Maximum Enrollees _____

Enrolment Deadline _____

Number Enrolled To-date _____

FIGURE 10.4 **Sample Employee/Course Screen for a Training Module of a Hypothetical HRMS**

EMPLOYEE/COURSE SCREEN

Employee Name   _____

Employee Number   _____

Course Title   _____

Course Number   _____

Status: Enrolled _____   Wait-Listed _____   Completed _____

Date Enrolled _____   Date Completed _____

Fees: Tuition Paid _____   Other Expenses Paid _____

End-Course Evaluation _____

_____

_____

_____

_____

_____

_____

In various combinations, data from the screens outlined above can be used for a broad range of training and development planning, management, and monitoring applications. An HRMS may be used to collect data and produce analyses and reports at many different levels in the training and development model depicted in Figure 10-1. It may be used, for example, for:

Data Storage

◆ Lists of courses available by subject area

◆ Training curricula

◆ Employee training and development plans

◆ Student course results

- Results of training
- Training location
- Course evaluations
- Training history
- Lists of instructors
- Survey results (e.g., from training needs analyses, career and organization development, attitudes)

Training Management
- Creating class rosters
- Course scheduling
- Creating training announcements and confirmation notices

Reports
- Training costs, by student, per course, by organizational unit, etc.
- Numbers of employees trained by course, per year, by organizational unit, etc.
- Numbers of individuals requiring specific kinds of training and development
- Course evaluations by topic area or by instructor

There is one aspect in the gathering and storage of training information that deserves highlighting; and that is the increasing need for organizations to be able to demonstrate that they have taken all reasonable precautions to safeguard the health and safety of the public, clients, and employees. This means that organizations must ensure that their employees are trained to recognize health and safety hazards, and to take corrective action. It also means that employees must be trained to respond appropriately when accidents happen.

For example, quick and appropriate action in medical resuscitation, in accident prevention, and in fire drills are critical in such health care and social services areas as nursing homes and residences for individuals with disabilities. Generally, serious medical incidents or accidents must be reported. Investigations are conducted to determine whether appropriate action has been taken by staff and others in the incident. The organization may be liable if it cannot demonstrate that it made all reasonable efforts to ensure that staff were qualified for the responsibilities that the organization was expecting them to perform (Belcourt and Wright, 1996). Similarly, all organizations in Canada must ensure that their employees are trained to carry out their responsibilities with respect to the Workplace Hazardous Materials Information Systems (WHIMS) (Belcourt et al., 1996). Again, not being able to demonstrate that the organization has conducted this training to a satisfactory level could render the organization liable to criminal and civil litigation.

Thus the organization is responsible for ensuring and demonstrating that it has taken all necessary health and safety precautions, including training, to ensure that employees understand their responsibilities and can carry them out. It is critical, therefore, that the HRMS be able to collect, store, and report health and safety training, as well as professional certification or other forms of qualifications, whether this follows formal training or not (Belcourt and Wright, 1996). These may take the form of certifications provided by authorized professional organizations or appropriate tests established by the organization itself.

◆ ◆ ◆
APPLICATION

No other sector of society spends as high a percentage of its budget on training and development, or coordinates these functions as closely with other human resources and operational functions, including strategic/operational planning, as do Western military forces. Demand requirements are translated into organizational or job requirements via formal occupational analyses. In the Canadian Forces this is done at a special directorate called the Directorate of Organizational Structures located in Canadian Forces headquarters in Ottawa. Occupational information is gathered in detailed survey form and analyzed by means of the software package, Comprehensive Occupational Data Analysis Programs (CODAP), mentioned in the previous chapter.

This information is then used to define the position/organizational component of the Canadian Forces Personnel Management Information System (as its HRMS is known). The "employee module" of this system contains all performance appraisal and related information. Comparisons between job requirements and the kinds and amounts of skills of individuals at all levels leads to planning for individual training and development. This information also leads to the determination of the kinds of training and development courses required to meet these demands.

Western military forces provide a broad variety of occupational and training courses leading to full employability in such varying functions as the combat arms, electronics, high performance flying, and management courses. University courses at both the undergraduate and graduate level are offered internally in the military college setting and at external universities. Formal courses are only a part of the training and development involved. Career managers schedule these courses as well as orchestrate a planned series of career moves to enhance each individual's knowledge, experience, and value to the organization. The results of training and development are closely monitored, both at the individual level and across trainees, to ensure that the training provided is both validated and efficient.

Other large organizations attempt to recruit individuals who are capable of fitting into the organization at almost any level, on the basis of knowledge and skills previously obtained through public education or experience in other organizations. However, many of these organizations find that they cannot recruit all of the required knowledge and skills externally, and that they must develop and maintain extensive in-house training programs.

Some of these organizations have found it necessary to maintain an extensive array of training programs, involving a broad range of technical, management, and administrative courses. In addition to allowing the organization to plan for training on the basis of identified need (both at the individual and organizational level), training management systems assist trainers in course scheduling, course loading, data gathering, preparing course reports, and training validation.

◆ ◆ ◆
ATTITUDE SURVEYS

Some organizations, such as the Canadian Imperial Bank of Commerce, International Business Machines, Xerox, and General Electric, which place a premium on employee training and development, complement their efforts by having their employees provide feedback on the perceived effectiveness of these programs along with other organizational issues. These organizations have found that upward communication can lead to reduced absenteeism and turnover, less waste and spoilage, improved safety records, increased productivity, and higher profits—if the result of such feedback is acted upon seriously and expeditiously (Belcourt et al., 1996).

As reported in Rampton and Innes (1985), for many years the Israeli Defence Forces (I.D.F.) have complemented their training programs with sociometric surveys to support the early identification of leadership and officer-like qualities. In addition, regularly administered paper and pencil surveys and interviews are held with personnel at all levels to provide feedback to commanders with respect to such issues as motivation and morale, perceived adequacy of training and equipment, confidence in leadership, and perceived operational readiness of the particular unit involved.

The results of these surveys are considered to be an important indicator of operational effectiveness and a source of problem identification and resolution of command by the various levels. Results are eagerly awaited by commanders at all levels, probably because a specific commander sees his results only in relation to those of the average of the companies in his battalion. He does not see the individual results of his fellow company commanders. Further, since the surveys are conducted regularly and maintained in automated form, a commander can trace the results of any leadership or training initiatives that were taken.

COMPUTER-ASSISTED LEARNING

The Hudson's Bay Company, the Ontario Government, and Canada Post are examples of organizations that make increasing use of computer-assisted training in which training courses are provided via personnel computers often at convenient time, place, and learning speed. Not only can such training programs be more cost effective than alternative methods, but the results of training can be monitored by and entered directly into the HRMS.

Computer-assisted training is flexible in that its use opens doors to a number of training options including integration with other training media for what has been termed as "multimedial presentations." Alternatively, core course modules may be integrated with other modules to track and record progress, provide special tutoring for slower students, and provide proof of knowledge and skills learned for legal purposes.

Keeping track of the above information, conducting and keeping track of survey results, and performing needs analysis by matching organizational requirements to the resources available, both at the individual level, and more broadly, require automation and integration with an effective HRMS.

◆ ◆ ◆
SUMMARY

With the advent of the information society coinciding with a decreasing labour force as baby boomers retire, skill shortages in key areas are predicted. Many organizations have already experienced these pressures and are responding by increasing the priority attached to employee training and development. This in turn is reflected in more resources being applied to training and development. As organizations place an increased emphasis on training and development, they are finding it necessary to implement automated procedures to manage these programs and to document the results of training for each trainee. This chapter has discussed the implementation and use of an HRMS in support of these goals.

EXERCISES

1. Why is it that training management information systems are becoming increasingly important, either as modules of a larger HRMS, or as "stand-alone" systems? What skills do you feel that training specialists need to use such tools successfully? What relationships and divisions of responsibility should exist between training specialists and human resources management information personnel with regard to training information? For example: Who should decide what data to gather? Who should be responsible for data input? Accessing data? Preparing reports? Should managers,

and others in the organization, have any responsibility for data input or access? Under what circumstances?

2. What factors might influence whether an organization would incorporate the training management module into the HRMS or keep it separate? Would any of the responses to Question 1 differ depending on whether the system was "integrated," or "stand-alone"? Are there any issues of confidentiality to be considered in making these decisions? If so, what are they, and how might they be resolved?

3. What primary considerations should be taken into account when evaluating

the cost effectiveness of training? What role should the HRMS have in this evaluation? Must separate analyses be conducted to take into account differences at the individual level, the department level, or the organization overall? Why, or why not? Who should perform the analyses at each level? Is there an inherent conflict of interest if the evaluation is performed solely by training specialists?

4. What issues should be considered when an organization is deciding whether to provide training in-house, or to contract it to external agencies? How might the HRMS be useful in

helping to make this decision? Would more or less reliance be placed on an HRMS if training were contracted out? Please explain.

5. Access to suitable training and development has been defined as very important in employment equity programs. How might an HRMS be used to monitor and facilitate employment equity with respect to training and development programs? Would having a "stand alone" training management information system make the coordination of information more difficult? What adjustments would have to be made?

References

Belcourt, M., A.W. Sherman, G.W. Bohlander, and S.A. Snell. 1996. *Managing Human Resources*, Canadian ed. Toronto: Nelson Canada.

————. and P. Wright. 1996. *Managing Performance Through Training and Development*. Toronto: Nelson Canada.

Bensu, J. 1991. "HRMS Training Applications." In A.L. Lederer, ed. *Handbook of Human Resource Information Systems*. New York: Warren, Gorham and Lamont.

Bernard, H.B., and C.A. Ingols. 1988. "Six Lessons for the Corporate

Classroom." *Harvard Business Review* (Sept.–Oct.): 40–46.

Canadian Labour Market and Productivity Centre. 1990. *A Framework for a National Training Board: the Report of the Phase II Committee on the Labour Force Development Strategy*. Ottawa (July).

Cascio, W.F., and J.W. Thacker. 1994. *Managing Human Resources*. Toronto: McGraw-Hill Ryerson.

Ceriello, V.R. 1991. *Human Resource Management Systems: Strategy, Tactics, and Techniques*. Toronto: Maxwell Macmillan.

Coates, J.F. 1990. *Change Requires Retraining: Success Depends on Workplace Skills*. Technical Report. Washington, D.C.: J.F. Coates Inc.

DeSouza, J. 1995. "Training: The Key Human Resources Issue for the 1990s." In *Human Resources Management in Canada*. Scarborough, Ont.: Prentice-Hall.

Downey, J., and D. McCamus. 1990. *To Be our Best: Learning for the Future*. Montreal, Que.: Corporate Higher Education Forum.

Geis, G. 1991. *As Training Moves Toward the Next Decade: a Needs Analysis of Professional Development for Trainers*. Toronto: Ontario Training Corporation Report (May).

Larson, P.E., and M.W. Blue. 1991. *Training and Development 1990: Expenditures and Policies* (Report 67-91). Ottawa: The Conference Board of Canada.

Human Resources Management in Canada. 1995. Scarborough, Ont.: Prentice-Hall.

Manion, J. 1985. *The Integration of Human Resources and Corporate Planning*. Address to the Ottawa Branch of the North American Society for Corporate Planning Inc. Ottawa.

McIntyre, D. 1991. *Training and Development 1991* (Report 85-92). Ottawa: The Conference Board of Canada.

Rampton, G.M., and L. Innes. 1995. "The Role of the Behavioural Scientist in Support of Future Military Operations." In J. Hunt and J. Blair, eds., *Leadership on the Future Battlefield*. Willowdale, Ont.: Pergamon-Brasseys.

Senge, P.M. 1990. *The Fifth Discipline*. New York: Doubleday.

Smith, M.E., and D.C. Brandenburg. 1991. "Summative Evaluation." *Performance Improvement Quarterly* 4, no. 2: 35–38.

II

Compensation and Payroll

♦♦♦
INTRODUCTION

This chapter discusses the use of an HRMS in support of the compensation and payroll functions of the organization. Historically, the need to handle large amounts of information accurately led to the early automation of payroll and related functions (Ceriello, 1991; Kavanagh et al., 1990; Lederer, 1991). Indeed, as pointed out in Chapter 1, many human resources management information systems evolved from adding a broader range of capabilities to what started out as payroll systems.

♦♦♦
COMPENSATION/PAYROLL MODEL

Figure 11-1 applies the human resources model to the compensation and payroll function. As in the previous applications, the upper level of the model refers to the global, strategic context. Level three refers to the practical, hands-on functions that we traditionally think of as human resources programs, for example: job evaluation, linking performance appraisal processes with pay-for-performance, and individual salary determination. Level two, between the strategic context and the hands-on programs, represents the planning and development programs which use information from the strategic context to shape and direct the form and operation of the human resources programs. Level four, as in the other models, reflects the monitoring and auditing processes that ensure that compensation/payroll programs, in support of and in conjunction with other functions in the organization, are operating as they should.

At the global level, an organization's compensation strategy is generally influenced by the following:

1. the organization's financial situation — how much it can pay;

2. the salary market — how much other organizations are paying for similar jobs;

FIGURE 11.1 Compensation and Payroll

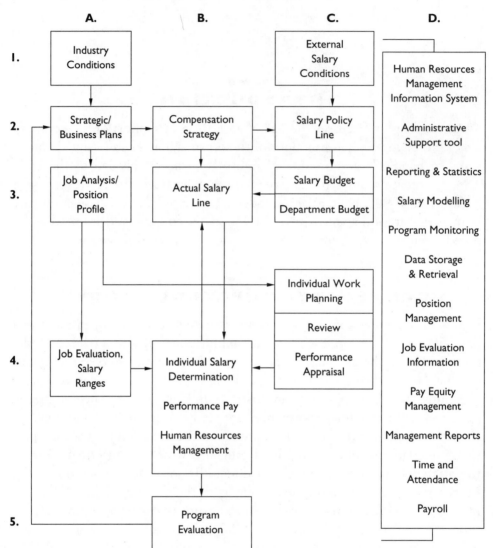

3. how much the organization wants to pay — some organizations want to be salary leaders and pay more than others in their sectors; others want merely to be competitive, and pay average salaries; while others prefer to pay less; and

4. how the organization is going to pay its employees — that is, the payroll function (Belcher and Achtison, 1987; Freedman et al., 1982; Theriault, 1992).

◆ ◆ ◆
SALARY MARKET SURVEYING

Many organizations keep track of the salary rates paid by others in and outside of their industrial sectors by participating in and subscribing to published salary surveys (Milkovich and Newman, 1990; Theriault, 1992). Other organizations prefer to conduct their own surveys. The information gathered may be entered into the HRMS and used as a context against which to conduct analyses to determine a salary policy line. A salary policy line outlines the salary that the organization wishes to pay at each job evaluation level (see Agarwal, 1986; Cascio and Thacker, 1994; Milkovich and Newman, 1990; Theriault, 1992).

The difference between the actual salary line (what the organization is actually paying at each job evaluation level) and the salary policy line represents the salary adjustments required to align actual salaries with the established salary policy line (see Figure 11-2).

◆ ◆ ◆
SALARY POLICY LINES

Salary policy lines may be established in different ways, for different purposes. Traditionally, however, they have been established by senior management, based on the organization's compensation strategy and knowledge of external salary conditions.

The organization's compensation strategy should be rooted in its strategic/business plans, since the salaries paid by the organization will reflect the quality and availability of human resources (Theriault, 1994). As a consequence, strategically, some organizations decide that they want to pay above average salaries for their sector, while others choose to pay average salaries.

FIGURE 11.2 Relation Between a Salary Policy Line and an Actual Salary Line Derived from Benchmark Salaries

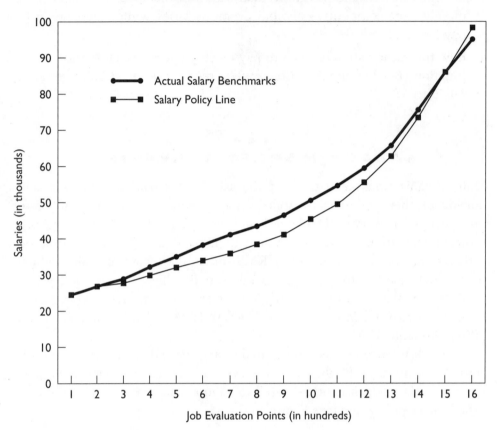

Economic and business conditions for some organizations may mean that they have to pay less than average salaries for their sector.

◆ ◆ ◆
JOB/POSITION DEFINITION

The same processes that are used to define bona fide occupational requirements for staffing purposes are generally used to define job requirements for job evaluation processes (Cascio and Thacker, 1994) in salary determination. As noted in Figure 11-1, job requirements derive from organizational requirements as reflected in strategic/business plans. Traditionally job requirements were documented in formatted job descriptions. Increasingly, however, job surveys are being used to gather this information. Well prepared job surveys can have the advantages of being more objective, requiring less time and effort to complete, and being more easily automated.

However gathered, job requirements information must be evaluated to determine the relative value of jobs, and thus, relative salary ranges. This is generally done by job evaluation committees according to established evaluation guidelines. Job surveys can produce automated information in weighted form that could be used directly to determine salary ranges; however, evaluation committees are most often used to evaluate the information derived from this source. Such committees can compensate for employees and supervisors who might tend to under- or over-represent the job described.

◆ ◆ ◆
WORK PLANNING AND REVIEW

The requirements of the job provide the context or mandate against which individual work goals may be developed. At the end of the performance period, performance may be measured against these goals and the assessment used to determine merit pay, in those organizations that use merit as a determinate of pay increases (Agarwal, 1986).

◆ ◆ ◆
PROGRAM EVALUATION

As with the other models, it is important that the effectiveness of the processes outlined above be monitored and upgraded continuously (Rampton and Doran, 1994).

◆ ◆ ◆
PAY EQUITY

Where pay equity legislation applies, a salary policy line may be determined by the pay rates of male-dominated jobs (Cascio and Thacker, 1994). In Ontario's pay equity legislation, for example, a comparator was defined to be the lowest paid male-dominated job class of equal value. When suitable comparators do not exist, then extrapolation across points in the salary line is possible. When too few male comparators exist even to do this (for instance, in highly female-dominated work-sites such as day-care settings),

◆

proxy comparators may be chosen from other settings to serve as points on the salary policy line. The salary adjustments required to bring the salaries of individuals in female-dominated job classes to the salary policy line represents the pay equity adjustments.

Obviously, one would prefer a smooth ascending curve when dollars (Y-axis) are plotted against job evaluation level (X-axis). A major problem with the job class to job class comparison method for determining pay equity in Ontario is that it is possible to get inversions in the curve when a highly paid male-dominated class has to be used as a comparator at one level, while a lower paid, but more highly evaluated male-dominated job is the comparator at a higher level. For example, the coaches of most professional hockey teams make less than their team captains, although the job of coach would probably rank higher than the job of team captain in most evaluation schemes. Therefore, if the jobs of coach and team captain were identified as two male comparator job classes, an inversion of the type mentioned would occur.

To establish internal equity within an organization, any such anomalies are usually resolved by smoothing out the salary policy line even when this means raising the line overall to compensate for these anomalies. Adjustments required to raise salaries to the policy line are made across all jobs at a given evaluation level, whether or not the job falls into a female, male, or neutral job class.

◆ ◆ ◆

HRMS REQUIREMENTS

In any organization consisting of more than a few hundred employees, organizing and maintaining all the current and historical information required to do salary determination and pay equity analyses requires the assistance of a sophisticated HRMS (Doran and Rampton, 1994). This has been found to be true in actual examples across a variety of organizations of various sizes, including:

1. small to medium-sized organizations—around 400 employees in the resources sector, and a social services agency;

2. medium to large-sized organizations—around 7000 employees at a large post-secondary education institution; and

3. very large organizations—from 50,000 to more than 100,000 employees at a large Crown corporation and in the federal government.

In these organizations, salary information on the HRMS was used in salary analysis and modelling exercises in preparation for such business processes as strategic planning, labour negotiations, and human resources planning. The HRMSs of all of the organizations had separate modules containing job/organization data and employee data. Some of the organizations also had pay-for-performance programs in which annual salary increases were based on assessed performance, as well as where each individual was placed within the salary scale for his or her job.

To manage these functions effectively, the respective HRMS needed the capabilities described below:

DATA ORGANIZATION For cost effective updating and ease of data handling, all major data elements should be "table driven," that is, the possible values of each data element should be defined in tables that can easily be referred to in ongoing applications and amended as changes are required. Such changes may be necessary because of evolving organizational requirements or new legislation (e.g., new taxes or new employment equity reporting requirements).

POSITION MANAGEMENT The HRMS must be position driven. Positions must be linked to a job to obtain salary and employment equity attributes.

JOB INFORMATION The HRMS must have a job class table to store salary information as well as NOC (national occupational code) and OC (occupational codes) used for coding jobs for employment equity purposes.

ORGANIZATION An organization table must link to positions and have the attributes necessary to track costs. A location table must also link to the employee to identify actual work and/or mailing location.

AFFILIATION An affiliation table is necessary to record the major affiliation(s) of each employee, whether this be employment function, professional affiliation, or union affiliation.

SENIORITY The HRMS must provide a field that can be updated manually to reflect seniority date.

ATTENDANCE MANAGEMENT The HRMS must provide sufficient fields and capacity to record all absences by type, date, paid/unpaid, etc. (See the discussion in the following section.)

EMPLOYEE/POSITION HISTORY The HRMS must track all individual appointments, showing all jobs held. It must also track who is, and has been, in each position.

PERFORMANCE EVALUATION The HRMS must provide for the tracking of goals and objectives, performance intervals, and evaluation.

EMPLOYMENT AND PAY EQUITY The HRMS must identify the key data elements associated with employment and pay equity as related to the positions and employees, and be able to report this information in formats required by provincial and federal governments.

PAYROLL

The basic requirements for contemporary HRMS payroll modules are similar, regardless of the size of the organization. Some of these areas are described below:

KEY DATA ELEMENTS An HRMS with a payroll module must be capable of maintaining a basic record on all employees, with a data element for each of the key variables linked to calculating pay for salaried and hourly employees. *Note*: A data dictionary must be developed for each of these essential data elements, so that the definition of each element is readily available for users.

DEDUCTIONS The system must be able to deduct and track all standard deductions, such as Canada Pension Plan, unemployment insurance, and tax.

SALARIED EMPLOYEES The payroll system must be capable of accurately calculating the pay for each salaried employee. Salary must be calculated according to the number of days (entitled to be paid) if the employee starts/stops work during a pay period. The HRMS must calculate additional pay if additional pay is earned. Adjustments must be able to be made accordingly.

HOURLY EMPLOYEES The system must be capable of accurately calculating the pay for each hourly paid employee according to the rate of pay and hours worked. A complication in some organizations for both salaried and hourly employees is that individuals may work at multiple jobs at multiple rates of pay for different cost centres during a pay period. The system must also:

1. produce, on demand, time sheets for each employee and/or work unit;
2. track and analyze shift pay differentials;
3. store and report on a variety of salary related data including leave of absences, sick leave, workers' compensation, union duty, and other union business including union education and vacation; and
4. have provision for extra fields for information that will be required in the future.

YEAR-TO-DATE INFORMATION The system must be able to accumulate earnings and deductions, and to display year-to-date information.

RECORD OF EMPLOYMENT The system must be able to produce accurate records of employment as required. The calculation of these records of employment for each individual must be based on actual history.

INCOME TAX STATEMENTS The system must be able to produce accurate income tax statements at year-end. In Canada these are known as T4s (statement of remuneration paid) or T4As (statement of pension, retirement, annuity, and other income). In addition to the paper forms provided to each individual at year end, the system must also be able to produce electronic records of all T4s for government purposes (i.e., Revenue Canada).

RETROACTIVE PAY The system must track all pay events and facilitate the calculation of retroactive pay.

HEALTH TAX In jurisdictions to which it applies, the payroll system must be able to calculate and remit payroll-related health tax. In the province of Ontario this was 1.95 percent of gross payroll for the year 1994.

LIEU TIME Where it applies, the system must be able to track time off in lieu of overtime. This must link to attendance management.

PENSION REPORTS The system must be able to track and report all pension deductions.

LEAVES OF ABSENCE The system must be able to track periods of leave of absence, with and without pay, maternity leave, and unpaid sick leave.

SHORT- AND LONG-TERM DISABILITY If applicable, the system must continue to pay the employee on short-term disability (STD) if the employee has sick leave accumulated. The system must be able to track and administer long-term disability (LTD) where this is required.

MASS CHANGES The payroll system must be capable of making mass changes of data, such as when pay increases are processed. Major data entities, such as organizations and jobs, must be table driven. A name change to an organization unit in a table will result in a name change of the organization of all employees linked to that organization.

SPREADSHEET INTERFACE The system must be able to interface with popular spreadsheets, such as Lotus 1-2-3, for downloading of pay information for analysis.

INTERFACING WITH OTHER SYSTEMS The HRMS containing the payroll system must be able to interface with accounting and other systems to ensure that most effective use is made of the organization's corporate information resources.

AUDIT TRAILS The payroll system must be able to provide a complete record of all pay transactions, including employee, amount paid, pay type, cost centre, date paid. Analytical reports must be set up to do "real vs. planned" comparisons.

TIME AND ATTENDANCE

As noted above, each payroll system must have the capability to accurately capture, analyze, and report attendance on the job, as well as the time worked in the various categories for which an individual is eligible. Because of the complexity of "time and attendance," many HRMSs have special modules for this purpose.

Figure 11-3 provides a graphic illustration of one such module and shows how the various types of employee time feed to the HRMS and other organization systems.

Several different time categories may be relevant, depending on the employee group in question. Included among these are:

1. *Available time.* This is the amount of time available to be worked by each type of employee. It is derived from union employment contracts, applicable legislation, and organization policies and practices and includes regular time and overtime.

FIGURE 11.3 Employee Time Model

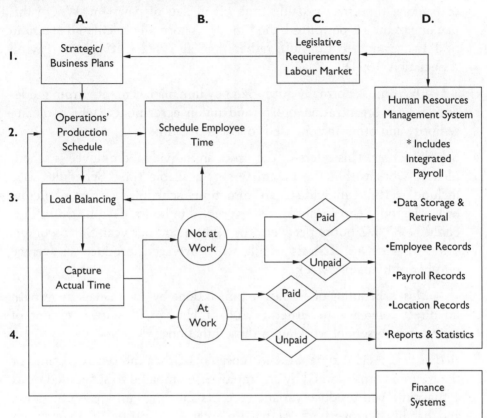

2. *Regular or standard time.* This refers to the number of hours/shifts an employee is normally expected to be at work in a given period. It will include direct and possibly indirect labour as well.

   Legislation varies widely by jurisdiction, but normally sets maximum allowable hours an employee is allowed to work regardless of overtime, and often specifies minimum hours of work for which an employee must be paid if called in to work (Canadian Payroll Association, 1994).

   The payroll group is usually charged with the responsibility of auditing actuals against legislative, contract, and organization limits.

3. *Overtime time.* This refers to time worked in excess of standard hours for which an additional payment is provided (most often 1 1/2 times the

regular hourly payment). In some jurisdictions a provision for building up or banking time may provide time off in lieu of payment. Where this banking of time is permitted, the time off is normally calculated at a ratio of 1:1, overtime to time off, rather than at 1 1/2:1 (Canadian Payroll Association, 1994).

Overtime is normally authorized by line management within guidelines set by organization policy and union agreements (which dictate seniority and other factors used to assign overtime).

4. *Scheduled time.* This refers to the times an individual employee is scheduled to work within the parameters of available time. Schedules may include overtime. Individuals are sometimes scheduled as part of a crew or work group. This is most often expressed in hours, days, or shifts. This could be 37 1/2 hours per week, or 1980 hours per year. Shift workers often work cycles of shifts which, when averaged, produce an average number of hours per week.

Most scheduling of employee time is done by line management with no direct reference to either Payroll or Human Resources, except of course, for personnel working in those functions.

5. *Actual time.* Actual time worked represents either the recorded time or the assumed time worked by an employee. Compared to scheduled time, actual time will produce variance reports showing employee utilization and liability for overtime. Actual time can be captured in many ways including several automated methods. McCallum (1996), for example, reports that employees at Niagara Paints in Hamilton, Ontario, use an electro-magnetic card to record hours of work and breaks. Entries from this card are automatically analyzed by the HRMS time and attendance/payroll modules. These can be entered into an HRMS for payroll, human resources, operational, and other purposes. Actual time is often broken into the following three components, particularly in heavy and resource industries:

(a) *Direct labour* generally reflects employee time spent at work in productive activity. It is often recorded against volume of output produced, machine utilization, and other such components. It often includes activities that are directly related to productivity such as set-up and wash-up times.

It is used by line management and finance groups to assign production costs and measure production efficiency, and is not normally a concern of Human Resources.

(b) *Indirect labour*. Indirect labour involves employee time spent at work but not in directly productive activities. Examples include training, union business, and time spent on performance appraisal or discipline. This time is separated from direct labour in order to provide a more accurate estimate of the cost of production. Operations and Finance are concerned with indirect labour, particularly in reducing it, but most indirect labour activities are also of concern to Human Resources.

6. *Not at work.* "Time not at work" may be for legitimate (e.g., leaves of absence (LOAs)) reasons or not (e.g., absence without permission to pursue personal interests). LOAs may be with or without pay depending on the nature and duration of the leave. It includes sick leave, short- and long-term disability, vacation, education leaves, and time off on personal business (bereavement, jury duty, voting, etc.) (Canadian Payroll Association, 1994).

Line management is often responsible for monitoring and dealing with poor attendance, usually expressed as a percentage of available hours, although Human Resources is sometimes responsible for managing an overall organizational absenteeism or attendance program, when one exists. Payroll concerns itself with the payment or nonpayment of time not at work, pursuant to input from operations and interpretation of employment contracts and legislation. Human Resources usually has a significant role in the management of LOAs and associated benefits administration, to ensure adherence and consistency of application with organization policies and collective agreements.

The responsibility for authorizing, monitoring, and documenting employee time and attendance has traditionally fallen into at least three responsibility areas: line management, Payroll, and Human Resources. In the 1960s, 1970s, and 1980s these separate functions often had separate computer systems. This functional separation was explained in several ways. In organizations that designed their own "stand-alone" functional systems the separation really occurred because "Personnel" or "Human Resources" was defined too narrowly. The larger concept, human resources management, had not yet been described and adopted. The scheduling of time was not seen by any level or function of management to be part of Human Resources so that:

1. Organizations that bought software found (and often continue to find) that human resources systems and integrated HRMSs lacked key capabilities required by either Operations or Payroll. The function of scheduling of time, for example, is often ignored by HRMSs, with the time cycle being picked up at the reporting of actuals.

2. The unsophisticated security that most of these systems contained meant that users could not be restricted to their particular area of interest; in this case, line management and Payroll could access confidential compensation and other human resources information on employees in their own or other areas for which they had no need or authority to access. Fortunately, with improved techniques for managing security, it is no longer a barrier to integrated systems.

3. The existence of multiple systems holding related information also led to duplicate data capture and entry. The time records of one employee could be captured by as many as four separate systems; the foreperson's paper record, production labour reports, Payroll, and Human Resources. In addition, in some instances the same supervisor would enter essentially the same data all four times.

4. The trend toward coordination of information systems holding time and attendance, and payroll information has forced those responsible for the design of work processes to consider how those processes might better be designed to be more integrated and reduce duplication.

◆ ◆ ◆
MANAGING TIME REPORTING

There are many different ways of handling the capture and reporting of time worked. Traditionally, the most common has been the use of time cards on which an individual employee's actual time at work (direct and indirect) is recorded. This card is then passed to production accounting where the values are entered for production purposes, and then passed to payroll for pay processing. Time cards can be manual or automated by use of mechanical time clocks, scanners, or direct computer entry.

It is desirable to collect all data as close to the source as possible, to minimize manual data entry, and to maximize access to the data. Many organizations collect employee time data for all actual time, but some organizations are making a strategic decision to move away from that level of detail to "exception reporting."

The use of exception reporting of employee time assumes that an employee works as scheduled unless otherwise reported. Exceptions, such as scheduled direct labour being attributed to indirect labour or daily sick leave, are still reported, but the volume of time information that must be collected and entered is significantly reduced. Exception reporting has been used for some time, but has normally been restricted to salaried, nonunionized employees.

New technological options for reporting time are also easing this task. Interactive voice response (IVR) systems utilizing touch-tone phones for entering into computer systems from remote sites are now being marketed. Using such equipment, the employee or supervisor can call the system from home, car, or office and use the phone keypad to enter the exception information. The IVR system is interfaced with the main HRMS so that the data is automatically transferred.

◆ ◆ ◆
SUMMARY

This chapter has discussed the use of an HRMS in support of the compensation and payroll functions of the organization. The interrelationship between these and other human resources functions—including an HRMS— were demonstrated with the assistance of a human resources model. Emphasis was placed on contemporary issues such as evolving strategic/business trends and pay equity. The capture of employee time as an important data component for several functional areas was also discussed. These areas have traditionally kept their data separately, but new strategic thinking and technology have combined to make it possible to collect and enter the data once and treat it as an organization-wide resource. Integration of these multiple data streams into one set of data within the HRMS provides an excellent example of the organization-wide applications of the HRMS. Such integration also provides concrete savings.

EXERCISES

1. Payroll and related costs can be the single largest component of many organization's annual operating budget. This being the case, establishment of the organizations salary policy can be a very important strategic/business issue, requiring that Human Resources work very closely with the organization's executives. What do you feel should be the role of Human Resources in this process? What part should the executive play? The HRMS? What other parties may feel that they should be involved in influencing salary/wage decisions?

2. Is it generally better for an organization to conduct its own salary surveys, to cooperate with other organizations in the same business sector, or to buy salary survey information from an agency that conducts such surveys annually or on contract for specific purposes? What considerations would lead an organization to decide upon one option or another?

3. As was mentioned earlier, in some organizations pay and employment equity information is maintained in systems separate from the HRMS. The reason for this is to maintain confidentiality with respect to the pay and employment equity data and to ensure that this data is not used as the basis for administrative decisions. Do you agree with this approach? Can you think of practical alternatives?

4. Why did the HRMS in many organizations evolve out of the automation of compensation and payroll processes, rather than from other HR functions?

5. In some organizations payroll is part of Finance, while in others it is contained within Human Resources. Please explain the pros and cons of having it report to either of these functions.

6. To what uses does the Operations group of an organization put time information? Are these uses changing?

7. What has stood in the way of integrating time information on a single organization-wide computer system?

8. Exception reporting seems to be gaining favour in some nontraditional areas. Explain why this might be.

References

Agarwal, N.C. 1986. "Wage and Salary Administration." In *Human Resources Management in Canada*. Scarborough, Ont.: Prentice Hall, 1995.

Belcher, D., and T.J. Achtison. 1987. *Compensation Administration*. Englewoods Cliffs, N.J.: Prentice-Hall.

Canadian Payroll Association. 1994. *Student Guide for Introduction to Payroll, Level I*, 3rd ed. Toronto.

Cascio, W.F., and J.W. Thacker. 1994. *Managing Human Resources*. Toronto: McGraw-Hill Ryerson.

Ceriello, V.R. *Human Resource Management Systems: Strategy, Tactics, and Techniques*. Toronto: Maxwell Macmillan.

Doran J.A., and G.M. Rampton. 1994. "Making a Business Case for a New Human Resources Management Information System." *Canadian Human Resources Systems Professionals Resource Magazine* (June): 4–8.

Freedman, S.M., J.R. Montanari, and R.T. Keller. 1982. "The Compensation Program: Balancing Organizational and Employee Needs." *Compensation Review* (2nd quarter): 47–54.

Kavanagh, M.J., H.G. Gueutal, and S.I. Tannenbaum. 1990. *Human Resource Information Systems: Development and Application*. Boston, Mass.: PWS-Kent.

Lederer, A.L. 1991. *Handbook of Human Resource Information Systems*. Boston, Mass.: Warren, Gorham and Lamont.

McCallum, T. 1996. "Embracing the Chip: State-of-the-Art Technology Propels HR into Strategy's Front Lines." *Human Resources Professional* (April): 13–16.

Milkovich, G.T., and J.M. Newman. 1990. *Compensation*. Homewood, Ill.: Richard D. Irwin.

Rampton, G.M., and J.A. Doran. 1994. "A Practitioner's Guide for a New HRIS." Unpublished paper presented at the 9th Annual CHRSP Conference (October): 4-7.

Theriault, R. 1994. "Mercer Compensation Manual: Theory and Practice." Unpublished paper presented at the 9th Annual CHRSP Conference (October): 4–7.

12

Benefits and Pension Programs

◆ ◆ ◆
INTRODUCTION

n Western industrial countries, organizations are expected to provide benefits and pension programs, particularly to their permanent, full-time employees (Cascio and Thacker, 1994; Coward, 1991; McCaffrey, 1988). These programs are expensive, typically involving 35 percent or more of an organization's total compensation package. Recently, many organizations have been extending some or all of their benefits packages to part-time employees (Stelluto and Klein, 1990). This trend has been stimulated, at least in part, by the recognition that women and members of minority groups tend to be overrepresented in the part-time component of the labour pool. Extending benefits to this group has become an employment equity issue (Cascio and Thacker, 1994), and will have the effect of further increasing benefits costs. An HRMS has a critical role in the cost-effective management of benefits and pension programs (see examples in Chapter 3). This chapter will discuss the requirements and application of an HRMS benefits and pension module.

◆ ◆ ◆
BENEFITS AND PENSION MODEL

Figure 12-1 shows the human resources model considered from the perspective of benefits and pension applications. As in the models presented in previous chapters, the top levels of the model reflect the global, strategic context in which the other benefits components exist. The next level denotes planning processes designed to translate information from the global strategic/business context into the practical human resources programs reflected at the third level. The bottom level in the diagram contains program evaluation processes designed to assess whether the programs are doing what they were designed to do, and to feed the findings of these analyses back into the system, so that continuous improvements may be made.

FIGURE 12.1 **Pension and benefits**

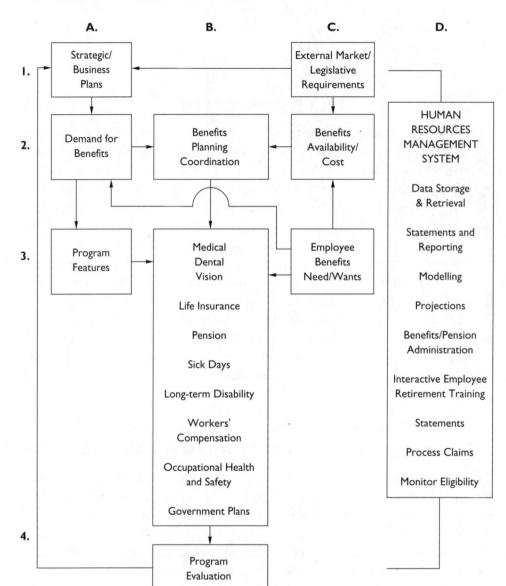

In deciding what benefit and pension programs to provide to employees, an organization will generally be interested in determining what it must (and can afford) provide to:

1. achieve the objectives of the organization;
2. remain competitive in terms of attracting and retaining employees;
3. satisfy employee requirements as defined through collective bargaining;
4. satisfy ever-changing government legislation (e.g., workers' compensation, maternity/paternity benefits, payroll taxes for health care);
5. fulfil its values/responsibilities as a good corporate citizen (Benefits Communication, 1992; McCaffrey, 1989; MacPherson and Wallace, 1992).

Information related to the first point derives from the strategic plan of the organization together with what employees expect or want, while information related to the second may derive from market surveys of what other organizations are providing to their employees (Cascio and Thacker, 1994). Pressure to satisfy employee wants or needs may be reflected in labour negotiations. Benefits supply derives from benefits that are available from carriers, government, and other sources.

Benefits planning and coordination is used to determine how the demand for benefits is to be satisfied with the supply. The demand for benefits becomes translated into the specific features of the various benefits programs, while benefits availability and cost will have a bearing on the employee needs and wants.

Benefits programs per se will be determined by a combination of benefits planning, program features, vacation/holidays, sick leave/personal time off, and employee wants and needs (Schuler, 1984). These programs may include *health-related plans* like medical, dental, and vision programs; *insured programs*, such as life insurance, short- and long-term disability, workers' compensation; *safety programs*, like occupational health and safety; and *pension plans*, whether defined benefits, money purchase, or mixed. Some organizations may also include such items as educational upgrading, top-up of maternity and paternity leave, stock options, financial counselling, employee assistance programs, day-care, and elder care. (Coward, 1991).

As with the other models, the last, but very important function depicted is program evaluation, in which the performance and administration of benefits programs are evaluated so that continuous improvements may be made (Cascio and Thacker, 1994).

◆ ◆ ◆
HRMS APPLICATIONS

Those searching for a new, fully integrated HRMS are well advised to note the criteria set for the benefits module of the programs they are contemplating. To be effective across organizations, such modules must be complicated, since the nature and requirements of benefits programs vary widely (Kelly, 1991). Growing legislative demands add to the complexity (Cascio and Thacker, 1994). It is difficult to create programs that can deal with these complexities effectively, while still being user friendly.

Some organizations have in fact found it more effective to develop their own benefits modules, or to buy separate ones that have been designed especially for benefits applications (Kelly, 1991). The complication then becomes how the interface between such modules and the other module in the HRMS is handled.

Whether a benefits module integrated within the larger HRMS, or a "stand-alone" module is purchased, the following capabilities will be important.

To meet an organization's internal needs an HRMS must:

1. identify all employees, both active and inactive, who are eligible for the various benefits;
2. allow for efficient enrolment of new members, preferably as a normal part of the staffing process;
3. accurately monitor benefits eligibility, whether on enrolment or on change in employment status;
4. accurately track benefits coverage for each employee especially as changes occur during an individual's career;
5. facilitate the accurate collection and storage of both current and historical benefits and pension data;
6. be easily updated to reflect legislative, union contract, and policy changes affecting employee benefits;
7. allow automated monitoring of claims performance;

8. interface with the databases of other functions that may or may not have been integrated into the HRMS, such as payroll, occupational health and safety, worker' compensation, and medical records;

9. process claims payments; and

10. automatically effect payroll deductions through the payroll function.

An HRMS must also allow the ready but secure transfer of information to and from relevant external parties, such as reports and returns on pension and benefits information to government agencies; pension and benefits cost data to and from actuaries, auditors, and outside consultants on contract to the organization; rate and coverage information to and from insurance carriers; and information on money available for investment, investment strategy, and investment performance from investment managers and plan trustees.

◆ ◆ ◆
MODELLING/ANALYSES

An HRMS must be able to:

1. provide information flexibly and quickly in formats tailored to the requirements of the situation. This can include information for senior management decision making, strategic planning, or labour negotiations;

2. support modelling and analyses of benefits data so that problem areas may be identified, and the implications of usage, cost, and other trends explored; and

3. support cost control by automating benefits administration, and providing the means for monitoring excess use, abuse, and inefficiencies, as well as the means for taking corrective action.

◆ ◆ ◆
TRENDS

Several examples of the way in which automating benefits and pension programs can provide for the more cost-effective administration of these programs were provided in Chapter 3. One of these examples involved the purchase of a pension administration system. This system replaced a partially automated system that had served the pension and benefits staff well for many years, but since it was based on outdated technology, was becoming increasingly difficult to maintain and use.

Benefits and pension plans can be complicated, especially in large organizations. Further, the trend is to greater complexity (Belcourt et al., 1996). The increased use "flexible benefits programs," leaves of absence, more and different categories of workers, special appointments, and other status changes can cause many variations in the status of compensation, benefits, and pension plans for any individual. All of these must be tracked and recorded if accurate estimates of pension status must be provided to members on an annual basis, as required by law; and accurate pension calculations must be done on retirement.

Prior to the implementation of a new pension administrative system, records in many pension programs must be cross-checked manually, with calculations reviewed at least once to ensure the accuracy of final pension calculations. This may take several hours for each individual. Organizations that have not automated these functions are well advised to consider doing so now or risk being at severe disadvantage as greater numbers of individuals retire with the aging of the baby boom generation.

COORDINATION OF BENEFITS

With increasing numbers of "dual career families," both spouses may be in organizations that provide benefit programs (Stelluto and Klein, 1990). This may lead to "double coverage" in that each employer may cover both spouses. It is obvious that, in medical or dental programs, for example, this can lead to unnecessary expenses since coverage by just one of the plans is required. Premiums in the other can be saved through coordination across plans. When both spouses are employees of the same organization it should be a relatively simple matter to ensure that this coordination occurs. The HRMS must also be able to provide information to pension and benefits staff (or insurance carriers acting on their behalf) so that contact may be made with organizations or insurance carriers responsible for the benefits programs of each employee's spouse (where such exist) to coordinate benefits programs across organizations. As pointed out in Chapter 3, there can be a considerable pay-back to the organization when this coordination is done effectively.

EXAMPLE: AUTOMATING THE PENSION SYSTEM

At one large Canadian university, the administrative work alone to process the retirements using the technology at hand was predicted to have required several additional staff at a time when the university was attempting to effect economies. Therefore, the decision was made to implement a new pension administration system that could provide:

• Annual pension statements

• Pension projections to plan members for planning purposes

• Accurate analysis of pension entitlements for retirees

• Accurate data to the university's actuary so that valuations may be done to determine the funding requirements of the plan

• Accurate reports for the plan's board of trustees

• Returns to meet government requirements

• Analysis/modelling capability to support potential plan changes for both active and retired employees

This pension system represented a heavy up-front investment in getting it up and running and then loading it with accurate data, especially since it had to be implemented and run parallel to the older system for a few months. System implementation and debugging were stressful for the pension staff, but proved worthwhile in that the system is now operating well and more than living up to the original expectations held for it.

FLEXIBLE BENEFITS

In an attempt to offer a greater range of benefits while controlling costs, some organizations are offering "flexible benefits" (also termed "cafeteria" programs) (Stonebraker, 1995) in which individuals are generally provided with a basic "core set of benefits" and then allowed to pick from a menu of additional benefits until the cost of the benefits chosen equals a predetermined amount. This enables employees to tailor their benefits program to their needs, by selecting those components that are most useful to them, and not being compelled to pay for others that are not. It also places more demands on the benefits module of an HRMS, which must be able to keep track of and report on what are, essentially, unique benefits programs for each employee.

In a traditional "defined benefits" program, usage and cost are balanced out over all participants. In a flexible benefits program, individuals will select the components that they feel will be most valuable to them in terms of frequency of usage and cost. Those developing a flexible benefits program must take this into account and build safeguards into the system, or risk increased overall costs.

In the design and development of a flexible benefits program, an HRMS benefits module must be able to support research (including employee surveys), analyses, and modelling to help predict employee usage of each of the benefits components. After the program has been implemented, regular and ad hoc HRMS reports will be important to ensure that the program is managed effectively, including achieving its objectives, within cost limitations.

◆ ◆ ◆

ON-LINE COMMUNICATIONS AND ADMINISTRATION OF BENEFITS PROGRAMS

Organizations are increasingly providing their employees with direct on-line computer access to selected HRMS information (see Chapter 14). This raises the possibility of allowing employees to access their benefits and pension information in forms that are designed to communicate what benefits the individual has, as well as what options are available. This may be done directly via screens that the individual calls up on a computer (with, of course, appropriate security safeguards under "password" protection), which may or may not be supplemented with "help menus," or automated tutorials. Employees may even be allowed to select benefits options in this way. Nolan (1995), for example, reports that NorTel used an interactive voice response system to allow its more than 13,000 employees to select options from its flexible benefits program. This information was then transferred in automated form directly to the organization's HRMS, thus saving a considerable amount of benefits' staff time and effort.

◆ ◆ ◆

SUMMARY

Benefits and pension plans in most organizations are complicated. Plan complexity of course tends to be greater in large organizations. However, there has been a general evolution toward greater complexity over time for all organizations, as employee expectations have increased and legislation has imposed further demands. Even relatively small organizations are consequently finding it necessary to use an HRMS to store and manipulate the information required to manage benefits and pension programs. This includes doing costing and other analyses required to reconcile the demand for benefits from various sources with what can be done within available cost constraints.

E X E R C I S E S

1. It was noted that cost savings may be realized through the coordination of benefits across plans in dual career families. What difficulties might be experienced in coordinating this coverage? What would be the role of the HRMS?

2. What are the advantages of flexible benefits programs? What complications do you see in the information requirements of this type of program over more traditional programs? What role might an HRMS play in meeting these requirements?

3. It is sometimes said that employers tend to emphasize the "cost of benefits," while employees are mainly concerned with their "value." Does this have implications for the way in which annual benefits statements should be formatted and presented? What about other methods of communication? What is the role of the HRMS likely to be in the communications process?

4. In some organizations employees have been given direct access (usually read only) to HRMS screens containing benefits and pension data via desktop workplace terminals or personal computers. In a few organizations this has been extended so that employees can initiate analyses to obtain pension projections, estimates of the consequences of electing various pension or benefits options, etc. Do you think that giving employees access to their benefits and pension information in this way is a good idea? What advantages or problems might it pose for HR personnel, employees, or the organization at large? How might one deal with each of these problems, and with the issue of confidentiality?

5. What benefits program monitoring and analysis capabilities are likely to be important in an HRMS? Do you feel that the presence or lack of such capabilities should be an important criterion in selecting a new HRMS? Why? How would one assess whether the HRMS can do all that is required in this area?

References

Belcourt, M., A.W. Sherman, G.W. Bohlander, and S.A. Snell. 1996. *Managing Human Resources*, Canadian ed. Toronto: Nelson Canada.

"Benefits Communication: Linking costs and commitment." 1992. *Canadian HR Reporter* (February): 13.

Cascio, W.F., and J.W. Thacker. 1994. *Managing Human Resources*. Toronto: McGraw-Hill Ryerson.

Coward, L.E. 1991. *Mercer Handbook of Canadian Pension and Benefit Plans*. Don Mills, Ont.: CCH Canadian Ltd.

Kelly, J.G. 1991. "Benefits Applications." In A.L. Lederer, ed., *Handbook of Human Resource Information Systems*. New York: Warren, Gorham and Lamont.

MacPherson, D.L., and J.T. Wallace. 1992. "Employee Benefits Plans." In *Human Resources Management in Canada*. Scarborough, Ont.: Prentice-Hall.

McCaffrey, R.M. 1988. *Employee Benefits Programs: a Total Compensation Perspective*. Boston, Mass.: PWS-Kent.

_____. 1989. "Organizational Performance and the Strategic Allocation of Indirect Compensation." *Human Resources Planning* 12, no. 3, 229–38.

Nolan, C. 1995. "Plugged In: Delivering the Benefits Message Goes Interactive." *Benefits Canada* (June): 34–35.

Schuler, R.S. 1984. *Personnel and Human Resources Management*, 2nd ed. New York: West Publishing.

Stelluto, G.L., and D.P. Klein. 1990. "Compensation Trends into the 21st Century." *Monthly Labour Review* 113, no. 2: 38–45.

Stonebraker, P.W. 1995. "Flexible and Incentive Benefits: a Guide to Program Development." *Compensation Review* 17, no. 2: 40–53.

13

Occupational
Health and
Safety

◆ ◆ ◆

INTRODUCTION

Occupational health and safety (H&S) is receiving increased workplace emphasis, fuelled by government legislation, pressures from organized labour, and increased awareness on behalf of many progressive organizations that healthy, safe working environments are cost-effective. As noted in Robertson (1992), H&S legislation has three major aims:

1. *Prevention*. Setting minimum standards in the workplace, together with the means of enforcing these standards.

2. *Employment security/Compensation*. Ensuring that injured workers receive appropriate Workers' Compensation, medical attention, rehabilitation support, a suitable job to return to, once they are able to work, or extended financial support if they are not.

3. *Employer liability*. Ensuring that the employer meets the established H&S standards, and is accountable when the standards are not met.

This chapter discusses the use of an HRMS in support of occupational health and safety. Readers searching for a more detailed account of occupational health and safety issues are referred to a companion text in this series (Montgomery, 1996).

◆ ◆ ◆

OCCUPATIONAL HEALTH AND SAFETY MODEL

Figure 13-1 applies the human resources model to occupational health and safety.

Occupational health and safety can be described as the identification, evaluation, and control of hazards associated with the work environment (Montgomery, 1996) and for the purposes of this text includes industrial

FIGURE 13.1 Occupational Health and Safety

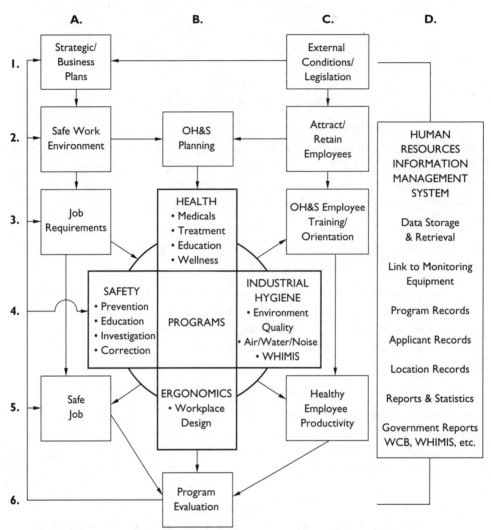

hygiene (environmental monitoring of air and water quality and noise levels), as well as ergonomics (Plog, 1988).

Other general activities covered under the heading of H&S include medical testing, medicals (pre-employment, during employment, post-employment), medical treatment, first aid, preventative measures (e.g., flu and travel shots), accident prevention and education, accident investigation, recommendations for correction of procedures, equipment, union and management committees, and workers' compensation boards.

Traditionally, hazards have included *physical hazards* such as falling objects, dangerous tools or machinery, footing, noise, light, temperature, radiation, and vibration; chemical hazards, including carcinogens; and biological hazards such as bacteria, viruses, and allergens (Firenze, 1978). More recently, ergonomic issues—appropriateness of work environment, tools, etc.—and workplace stress have gained prominence (Belcourt et al., 1996).

◆ ◆ ◆
LEGISLATION

In Canada, H&S is a provincial responsibility, except in federally regulated settings like the federal public service, Crown corporations, broadcasting and transportation companies, banks, grain elevators, and the Canadian Forces (Montgomery, 1996). Whereas in the United States H&S is regulated by the federal Occupational Safety and Health Act, separate legislation exists in each of the 10 Canadian provinces and there is federal legislation as well. In specific areas, such as the Workplace Hazardous Materials Information System (WHMIS), the federal government and the provinces have cooperated to establish common standards.

Readers are directed to Montgomery (1996) and Robertson (1992) for listings of H&S legislation in Canada, and more detailed discussions of the application of this legislation in the workplace.

As pointed out in Chapter 10, legislation in all Canadian jurisdictions requires that organizations show "due diligence" in protecting clients, workers, and others on the organization's property, using the organization's property, or acting on the organization's behalf. This means that all reasonable precautions have to be taken to ensure that the workplace and property are safe, and that workers are trained and skilled in doing their jobs safely (Montgomery, 1996).

The following criteria are likely to be used to determine "due diligence" in the case of an investigation of an accident or unsafe working conditions:

1. Whether appropriate H&S policies and procedures exist (see Robertson, 1992), based in substantial part on applicable H&S legislation, but also on the genuine will of the organization to maintain a healthy and safe workplace.

2. Whether legislation, policies, and procedures are translated into effective H&S programs, including written information, training for management and staff at all levels (including orientation training for new employees), joint health and safety committees (which meet regularly, and are qualified and empowered to conduct accident investigations and workplace health and safety inspections), and clear evidence of the commitment of the organization's board of directors and executive to H&S, including the commitment of necessary resources.

3. Whether H&S legislation, policies, procedures, and programs are understood, applied, and monitored throughout the organization, and whether appropriate follow-up action, including discipline, when appropriate, is taken for noncompliance.

◆ ◆ ◆
APPLICATION

The Pulp and Paper Research Institute of Canada, with a number of sites across Canada, conducts research using a large number of potentially hazardous equipment and chemicals. Occupational health and safety must be a priority of employees at all levels of the various laboratories and research sites included in this research. A copy of the preface of the Institute's H&S manual (Pulp and Paper Research Institute of Canada, 1996) is provided below to illustrate how an organization can demonstrate its commitment to health and safety:

> *Safe working conditions and a healthy workplace environment are important for all of us. These conditions do not just occur automatically—they require thoughtful, conscientious effort to ensure that safety is a routine part of our work. To assist employees, Paprican has developed this Occupational Health and Safety Manual. It provides guidelines and procedures aimed at helping us to work safely. I urge all employees to read this manual carefully and to become familiar with the sections that apply to their work area.*

Despite these precautions, we are all aware that many of our research activities are not routine in nature. Therefore, we must also rely on common sense and a spirit of cooperation to help prevent potentially hazardous situations. All employees, whether they be officers, research management, supervisors, researchers, technical or support staff, must work together to identify potential hazards by appropriately analyzing operations, planning experiments, and installing equipment with safety in mind. Inspections by the Safety Committee and investigations of incidents and accidents are also important milestones in our ongoing commitment to safety. Clear, direct communication and a willingness to share information openly and to discuss issues frankly and objectively are essential.

Compliance with our safety guidelines and regulations, whether contained within this document or otherwise communicated, is not optional—it is a condition of employment. Failure to respect safety procedures could endanger not only your life but the lives of your fellow workers. It should be understood that wilful infractions will result in disciplinary action.

All employees should feel free to discuss any aspect of safety with their supervisor or safety representative. Health and safety are the right and responsibility of each employee (p. i).

An organization's HRMS has a key role to play in collecting, storing, and reporting of information to assist personnel at all levels of the organization carry out their H&S responsibilities (Belcourt et al., 1996). An HRMS can be used, for example, to:

1. keep a roster of safety inspections, maintain the results of such inspections, and conduct analyses to identify either particularly good (to be rewarded) or problem areas (for corrective action);

2. maintain the results of accident investigations, as well as identify and report on trends;

3. maintain a roster of employees that have received H&S training and/or certification (see Chapter 10) or have otherwise passed or met specific knowledge targets, as well as individuals who are qualified to provide H&S training; and

4. collect information and provide regular reports on injuries, medical time-off, and workers' compensation statistics so that the organization can identify trends; compare and manage costs (see Chapter 3); identify priority areas for joint safety committee attention; allow comparisons with other organizations in the same sector; and provide reports and returns both for the government and for internal use, quickly and efficiently.

Information for the reports and returns mentioned in points 1 to 4, above, should be available from the results of formal health and safety inspections, accident and hazard investigations, workers' compensation reports, and other HRMS modules, such as training or benefits, discussed in previous chapters.

◆ ◆ ◆
RELATIONSHIPS BETWEEN H&S AND HRM DATA

The following list shows some of the areas that either share information with H&S, or share closely related information.

1. Staffing
   - Pre-employment health declaration
   - Pre-employment medical

2. Benefits
   - Medical and drug requirements

3. Attendance Management
   - Medical/health reasons for absence
   - Accident investigation
   - First aid

4. Wellness Programs
   - Preventative measures

- ◆ Periodic medical testing
- ◆ Education
- ◆ Safety inspections
- ◆ Industrial hygiene programs
- ◆ Employee Assistance Program (EAP)
5. Employee Relations
    - ◆ H&S union or management committees
    - ◆ Incident reports

Selected HRMS data may be required in specific H&S programs. For example, administration of an employee assistance program (EAP) could require the following HRM data elements for each worker, his or her significant other, and immediate family:

- ◆ Name
- ◆ Address
- ◆ Phone
- ◆ Date of birth
- ◆ Social Insurance Number
- ◆ Emergency contact(s)
- ◆ Work location
- ◆ Job title
- ◆ Level of benefits
- ◆ Medical history
- ◆ Job performance records

◆ ◆ ◆

OCCUPATIONAL HEALTH AND SAFETY INSPECTIONS

These inspections are often the responsibility of joint (union/management) occupational health and safety committees (Montgomery, 1996). Inspections should be conducted systematically, according to an established checklist (Laing, 1992). The following items will generally be covered in such a checklist:

1. Safe use and maintenance of machinery, tools, and equipment.

2. Environmental factors such as noise, atmosphere, and temperature.

3. State of storage areas and facilities, especially as pertaining to hazardous materials.

4. Storage and use of hazardous materials. (Do material safety data sheets exist, and are the materials concerned being stored and used properly? Has training been completed in accordance with WHMIS?)

5. Existence and quality of personal protective equipment.

6. State of working and walking surfaces.

7. Adherence to safe working practices.

8. State and quality of emergency facilities and equipment.

In each of the above areas the HRMS should be able to document and report on the following:

1. Department inspected, date, time.

2. Name of inspectors.

3. Hazards observed.

4. Recommended action, date action taken.

5. Result of follow-up review by safety committee, date of follow-up.

6. Safety committee sign-off.

◆ ◆ ◆
ACCIDENT REPORTING

An HRMS health and safety module should contain accident report information such as the following (Biggs, 1991):

1. Description of accident, location, date, time.

2. Machinery, tools, equipment involved.

3. Any mitigating environmental conditions (lighting, atmosphere, chemicals, working surfaces).

4. Name of person(s) involved.

5. Description of injury.

6. Job being performed.

7. Analysis of causes.

8. Recommendations.

9. Name and signature of investigator, date.

10. Follow-up action taken, date.

Figure 13-2 illustrates common steps that occur after an accident at work, and the way in which an HRMS may be used to capture, analyze, and report significant data about these steps.

The effect of these steps on human resources tasks are described below:

1. Time lost from work due to an accident often triggers the requirement for either a replacement worker or overtime. In unionized settings, seniority usually governs who is to be engaged as a replacement or to be given overtime. Seniority is generally calculated and maintained on the HRMS by Human Resources.

2. An injured employee's progression through sick leave, short-term disability, long-term disability, workers' compensation, restricted return to work and unrestricted return to work, must be tracked, preferably with the HRMS.

FIGURE 13.2 Accident/Injury Process Flow

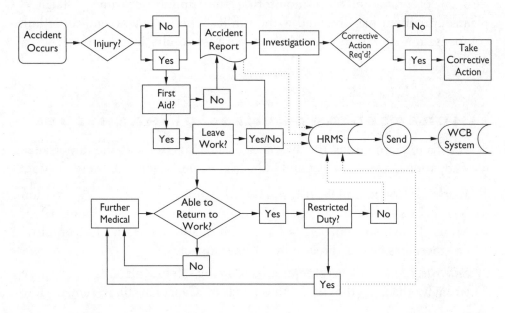

3. External agencies (i.e., Workers' Compensation Boards) and contractors (such as health case workers) both require and generate data. Most of this information should come from and/or be entered into an HRMS.

4. Depending on the nature and cause of an accident, labour relations issues may arise, up to and including strike action. Information regarding other accidents in the same location, or of the same nature or cause, would normally be required by all parties to such a dispute.

5. Additional benefits or levels of benefits may be triggered for an injured employee and, depending on the nature of the employer's coverage, there could be increased costs for the employer and/or employee. Overall bene-fit plan costs are normally based on the prior period experience so that close monitoring and control of accidents and workers' compensation benefits can result in significantly reduced costs to the organization (Hunt, 1995; see also Chapter 3).

Other occupational health and safety programs have much in common with Human Resources' domain. As noted in Chapter 10, programs such as employer wellness programs, designed to prevent health problems and acci-dents through education, should be monitored to determine their direct and indirect effects and cost-effectiveness.

Many organizations work on creating a more positive H&S culture through programs such as monitoring the amount of time a facility/ plant/department has operated without a lost time accident, and some link compensation or reward programs to positive results in this area (Moser, 1995).

◆ ◆ ◆
INCREASED AWARENESS OF H&S ISSUES

Several factors are raising the awareness of managers about the importance of occupational health, safety, and industrial hygiene. Some of these include:

1. *Workers' Compensation Board (WCB) Costs.* Workers' compensation board costs have risen dramatically over the last few years (Hunt, 1995; Moser, 1995). Since these costs are traditionally charged back to employ-ers, there has been a direct bottom-line impact.

2. *Safety legislation.* Governments are enforcing safety violations much more strongly than in the past. Nevertheless, Canadian fines remain low

compared to those in the United States (the largest fine handed out in New Brunswick, for example was just $7500) (Moser, 1995). There is, however, in addition, considerable negative publicity surrounding a company involved in serious safety problems (such as the Westray Mining disaster on Canada's East coast a few years ago).

3. *Increasing health care costs.* In Canada, health care has been paid for by provincial governments under the umbrella of a national plan. Increasing health care costs, reduced federal government transfer payments to the provinces, and burgeoning debt at all government levels have combined to produce a different payment strategy. Several provinces have enacted employer health tax legislation which shifts an increasing amount of the burden to employers.

4. *Trends in health care responsibility.* As costs rise and are shifted to employers, the future offers little hope of relief. Frantisak (1993) predicts that an illness will more often be determined to be caused by an individual's prior exposures at work (i.e., exposure to asbestos prior to the 1980s when precautions began to be taken). The implications are significant. It appears likely that prudent employers will increase the amount of health data they collect about workers (before, during, and after employment) and their environment, and retain that data for a lifetime.

5. *Technology.* Advances in technology have made telecommuting—working from home, or a remote location, and only rarely, if ever, appearing "at the office"—a reality, and has raised an interesting question. Is an employer responsible for worker safety in the home (Currie, 1995)? In some jurisdictions, such as Manitoba and Nova Scotia, employers may be faced with responsibility for independent contractors. How they are expected to manage this responsibility, track this potentially new and different data, and what the impact on an HRMS or other systems will be, are questions that have not yet been fully answered. The Canadian government recently conducted a three-year study (1992–95) named "Telework" (Currie, 1995). Home H&S concerns were carefully addressed, as were ergonomics, the validity of home insurance, and even potential zoning issues. The study concluded that while telework was increasing rapidly, the administrative framework in which these workers function (including health & safety) has not kept pace. The questions it raises about employer liability for health or safety issues within the home while the employee is teleworking, have yet to be fully explored and resolved.

An examination of various models of human resources management (HRM) reveals that the HR community is split as to whether H&S is or is not part of that community. The Canadian Council of Human Resources Associations (CCHRA), however, includes H&S in its model of HRM.

There are both clear differences and connections between H&S and the rest of the HRM community. Most HRM professionals rarely have specialized training or experience with occupational health, safety, or industrial hygiene. H&S professionals include medical (occupational health nurses, doctors—including specialists in occupational medicine, registered occupational hygienists), safety professionals, and other specialists. There appears to be little cross-over from these professions or avocations to HRM and so the two functions have often remained separate, even when a common reporting relationship exists. Safety professionals, for example, represent several disciplines, including engineering, psychology, preventative medicine, and industrial hygiene (Montgomery, 1996). However, many H&S activities serve as the starting point for HRM data, or provide parts of the record. For example, HRMS subsystems such as time and attendance and employee benefits are closely tied to H&S related events, such as employee accident, first aid, medical treatment, workers' compensation, and restricted work duty.

As noted in Chapter 5, the HR_Matrix published by HRMS Directions, provides a comparison of HRMS, benefits, payroll, and related systems (Heinen, 1994). A review of the 1995 version of the HR_Matrix reveals that H&S modules are not generally well handled by commercial HRMS packages. Many HRMSs offer no or limited H&S capability; very few offer a complete H&S module. This is probably because of a perception that occupational health, safety, and industrial hygiene are not part of human resources responsibilities.

Take, for example, the case of a mine and process operation located in the Canadian Maritime provinces. The organization chart of this operation reflects not only the separation of various occupational health and safety activities and responsibilities from human resources, but also the disjointed manner in which this organization (and many others) deals with this functional area.

The organizational structure illustrated in Figure 13.3 should not be judged as wrong or inadequate as long as it works to meet the organization's needs. However, because it is fragmented, duplication of roles and responsibilities seems highly likely. Here we have further proof that traditional

FIGURE 13.3 Organization Chart of Occupational Health

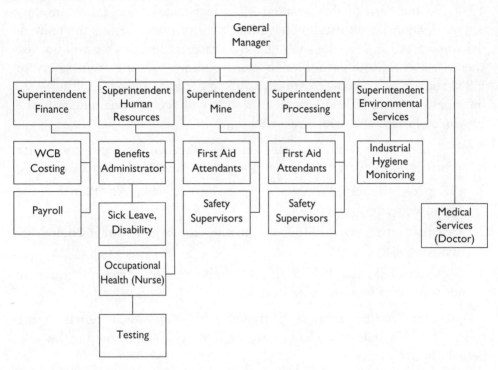

human resources functions need to be placed in a broader strategic context, and evidence of the need for an organizational structure that draws together disparate tasks into one functional group.

◆ ◆ ◆
SECURITY AND PRIVACY

Organizations that designed their own functional "stand-alone" systems may have done so because H&S was not seen as a part of Human Resources, while those that bought HRMS software found (and continue to find) that HRMSs did not have all of the capabilities required by H&S professionals. Functional separation may also have been due to the fact that access to the organization's separate information systems could not be restricted to a particular area of interest, and both H&S and HR personnel were concerned about (and perhaps jealous of) the confidentiality and security of information, which each regarded as sensitive.

Maintaining the confidentiality of health records is a problem (Cann, 1994). At the heart of this problem is the fact that, while paid by employers, occupational health staff believe that their primary client is the individual worker, and that workers who have no assurance of privacy will not use their services. Health professionals can be under pressure from safety or HRM staff, or an employee's supervisor to provide employee health-related information. Cann (1994) reports on a survey of occupational nurses in the province of Manitoba, which revealed that:

1. 62.7 percent of those surveyed reported receiving requests for health information from a worker's direct supervisor within the last six months;

2. 49.3 percent reported receiving requests from a manager other than the employee's direct supervisor;

3. 45.3 percent received requests from the employer's worker compensation specialist;

4. 48 percent reported that 75 percent of all requests for information were not supported by written authorization.

It would not be surprising if these health professionals resisted using general HRMSs unless they had assurance that health data could and would be held in confidence.

Fortunately, improved techniques for managing security means that this is no longer a barrier to integrating a broad range of organizational functions into one system, or developing a coordinated network of subsystems that can act as an integrated system.

◆ ◆ ◆
SUMMARY

Recent significant increases in health care and benefit costs and the trend to shift the funding of health care to employers have served to intensify the focus on occupational health and safety issues. This, in turn, has created an increased need for reliable, available data on which to make decisions.

A general lack of sophistication and integration of occupational health and safety records with HRMS and other information systems is seen as preventing this data from being readily available, and management is looking for alternatives. One solution being explored is to integrate occupational health and safety processes and information systems with those in Human

Resources. This chapter has discussed some of these process links and the potential benefits the use of an HRMS could offer.

EXERCISES

1. What are some of the factors causing occupational health and safety to be the target of increased management attention?

2. For what reasons have H&S modules often not been included in HRMSs in the past? Has anything changed to make inclusion of occupational health and safety issues in an HRMS more likely?

3. In what ways do occupational health and safety issues affect human resources management?

4. Occupational health and safety data has many links to other human resources management data. Give at least two examples and discuss the relationships between traditional H&S data and HRM data.

5. Many health professionals believe that their first duty is to the individual worker, not to the employer. Discuss the varying perspectives on this issue, and comment on the way in which the different positions could affect the nature of the supporting information systems.

References

Belcourt, M., A.W. Sherman, G.W. Bohlander, and S.A. Snell, 1996. *Managing Human Resources*, Canadian ed. Toronto: Nelson Canada.

Biggs, F. 1991. *Guide to Health and Safety Management*. Don Mills, Ont.: Southam Business Publications.

Cann, B.J. 1994. "Maintaining Confidentiality." *Occupational Health and Safety Canada* (September/October): 90–92.

Currie, M.B. 1995. "There's No Place like Home." *Occupational Health and Safety Canada* (March/April): 30–31.

Firenze, W.J. 1978. *The Process of Hazard Control*. Dubuque, Iowa: Kendall/Hunt.

Frantisak, F. 1993. "The Future of Occupational Health and Safety." Presentation to Noranda Minerals: Montreal.

Heinen, J.C. 1994. "Automating the Process for HRIS Selection." *Employment Relations Today* 21, no. 4 (Winter): 371–80.

Hunt, S. 1995. "Twenty Cost-Cutting Tips." *Occupational Health and Safety Canada* (July/August): 44–50.

Laing, P. 1992. *Accident Prevention Manual for Business and Industry: Administration and Programs*, 10th ed. Washington, D.C.: National Safety Council.

Montgomery, J. 1996. *Occupational Health and Safety*. Toronto: Nelson Canada.

Moser, C. 1995. "Our Changing Workplaces." *Occupational Health and Safety Canada* (July/August): 26–31.

Plog, B. 1988. *Fundamentals of Industrial Hygiene*, 3rd ed. Chicago, Ill.: National Safety Council.

Pulp and Paper Research Institute of Canada. 1996. *Occupational Health and Safety Manual*. Pointe Claire, Que.

Robertson, D. 1992. "Occupational Health and Safety." In *Human Resources Management in Canada*. 1995. Toronto: Prentice-Hall.

14

Trends in HRMS

◆ ◆ ◆

INTRODUCTION

There is a new reality in business today, one that has grown out of a number of social and economic trends, and that overlies the business community worldwide. Organizations are still trying to adjust to this reality, with mixed results.

Some of the parameters of the ever-increasing pace of change facing society in general, and organizations in particular, were documented in Chapter 1. This chapter discusses the implications of these changes on information systems technology, as well as how such technology may be used in human resources management and the organizational functions which it, in turn, supports.

◆ ◆ ◆

THE NEW ECONOMY

Beck (1992) suggests that key driving forces in organizational processes may be defined as having passed through the following three phases over the past 150 years. In historical order, there are:

◆ Commodity-driven processes

◆ Manufacturing-driven processes

◆ Technology-driven processes

Beck (1992) states:

> *Every era has its engines—a handful of strategic industries that drive the entire economy and typically have risen rapidly out of humble origins ... The high-growth strategic businesses—the engines—(today) fall into four categories:*

- *computers and semi-conductors (including software and information services)*
- *health and medical care (including drugs, biomedicine)*
- *communications and telecommunications*
- *instrumentation*

Industries like cars, steel, petroleum and housing, which were once the driving force of the economy, still dominate the headlines with their continuing troubles, but they are simply no longer as important as they once were (p. 20).

Some of the features of this new economy are:

- Globalization
- Outsourcing
- Restructuring work
- Technological advances
- Access to information
- Information management
- Human Resources management

Each of these will be discussed in more detail below.

◆ ◆ ◆

GLOBALIZATION

High speed communications and transportation networks mean that a competitor may be just down the block or on the other side of the world. Businesses have discovered that operating in third-world countries offers the competitive advantage of low pay rates, which translates directly into lower product prices. This has created pressure on North American business to be more competitive. With labour laws blocking reduced pay, many organizations have responded by reducing human resources costs in other ways, first through downsizing, and more recently by rethinking the fundamental concepts of what makes an organization.

◆ ◆ ◆
OUTSOURCING/CONTRACTING OUT

Increases in the number of competent but unemployed professionals, along with organizations' need to reduce the number of full-time employees, has led to an increased use of contract employees and consultants who are available for specific projects or for a set duration of time but remain off the permanent payroll. Rivard (1995) lists the advantages of using such a temporary "external workforce" as reducing employee turnover, easing legislative compliance, reducing health care benefit costs and Workers' Compensation Board (WCB) costs and, most importantly, moving these HRM services from unvalued overhead to measurable expenses that add value.

Outsourcing human resources is just one option. Another is to outsource technology resources, a trend that grew from 63 percent in 1992 to 72 percent in 1993 (Slofstra, 1994). Almost all technology resources that now exist in-house can be outsourced, whether these resources are applied to system development, system operation, or system maintenance. Mainframes, or servers on which the systems operate, can also be leased from agencies operating across town, or across the country. Communications networks can be leased, as can other hardware. Sookman (1994) cautions that this option is not without risks (e.g., being locked into pricing arrangements, unexpected licensing and leasing costs, loss of control) which must be carefully weighed before a decision to outsource human resources or technical services is made.

◆ ◆ ◆
RESTRUCTURING WORK

Various techniques—such as business process engineering/re-engineering (see Chapter 4)—are and will continue to be used to restructure or eliminate work processes and to establish new, more cost-effective ways of doing things. The net effect will usually involve the use of fewer people, combined with new or better use of technology.

A 1994 survey of 500+ IS managers by Computer Sciences Corp listed re-engineering of business processes as the number one challenge (Daniel, 1994). The survey listed two key enablers of re-engineering: technology and human resources.

◆ ◆ ◆
TECHNOLOGICAL ADVANCES

Beck (1992) has defined our era as the technological era. Harry Copperman, vice-president, Digital Systems's Business unit, recently used an analogy to illustrate the degree of technological change: "If air travel had changed as dramatically as information systems in the last ten years, a trip from San Francisco to New York would take four minutes and the plane would be only three inches long (Copperman, 1996)." The impact of today's technology and its rate of change may be more dramatic than anything since the invention of the printing press or of gunpowder.

History is full of examples of people who ignored change with devastating results; sword makers who thought firearms were not a competitive threat, buggy whip makers who thought automobiles were a passing fad.

Burrus (1993) states:

> *First, in a broad and general way, it is necessary to understand the nature of the profound technological changes that are under way. There's never been anything comparable in all of human history! Second, just as our ancestors—and we in turn—learned to use basic tools like hammers and crowbars, it is time to understand that no matter how complex the specific technology may appear to be, it too is a tool that must be mastered. And third, with new tools come new rules that determine how institutions and individuals function effectively (p. xii).*

Many people are overwhelmed by the perceived complexity of information technology, when they should be concentrating on its functional applications. It is not necessary to know how a telephone or telephone networks are designed in order to make a telephone call, nor does the lack of knowledge about the inner workings of television seem to dampen its use. The same is true of modern computer-based information technology.

Burrus (1993) suggests that:

The status quo has been shattered by technological change. As a result, success or failure hang in the balance for the remainder of the 1990s and the twenty-first century. Ignoring this reality would be tantamount to having shrugged off the development of water and steam power and the invention of the steam engine. Many of those who did were left behind by the modern age, marooned in pockets of poverty and despair, deprived of the sustenance of the past and denied the promise of the future. Those who repeat the same mistake in our era are doomed to a similar fate (p. xii).

While many people are afraid of technology and its implications, there are also dangers in embracing change too quickly. Hardware and software suppliers sell the concept of "the leading edge," to describe the latest and greatest innovation. To this has been added the concept of "the bleeding edge," which graphically describes the experience of using untried or under-tested technology.

◆ ◆ ◆
FLEXIBILITY

Ten years ago most software was designed to operate on one type of computer. But, as *The Arthur D. Little Forecast on Information Technology and Productivity* (Weizer et al., 1991) predicted, users demanded the ability to share data and programs, regardless of what kind of computer they possess. Today the concept of "open systems" means that software can (or should be able to) operate on many different makes of computers, databases, and communications networks.

The need for software programs that can run on many different types of computers has led to much more competition in computer hardware. As the performance of various makers' products keep pace, the costs, reliability, and service that software suppliers are able to offer becomes more important than the make of the equipment per se in many customers' choice of computers and ancillary equipment. The job of software developers has become more complicated, as they struggle to ensure that their programs are operational on the many types of equipment that are available. User demand for flexibility of this sort is unlikely to abate.

◆ ◆ ◆
OTHER TECHNICAL ISSUES

Other notable trends that are affecting the development and use of HRMSs are described below:

CLIENT-SERVER (C/S) The concept of client-server is that one computer, or server (sometimes also referred to as a host), can work with many other computers, often referred to as clients (Miracle, 1993) (see Figure 14.1). The data resides in the server—which can be any computer, from a laptop to a mainframe—as does a portion of the application software. The client holds the rest of the application software and has its own processing power. Colour capabilities and graphical user interfaces (GUIs) are used to make the system as user friendly and efficient as possible.

This distribution shares the processing power between the client and the server, utilizing each to maximum advantage, and (hopefully) reducing costs, while increasing speed.

The concept of client-server is currently very popular in software design. Bartholomew (1995) states that client-server accounting systems account for almost 50 percent of today's multibillion-dollar worldwide financial services market.

INTERACTIVE VOICE RESPONSE (IVR) IVR is the use of touch-tone telephones to access and provide information verbally/orally. Although no longer considered new technology, IVR offers considerable untapped potential and is likely to gain in prominence in the future.

IMAGING Scanning technology or imaging acts much like a photocopier, except that the result, instead of a piece of paper, is an image represented by bites and bytes in a computer. Documents or pictures can be scanned and then stored electronically, reducing paper and paper-filing systems, while also being available to be added to other documents or transmitted via e-mail or Internet. Over the past several years the process has become cheaper and faster, with colour scanners now available. At the same time, quality, measured in dots-per-inch (DPI), has improved. These trends should all continue, making the movement of data from paper into electronic form easier and cheaper.

FIGURE 14.1 Client-Server

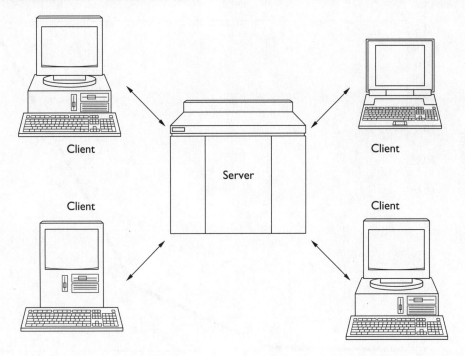

◆ ◆ ◆
ACCESS TO INFORMATION

We are frequently told that we live in the information age. Certainly the volume and variety of information available to everyone has mushroomed, and this trend should continue. It is perhaps best characterized by the Internet.

From a network that was started by the American military under the acronym of ARDANET, and for a number of years was little known outside of higher education and some government agencies, the Internet, "Cyberspace," or the "Information Highway" has grown dramatically: from 30,000 connected computers in 1987, to 1.3 million in 170 countries in 1993, to approximately 20 million users today, with a projection of 100 million by the turn of the century (Prociuk, 1996). Figure 14-2 provides a graphical representation of this growth.

The Internet gives users access to a system of electronic mail (e-mail) around the world, often within seconds, with no long distance or special

FIGURE 14.2 Internet Users

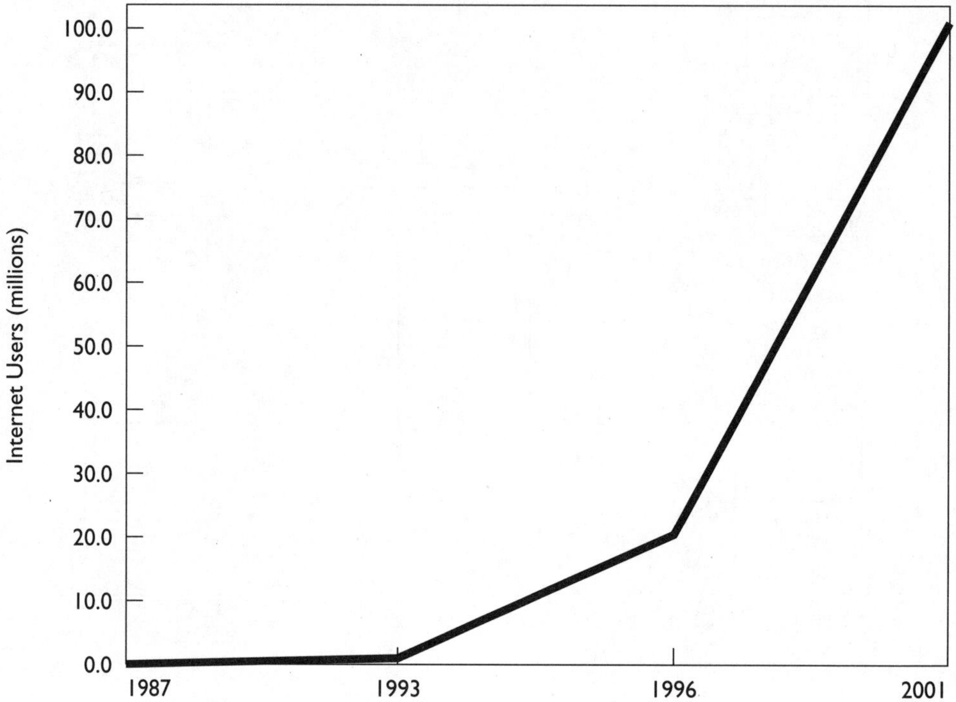

charges. It also gives access to the World-Wide Web (WWW); literally a web of information sites where anyone can access libraries anywhere from their computer—at the office, at home, in the car, or on a mountain-top.

Several human resources information management systems today recognize the power and potential of the "Net" by offering easy ways to receive and send information from an HRMS via the Internet. One good example of the use of this tool is advertising job openings. Many jobs are now advertised on the Internet, and many firms allow or encourage applications and résumés to be sent via the Internet instead of by fax or regular mail. Once in the organization's own electronic network these résumés can be saved electronically, searched for, e-mailed from desk to desk, annotated, and, if necessary, translated into hard-copy via a printer.

These uses have led to the concept of "Intranet," or use of the Internet within the walls of one organization for employee communications. Benefit plans, job openings, organization policy manuals, and new energized versions of the company bulletin board all appear in this new environment.

The now familiar fax machine was in limited use in the mid-1970s, gained prominence in business in the mid-1980s, and now occupies a place in many homes. Children fax each other homework assignments, and many children's television shows offer fax more often than voice telephone numbers or regular mail service addresses. But faxes cost money to send by long distance telephone, while Internet e-mail messages do not, and many feel that the Internet is easier to use.

Improvements in computer supported technology include:

1. Computers are becoming more powerful, and that power grows cheaper daily.

2. Components are getting smaller, encouraging a move away from "desktop" computers to "laptops," "notebooks," "subnotebooks," "palmtops," and "Personal Digital Assistants" (PDAs).

3. Batteries are lasting longer and getting lighter—both boons to the portable computer user.

4. Other than batteries, power can come from many sources including a car cigarette lighter, or solar power.

5. Linkage between computers can still be "hard-wired," but it can also be accomplished via infrared, cellular phone, or satellite.

◆ ◆ ◆
INFORMATION MANAGEMENT

Directly flowing from the increased access to information is the need to better manage information, otherwise, "information overload" becomes a significant problem. Users can drown in facts that are not always relevant.

Organizations are finding that there is a strategic advantage in being able to access the right information at the right time, and to share it properly within an organization's own Human Resources. Many things will combine to make this possible.

"Groupware" is one key. Groupware is software that permits groups of people to share data and applications. Caldwell (1995) states that:

Major consulting firms and systems integrators are focusing their information technology efforts on groupware and, increasingly, the Internet. The strategies enable them to share as much information as possible with their customers. Groupware is a near-universal effort in the industry, helping professional firms identify the human resources needed for client services. At the same time firms are boosting their mobile computing abilities, providing staff with remote access to database and electronic-mail servers so that they can work at customer sites and still have needed resources at hand. Mobile computing helps keep overhead costs low by reducing the need for office space (p. 57).

"Telecommuting"—linking to work via telecommunications devices which range from pagers to laptops and videoconferencing—is seen as contributing to the growing trend toward more people working at home, and is applauded for reducing air pollution, corporate office space, and the need to hire key talent (Baig, 1995a; 1995b).

◆ ◆ ◆
HUMAN RESOURCES MANAGEMENT

The general business and technological trends outlined above have an enormous impact on the way organizations of every size manage their human resources. In theory, the transition of the HR function from recordkeeper to strategic manager was accomplished some years ago but the reality may still be tantalizingly out of reach for many human resources professionals (Campbell and Matthews 1995)

One basic change has been the definition of human resources. Once defined as "employee," perhaps including part-time as well as full-time employees, an organization's human resources today can include retirees, contract employees, consultants, the families of these groups, and customers. Payment of those nonemployee human resources, and ad hoc payments to employees, such as expenses, can be made through payroll, relieving the burden on accounts payable. Advancing technology such as relational databases has made it possible for an HRMS to accommodate this broadening to human resources.

Traditionally, human resources has been driven by the need to conduct such functions as hiring, firing, and salary changes. Today business goals and the value that HR adds to those goals are becoming more important. So too is a new recognition of the importance of line management taking a more direct role in managing human resources and accessing the HRMS to do so, thus, assuming some of the functions that were previously performed by human resources personnel. Traditional HR systems do not allow line mangers to perform these functions, because direct access to critical human resources information is often only available to human resources staff (Mueller, 1994).

Recent technological advances, however, are leading to the following changes:

- Much-improved security in relational database structures allows users to access only their own "need-to-know" data. Client-server systems make an HRMS much more usable by casual users such as line managers.

- Operational supervisors are no longer tied to an office. Laptops and clip-board style computers give supervisors the freedom to travel within the warehouse, mine, factory, and forest, and still be able to access and modify records.

- Cellular phones and modems allow almost worldwide access to an HRMS.

- Work flow automates more of the business process, thus, directly engaging line management in an automated process and allowing them to interact more closely with an HRMS.

- Scanning/imaging makes it possible to integrate paper records into one electronic file, making central files more complete and removing that administrative burden from line management.

- Interactive voice response (IVR) can give line managers access to employee absenteeism (and other) records from their phone or in the car.

The relatively new profession of human resources information specialists combines technical and human resources management skills and knowledge. It represents a departure from the norm of having two distinct groups—information technology specialists and human resources practitioners—with distinct skill sets. Also, it represents a bridge to future organizational structures required by organizations operating in today's new economy.

As we pointed out in Chapter 1, the need to respond to quickly changing organizational requirements means new ways of doing business. The argument has also been made that now, as never before, the human resources function, supported by effective HRMSs, can have a critical strategic role in supporting the adaptation of new and more effective organizational structures and processes.

Almost a decade ago Davis (1987) wrote:

> It wasn't until the 1920s that Sloan developed at General Motors what was to become the basic model for industrial organization—a decentralized operating system combined with centralized policy and financial control. This was more than one hundred and sixty years after the industrial revolution began in England, and sixty years after it had transformed America from an agrarian to an industrial economy. It was not introduced, in other words, until the twilight of the epoch, just twenty years before the industrial period drew to a close. Now, thirty or forty years into a new, post-industrial economy, we find that Sloan's industrial model is still the major one used for organizing corporate America. We have industrially modelled organizations running post-industrial businesses. It is no wonder that we manage our way to economic decline. Our managerial models, the "context" in which we manage, don't suit the "content" of today's business (pp. 5–6).

The above quotation was written before the rapid spread of personal computers in the home, and before the Internet became more than the almost exclusive reserve of government employees and academics. Today we are just beginning to see organizations responding to the demands of post-industrialism.

NONTRADITIONAL HRM APPROACHES

Huva (1995) points out that systems to help understand and use human resources more effectively are becoming increasingly important, and that we must look beyond the traditional approaches because we have new work methods and organization patterns. Three nontraditional HRM concepts that are gaining acceptance are Competencies, Work Flow, and Teams.

COMPETENCIES

Spencer and Spencer (1993) report that the job-competency approach emphasizes validated criteria which cause and predict superior performance. "Competencies are underlying characteristics of people (p. 9)," and include motives, traits, self-concept, knowledge, and skill. Thus the traditional HRM activities of staffing and job design may translate to finding people with specific competencies, to fill positions with required competencies.

The demands on the HRMS will be to provide appropriate data elements and comparative tools to facilitate and document this process in much more detail than is now usually the case. One example of technology supporting the competency approach is computer-based training (CBT). Belcourt and Wright (1995) point out several advantages of CBT over traditional training, including greater mastery, reduced learning time, scheduling flexibility (self-paced learning available 24 hours per day), and tests that can provide proof of competency where required by law.

WORKFLOW

Dunivan (1996) defines workflow as automation of information flow, typically without imbedded business rules:

> *The distribution of memos represents a traditional workflow,*
> *one that we now take for granted in the form of electronic mail.*
> *It automates the physical tasks of carrying a document to a*
> *photocopier, making a copy, and delivering it (p. 11).*

The concept of a flow of work has taken on new perspectives with the growth and use of technology. Business process re-engineering (BPR) has supported the implementation of technology, and technology is beginning to return the favour with the development of computerized tools to help sequence processes into workflow.

Dunivan (1996) suggests that both of the concepts of BPR and workflow are immature, but today's new modelling tools and techniques will help to integrate the two. Workflow technology has much in common with the Groupware mentioned earlier in this chapter, and the flow chart tools mentioned in Chapter 5, and it supports the new focus on work teams.

TEAMS

People have always worked together, but HRM practices over the last decades have focused on the individual. Compensation, performance standards, measurement or appraisal, training and development have all dealt with people as single entities, but:

> *To review the performance of an employee assigned to multiple teams working on various projects overlapping several divisions, one needs to go beyond a traditional single-manager, single-profile evaluation model (Bryant, 1996, 17).*

The current trend is to focus on teamwork (Denton, 1992; Parker, 1994) in an attempt to increase organizational flexibility (including the ability to respond quickly to change), employee effectiveness, productivity and accountability, and to decrease administrative overhead. It is thus becoming *avant garde* to have "multiskilled workers" employed in "self-directed" work teams, in "flat, flexible" organizational structures (Irwin and Rocine, 1994; Stewart, 1992).

As with other management concepts that have become prominent over the past few decades, some of these will undoubtedly have a lasting beneficial impact, although their effects are unlikely to be as significant as their advocates predict (Lasden, 1985). In the meantime, they are certainly influencing the way in which organizations are structured and operate, and thus will influence the development, implementation, and operation of HRMSs, at least in the short term. It is important, therefore, that HR staff generally, and those responsible for the HRMS, understand these concepts and their implications.

DOWNSIZING

The need to maintain profits in a highly competitive, increasingly global business environment has led organizations to restructure their operations to try and maintain the productivity and quality of what they produce with fewer employees. This is often referred to as downsizing or rightsizing (Belcourt et al., 1996), and has been greatly aided by efficiencies offered by computer automation.

However, Tomasko (1993) reports that downsizing is not the answer to the many challenges facing organizations today. In a survey of over 1000 American firms that had downsized, the report of achievements vs. goals was bleak. This study found, for example, that:

1. Almost 90 percent wanted to reduce expenses; fewer than half actually did.

2. About 75 percent hoped for productivity improvements; only 22 percent achieved them.

3. More than half wanted to improve cash flow or increase shareholders' return on investment; fewer than 25 percent were able to do so.

4. More than half expected to reduce bureaucracy or speed up decision making; only 15 percent achieved these goals.

5. Many sought improvements in customer satisfaction and product quality. Others expected to become innovative or better able to utilize new technologies. But fewer than 10 percent felt that they had met their goals in these key areas.

These goals—to gain competitive advantage by reducing staff and reorganizing work—will clearly continue. The question yet to be answered is, how are they to be reached?

◆ ◆ ◆

HUMAN RESOURCES INFORMATION MANAGEMENT

The development of HRMSs is clearly tied to the current economic climate, current technology, and contemporary trends in human resources management. But it also reflects the history of HR. The 1995 survey of HRMS users reveals some interesting facts and speculation (Campbell and Matthews, 1995).

TABLE 14.1 MOST IMPORTANT HR APPLICATIONS

Now	Next 3–5 Years
◆ Employee Records	◆ Competency Profiling
◆ General HR Records	◆ HR Planning
◆ Payroll	◆ Attendance Management
◆ Attendance Management	◆ Career Management
◆ Pensions	◆ Succession Planning
◆ HR Planning	◆ Skills Matching
◆ Career Management	◆ Performance Management

There is a clear indication that HRMS users want to see a shift away from recordkeeping to what might be termed as "value-added management," but, as Table 14.1 illustrates, today's reality shows that few such systems are used for more than fundamental human resources functions and payroll recordkeeping.

However, competency profiling was seen as the top priority over the next three to five years. (It is even among the top 10 today). This fact, together with the projected importance of succession, career, and HR planning, demonstrates an awareness of the importance of creating an effective means of gathering, storing, and analyzing human resources information for all types of organizations.

As the 1995 *End User Survey* revealed, a clear focus for HR and HRMSs in the future is the empowerment of line management to use human resources information effectively. In part this will be accomplished by giving line managers more direct access to HRMSs. Richards-Carpenter (1994) points out that delayering tiers of management devolving the HRM function to business units, and empowering management all combine to make traditional computerized personnel information systems for the use of human resources alone completely inadequate.

The survey further indicates that cost justification is seen as the most significant barrier to acquiring new HRM systems, followed by a lack of top management commitment, a lack of a clear HRM strategy, outdated business processes, and a lack of computer skills. Campbell and Mathews (1995) lay the blame on a failure to justify the need for the new system in language that is persuasive to other managers, including the organization's executive. Generally this means being able to demonstrate that the HRMS contributes

TABLE 14.2 BENEFITS OF AN HRMS

- Improved management of HR operations
- Eliminate nonvalue-added work in HR
- Improved HRM productivity
- Improved management of Payroll operations
- Improved Payroll productivity
- Eliminate nonvalue-added work in Payroll
- Integrated HR/Payroll systems/processes

- Empowering line management
- Improved management of HR operations
- Integrated HR/Payroll systems/processes
- Improved HRM productivity
- Eliminate nonvalue-added work in HR
- Eliminate nonvalue-added work in Payroll
- Improved Payroll productivity

to the organization's competitive advantage (see Table 14.2) to specify what value is added through better management information, and to demonstrate potential savings in administrative costs (see also Chapter 3).

HRM practitioners must ask themselves how they can best help HR management to accomplish this in the years ahead.

Some other trends in HRM will include:

1. *User caution.* Some users will continue to be slow to invest in the latest technological trends, while insisting that their functional needs have top priority. The speed with which key technologies advance leave many wondering if there is ever a right time to buy a new computer or new software (Wetherbe et al., 1994) .

2. *Integration.* The integration of software has been a trend for several years. This is mirrored by the integration of human resources functions. As discussed in previous chapters, nontraditional HR management functions such as payroll, occupational health and safety, and time and attendance need to be integrated with other human resources functions and to be considered strategically within the larger organizational context. This integration, in turn, must be reflected in the HRMS. Fortunately, open systems provide opportunities to integrate separate software packages if a "fully integrated" HRMS is not available.

3. *Privacy/Security.* Although often used as synonyms for one another, these are two distinct and equally important issues. The *Personnel Journal*

(1994) emphasized the distinctions between database security and privacy. Security relates to proprietary, company-owned human resources data and systems, which are investments to be protected from theft or damage. Privacy is completely different; it concerns data contained in an HRMS that should not be made universally available. Security management policies and procedures can help resolve the privacy problems posed by the increased number of data elements and greater access, the latter being largely created by a new view of who the "users" of a system should be.

◆ ◆ ◆
SUMMARY

A new business climate has evolved that, combined with trends in technology and human resources management, will have a significant effect on the future of HRMSs.

Technology is expanding exponentially, and in doing so, it is shrinking the world, making globalization easier and faster. Organizations built to prosper in old environments must restructure or perish. Human resources must consequently be reinvented as a strategic and valued operational asset (Bryant, 1996). Although the tools to build new organizations are not entirely clear, effective HRMSs will be increasingly important in many organizations as they strive to better manage their human resources to meet their business goals.

To meet new requirements, however, HRMSs, built on the two towers of human resources management and technology, must change as well.

EXERCISES

1. What options have organizations explored in reshaping themselves? Which have proven most successful? Which were least successful?

2. What is the impact of globalization? Do you expect globalization to increase or decrease? Why? List two specific effects globalization has on the design of an HRMS.

3. Do you feel that technological changes are making employees' working lives more or less difficult? How do these

changes manifest themselves? How might any harmful effects of technological changes be reduced, without losing the benefits?

4. On what aspects of technology should nontechnical people concentrate? How can they do this?

5. Do you think it is a good idea for HRMS professionals to exist as a group apart from HR, Payroll, or Information Technology? Discuss the relative merits of the existence of an HRMS group.

6. Why do you think the Internet has become so popular. What is the future for this tool? Can you think of applications for the Internet with respect to HR and HRM?

7. What important trends in HRM are likely to affect HRMS development and use? More specifically, which do you believe will most affect the daily life of an HR manager, and therefore the demands on the HRMS?

References

Bartholomew, D. 1995. "Better Systems, Brighter Numbers." *Informationweek*, no. 516 (February): 66–72.

Baig, E.C. 1995. "Welcome to the Officeless Office." *Business Week*, no. 3430 (June 26): 104–6.

_____. 1995a. "Taking Care of Business—Without Leaving Home." *Business Week*, no. 3420 (April): 106–7.

Beck, N. 1992. *Shifting Gears*. Toronto: HarperCollins.

Belcourt, M., A.W. Sherman, G.W. Bohlander, and S.A. Snell. 1996. *Managing Human Resources*, Canadian ed. Toronto: Nelson Canada.

_____. and P. Wright. 1995. *Managing Performance through Training and Development*. Toronto: Nelson Canada.

Bryant, J. 1996. "Human Resources: Defining and Assessing Soft Skills." *The RESOURCE* (March): 16–18.

Burrus, D., with R. Gittines. 1993. *Technotrends*. New York: HarperBusiness.

Caldwell, B. 1995. "Making IT a Group Effort." *Information Week*, no. 545 (September 18): 170–74.

Campbell, I., and J. Matthews. 1995. *1995 End User Survey*. Softworld Report and Directory for Personnel and Human

Resources Information Systems Infact Research and Interactive Information Services Ltd. London, England (September).

Copperman, H. 1995. Presentation to the International User Group Meeting of Ross Systems Inc. San Francisco (May 15).

Daniel, D. 1994. "A Whole New Way of Thinking Computing Canada." *Computing Canada* 20, no. 7 (March 30): 17.

Davis, S.M. 1987. *Future Perfect.* New York: Addison-Wesley Publishing.

Denton, D.K. 1992. "Multiskilled Teams replace Old Systems." *HR Magazine* 37, no. 9 (September): 40–50.

Dunivan, L. 1996. "Workflow Technology." *The RESOURCE* (March): 11.

Huva, W. 1995. "Globalization and the HRMS." *The RESOURCE* (September): 28–30.

Irwin, D., and V. Rocine. 1994. "Self-Directed Work Teams: Coming Soon to an Organization near You." *CMA Magazine* (September): 13–14.

Lasden, M. 1985. "Fad In, Fad Out." *Computer Decisions* (May): 74–88.

Miracle, M. 1993. "The Trend to Client/Server is Maturing into Acceptance." *National Underwriter*

Life/Health/Financial Services 97, no. 45 (November): 2–8.

Mueller, B. 1994. "Changing Attitudes Help Shape HR Systems." *Systems Management (*March).

"New product news supplement." 1994. *Personnel Journal* (November): 16.

Parker, G. 1994. *Cross-Funcional Teams: Ways to Work with Allies, Enemies, and Strangers.* Bristol, V.I.: Soundview Executive Book Summaries.

Prociuk, H. 1996. "The Electronic Highway May Be the Dominant Information Tool of the Future. How Do HR Departments Get Up to Speed?" *Human Resources Professional* (April): 7–8.

Richards-Carpenter, C. 1994. "Personnel Takes Pragmatic Approach to Technology." *Personnel Management* 26, no. 7 (July): 55–56.

Rivard, J. 1995. "Why is Outsourcing a Choice?" *RESOURCE* 4, no. 1 (March): 14.

Slofstra, M. 1994. "A Positive New Image in the Works." *Computing Canada* 20, no. 16 (August): 27.

Sookman, B. 1994. "The Legal Issues Abound." *Computing Canada* 20, no. 16 (August): 29.

Spencer, L.M., Jr., and S.M. Spencer. 1993. *Competence at Work—Models for*

Superior Performance. Toronto: John Wiley and Sons, Inc.

Stewart, T. 1992. "Looking Ahead: the Search for the Organization of Tomorrow." *Fortune* (May 18): 93–98.

Tomasko, R.M. 1993. *Rethinking the Corporation—The Architecture of Change.* New York: The American Management Association.

Weizer, N., G. Gardner III, S. Lipoff, M.F. Roetter, and F.G. Withington. 1991. *The Arthur D. Little Forecast on Information Technology and Productivity.* New York: John Wiley and Sons.

Wetherbe, J.C., N.P. Vitalari, and A. Milner. 1994. "Key Trends in Systems Development in Europe and North America." *Journal of Global Informations Management* 2, no. 2 (Spring): 5–20.

Index

◆

To the owner of this book

We hope that you have enjoyed *Human Resources Management Systems*, and we would like to know as much about your experiences with this text as you would care to offer. Only through your comments and those of others can we learn how to make this a better text for future readers.

School _____   Your instructor's name _____

Course _____   Was the text required? _____   Recommended? _____

1. What did you like the most about *Human Resources Management Systems?*

_____

_____

_____

2. How useful was this text for your course?

_____

_____

_____

3. Do you have any recommendations for ways to improve the next edition of this text?

_____

_____

_____

4. In the space below or in a separate letter, please write any other comments you have about the book. (For example, please feel free to comment on reading level, writing style, terminology, design features, and learning aids.)

_____

_____

_____

_____

Optional

Your name _____   Date _____

May ITP Nelson quote you, either in promotion for *Human Resources Management Systems* or in future publishing ventures?

Yes _____   No _____

Thanks!

PLEASE TAPE SHUT. DO NOT STAPLE.

TAPE SHUT

TAPE SHUT

FOLD HERE

TAPE SHUT

TAPE SHUT

MAIL **POSTE**

Canada Post Corporation
Société canadienne des postes

Postage paid   Port payé
if mailed in Canada   si posté au Canada
Business Reply   **Réponse d'affaires**

0066102399   **01**

Nelson

0066102399-M1K5G4-BR01

ITP NELSON
MARKET AND PRODUCT DEVELOPMENT
PO BOX 60225 STN BRM B
TORONTO ON M7Y 2H1